D1646260

This very readable account of the 1859 on extensive and detailed historical res political and religious context of the day. Contemporary abound of the startling, immediate effects of this divine visitation, with the description of the impact made on the Orange Order and the observance of the Twelfth of July that year being of particular interest. The long-term influence of the revival is realistically analysed – the membership statistics of the various churches, both before and after 1859, making especially sobering reading. Altogether, this volume provides a penetrating insight into a fascinating instance of the strange and wonderful workings of God.

Rev C. Jonathan Stephen,
Principal, Wales Evangelical School of Theology, Bridgend, Wales

Revival on the Causeway Coast is a fascinating and gripping story retold by an author whose insights and conclusions are refreshingly open and honest. He pays eloquent tribute to the sensational grace of God in the lives of boringly ordinary people ... the same people that God used to set hearts on fire in the northwest of the Province. An absorbing read, this well-researched volume is one that I found impossible to put down – nothing dry or dusty here. May the sovereign Lord who has done it before be pleased to revive us again!

Dr Sam Gordon
Director of Ministries, *Messianic Testimony*

Nicholas Railton's work allows the Coleraine Revival of 1859 to come alive for us a century and a half later. This book is well documented, utilizing numerous primary sources to trace the history of the revival as well as the ensuing controversy. Railton's observations and conclusions about the 'causes', the progress, and the ending of the revival are balanced and helpful.

This work is a valuable addition to the literature on this 'season of revival', a revival that Harvard historian Perry Miller called 'The Event of the Century.' I heartily endorse it!

Dr Timothy Beougher
Billy Graham Professor of Evangelism,
Southern Baptist Theological Seminary, Louisville, Kentucky

Here is information about transformation. In this fascinating study of the 1859 Revival in the Causeway Coast area of Northern Ireland Nicholas Railton gives historical details which inform the mind and stir the heart. He earths the revival in the historical social and religious life of the mid 19th Century. He paints a broader picture of both the context of the revival and the impact of the revival. He gives fascinating personal details of lives changed, hearts renewed and families transformed. He gives social details of everyday life which provide an essential backdrop to remarkable events.

This is no dry historical study to be archived on a bookshelf. Here is an historical record which will focus the mind and revive the soul. It is God's story, for revival always is. It is a human story of repentance, forgiveness, hope and new life. The Gospel is not about impotence but about impact and permanent eternal change. This study is about an injection of Gospel truth and life which the Church and the world desperately need today. May it be widely read, thoroughly enjoyed and more importantly used by God to light flames of revival which will spread like Divine fire into dry and hard hearts. In this year of the 150th anniversary of the 1859 Revival here is a timely reminder of the greatness, holiness and power of God. This is a story of hope. It should come with a health warning ... that when God moves, nothing can stop Him! We have been warned! Hallelujah!

Bishop Ken Clarke,

Revival
on the
Causeway Coast

The 1859 Revival in and around Coleraine

Nicholas M. Railton

_____

CHRISTIAN
FOCUS

Scripture quotations marked 'KJV' are taken from the *King James Version.*

Nicholas M. Railton is a German lecturer at the University of Ulster since 1994 and a member of the local historical society – the Coleraine Historical Society. He has specialised in German ecclesiastical history and has extensively studied the relations of Christianity of both Germany and Ireland (and Great Britain).

Copyright © Nicholas M. Railton 2009

ISBN 978-1-84550-493-9

10 9 8 7 6 5 4 3 2 1

First published in 2009

by
Christian Focus Publications Ltd.,
Geanies House, Fearn, Ross-shire,
IV20 1TW, Scotland, Great Britain

www.christianfocus.com

Cover design by Daniel van Straaten
Printed by Bell & Bain, Glasgow

Mixed Sources
Product group from well-managed
forests and other controlled sources
www.fsc.org   Cert no. TT-COC-002769
© 1996 Forest Stewardship Council

Contents

Map of the Spread of the Revival in 1859

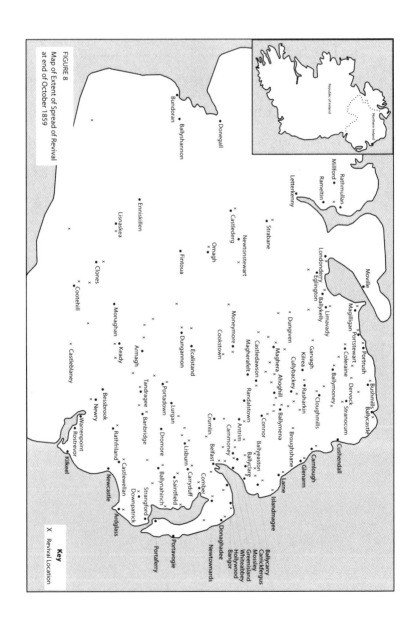

FIGURE 8
Map of Extent of Spread of Revival
at end of October 1859

Key
X Revival Location

Preface

In a sermon in 1959, commemorating the revival, Martyn Lloyd-Jones made the point emphatically that 'you cannot stop a revival any more than you can start it'. In his view, each and every revival is a sovereign work of God, for which humans cannot and should not take responsibility[1]. A revival cannot be organised in the way, say, a church might organise an evangelistic campaign. This may be seen by comparing responses to revival in 1833 and 1859. At the General Synod of Ulster, meeting in Coleraine in 1830, deep feelings and much debate were excited by a letter from the General Assembly of the Presbyterian Church in the USA containing news of an 'all-important' spiritual change in that country[2]. When news of the revival became known throughout Ireland in the early 1830s meetings were organised, as there would be in 1859, to deliberate upon the surprising events taking place on the other side of the Atlantic. In Belfast, for example, a meeting was held at which ministers discussed the propriety of uniting with their American colleagues in a day of prayer and fasting (7 January 1833 was the date set). This was to implore the blessing of God on the preaching of the gospel and to pray for 'the out-pouring of the Holy Spirit for the extension of religion throughout the world'. Four different meetings

1. Martyn Lloyd-Jones, *Revival. Can We Make It Happen?* London 1992, p. 236.
2. *The Orthodox Presbyterian*, No. XXIII, August 1831, pp. 378–81.

took place – at the Presbyterian churches in May Street, Fisherwick Place and Berry Street, as well as in the Independent meeting house in Donegall Street – and all were attended by large numbers of people. A follow-up meeting was planned for a couple of weeks later and organisers expected some permanent arrangement to be made to continue these meetings into the future[3]. What became of these meetings is unknown. What we do know is that no widespread revival took place either in Belfast or anywhere else in the north of Ireland as it would do, in a similarly expectant and prayerful atmosphere, in 1859.

Nevertheless, God has determined to use humans to preach the gospel and provides in His Word much encouragement to people to plead with Him for the souls of others. Strangely, there has probably never been a revival that has originated, from the human point of view, from within a church hierarchy. Indeed, quite frequently in church history, revivals have taken place almost against the wishes of those in authority. It is not unusual for church leaders to dislike and oppose them, or at least aspects of them. To their credit church hierarchies generally welcomed the revival of interest in spiritual matters in the north of Ireland in 1859. They were the first to admit the origin of the latter movement had little to do with them.

Historians seek to unearth the socio-political, economic and cultural causes of religious revivals. More often than not, the goal is to explain away the divine work. One must admire their creative ingenuity, though it would be fatal to overlook the hidden agenda. Historians fail, moreover, to provide reasons for the end of revival, which comes as suddenly as it had once appeared on the horizon. For believers in the historical truth of the New Testament Scriptures a revival is something sent periodically by God to refresh His people. A clear vision of His glory is the hard

---

3. *The Orthodox Presbyterian*, No. XL, January 1833, p. 143.

core of that revival. In the study which follows factors are discussed that accompanied and seem to have facilitated the human response to the unexpected, sudden move of God's Holy Spirit in the northern counties of Ireland. These factors do not fully explain that move; they were not the cause of the movement. The Christian must accept that the start and end of revival are sovereign, uncontrollable activities of the Holy Spirit.

Yet it is equally clear from reading the Pauline epistles that the Spirit can be grieved (Eph. 4:30) and quenched (1 Thess. 5:19). This points to the crucial importance of a correct human response to the leading and movements of the Holy Spirit. In the context of these verses it would seem that the way Christians speak about and to one another and the way they respond to prophetic utterances can lead to the withdrawal of God's Spirit. Put another way, when individuals or home groups of a congregation fail to reflect the nature of the Divine Spirit in their relationships, or when behavioural patterns inimical to God's character are tolerated, then, inevitably, the Spirit's operations are quenched.

Most revivals have thrown up many questions which Christians and non-Christians have struggled with. The 1859 revival is no exception. How is one to explain the apparent disorder that manifests itself during periods of revival? Is God not a God of order and is not everything to be done in an orderly manner? How should leaders deal with the unbounded enthusiasm shown by young converts? In every revival people stand aghast and ask: What is this? There are always mockers and scoffers wanting to quench all kinds of enthusiasm. Here Martyn Lloyd-Jones, a man hardly known for charismatic exuberance, warned his congregation in 1959 when he said that opposition to enthusiasm could be one of the greatest hindrances of all to revival[4].

---

4. *The Orthodox Presbyterian*, p. 73.

It is difficult, however, not to have some sympathy with the critics as well as with leaders who have, at times, a difficult balancing act to perform: managing events without stamping out the fires of revival. When the revival comes to an end there are more questions to answer. There is something intangible and inexplicable about every revival. The veil cannot be fully lifted on the whys and wherefores. People are left a little stunned, bewildered, overjoyed and yet full of questions – and a desire for more of the same. For Christians who can say 'This is what was spoken of, this is what God meant when He said: "I will pour out my Spirit upon all flesh"' the appropriate attitude to a revival should surely be one of worship and thankfulness. In each revival God again calls attention to Himself and His power. It is as if He were saying: 'I haven't gone away, you know.'

The 1859 revival in Ulster still holds a hallowed place in the hearts of Irish Christians. It impacted evangelicalism profoundly and one might say people are still enjoying the fruit of that movement. No single denomination monopolised revivalism in the Coleraine area. Evangelicalism was, and is, not bound by denominational labels and doctrines. The declared purposes of the revival meetings were never denominational reform of one kind or another, but rather the awakening of people's minds and hearts to their religious state. The agents of the Ulster revival came from all denominational backgrounds and none; they came from Reformed communities in Ireland, Britain and the USA. The focus of the revival in Coleraine was certainly the daily prayer meeting, which united Christians of various persuasions. In other words, focusing on theological developments within any one specific denomination seems to be inadequate as a way of explaining the 'awakening' of whole communities in 1859. In this study a pan-evangelical approach is taken.

Chapter 1: The Setting

The 1859 revival took place at a time of change and upheaval. Britain could still lay claim to being the world's superpower, its economic base providing the resources which facilitated expansion in all directions. The Industrial Revolution was ravishing the countryside and turning multitudes into appendages of machines. Charles Dickens drew the attention of the readers of literature to the appalling consequences of human greed. His *Tale of Two Cities* was first published in 1859. The British naturalist Charles Darwin published his groundbreaking *The Origin of Species* in November 1859[1]; he argued that organisms evolved gradually through a process called natural selection. Trinity College, Cambridge, banned the book. Clerics up and down the country, no doubt worried about the impact of a materialist interpretation of history, attacked the work and its author in a merciless fashion.

FEMALE PREACHERS

In *Adam Bede*, published in 1859, George Eliot told the story of a dairymaid who was seduced by a squire. The lives of ordinary working-class people are portrayed. Eliot fills the text with many Biblical allusions which reflected her own evangelical background. There are references in the story

---

1.   The book was being sold in Coleraine for 14 shillings by S. Eccles, whose shop was on the Diamond. *Coleraine Chronicle,*, 17 November 1860.

to a Wesleyan Methodist female preacher by the name of Dinah Morris who had started preaching at the age of twenty-one. This is how Eliot describes Morris's calling to the preaching ministry:

> [A]s I passed along by the cottages and saw the aged and trembling women at the doors, and the hard looks of the men, who seemed to have their eyes no more filled with the sight of the Sabbath morning than if they had been dumb oxen that never looked up to the sky, I felt a great movement in my soul, and I trembled as if I was shaken by a strong spirit entering into my weak body. And I went to where the little flock of people was gathered together, and I stepped on the low wall that was built against the green hillside, and I spoke the words that were given to me abundantly. And they all came round me out of all the cottages and many wept over their sins, and have since been joined to the Lord. That was the beginning of my preaching, sir, and I've preached ever since.

> Dinah had let her work fall during this narrative, which she uttered in her usual simple way, but with that sincere, articulate thrilling treble, by which she always mastered her audience.

Much of the work done by preachers in 1859 will have resembled the situation described here by Eliot: simple people communicating a simple message in simple words. Indeed, it is worth mentioning here that a goodly number of women did, in fact, help to promote the revival in Ulster. A Miss Witherow was an American who preached near Garvagh on 23 July 1859, giving an account of the state of Irish emigrants in the USA[2]. On 23 February 1859 a Miss McKinney delivered 'an earnest and impressive discourse' on 1 Peter 5:10 before a large inter-denominational gathering

---

2.   *Londonderry Sentinel*, 29 July 1859.

in Malin[3]. The same woman preached in Corporation Hall in Derry on 6 October 1859. 'The novelty of hearing a female preacher attracted a large audience, the hall being crowded to excess,' reported the Londonderry Sentinel[4]. In reality, Dinah Morris was in all likelihood a Primitive Methodist rather than a Wesleyan.

POLITICS

Other books published in 1859 had a greater impact than Eliot's on society and social mores. John Stuart Mill's *On Liberty* became one of the primary and most influential political texts of the nineteenth century. Mill had once worked as an administrator in the East India Company. He retired when the Company's functions were taken over by the British government following the Mutiny of 1857. For him fear of mob rule was married to a love of freedom. Another individualist approach to societal change was taught by Samuel Smiles. He lauded the virtues of 'self help' in a book of that title. Smiles completely abandoned his earlier interest in parliamentary reform and began to argue that industry, thrift and self-improvement provided the best way forward for society. A more radical approach was taken by a political refugee living in London, Karl Marx. In 1859 he published his *A Contribution to the Critique of Political Economy*, in the preface of which the key elements of historical materialism were outlined. For Marx change in economic structures over time, to better accommodate the continued development of the forces of production, was inevitable.

The jewel in Queen Victoria's crown nearly fell out when the Bengal army mutinied in May 1857. British guns restored what administrators might refer to as peace and order, but only for a time. In Europe too there were wars

---

3.   *Londonderry Sentinel*, 25 February 1859.
4.   Ibid., 7 October 1859. Miss McKinney was from Fintona, near Omagh in County Tyrone.

and rumours of wars: the Franco-Austrian war began in April 1859. On June 8 the French won a victory over the Austrians at the battle of Marignaro. At this time Garibaldi and his chivalrous volunteers landed in Sicily and would soon be compared with William of Orange by MPs in the House of Commons. Politicians, indeed all Londoners, were privileged to be the first to hear the peals of Big Ben, which had become fully operational on 7 September 1859.

International events as well as debates in the parliamentary chamber were reported in some detail in Coleraine's local paper, the *Coleraine Chronicle*. Viscount Palmerston formed his second Cabinet the month the revival fires erupted in the town. Gladstone was Chancellor of the Exchequer. The educated middle class in the north of Ireland would have been well aware of political and economic developments, though the majority of the population were more likely to be either ignorant of events further afield or simply uncaring. They were simply intent on surviving.

DEMOGRAPHICS

Ulster, just like the rest of Ireland, had long been losing its population. Indeed, the numbers leaving the province increased throughout the second half of the 1850s; nearly half the emigrants from Ireland in 1859 (38,000 out of 84,600) came from Ulster and this followed a decrease in population of 16 per cent between 1841 and 1851. Ulster lost 10,000 more people in 1859 compared with the previous year[5]. People from Coleraine left for Scotland, Australia, England, Canada and, of course, the United States. Relatives resident in America were probably the first to inform their families in Ireland of the religious revival spreading across the eastern states in 1857–8. Some would see the Ulster revival as perhaps the most explosive repercussion of the American revival. More will be said about this later. Relatives

---

5.   *Coleraine Chronicle,,* 14 April 1860.

not only sent back letters from the New World; just as importantly, they remitted money. Between 1848 and 1857 over $18.6 million was sent to Ireland by Irishmen resident in America. In 1858 alone $2.36 million was forwarded, often to help others to emigrate[6].

ECONOMICS

Coleraine's population had dropped from 6,255 inhabitants in 1841 to 5,631 in 1861 – a 10 per cent drop. People were leaving Ulster in spite of growing prosperity. The numbers of Irish paupers who received relief either in or out of workhouses dropped from 1.17 million in 1850 to under 160,000 in 1859[7]. In the revival month of June 1859 there was one pauper for every 140 of the population: in England the ratio was 1:25 and in Scotland 1:24[8]. In Coleraine itself there were 171 people in the workhouse on 4 June 1859, compared to 574 on 16 December 1848.

The lowest level of pauperism was reached in August 1859 when there were only 34,000 inmates in Irish workhouses[9]. The revival took place at a time when abject poverty was decreasing. Only at the beginning of 1860 did numbers of paupers begin to increase again.

Wealth was, then as now, unevenly distributed. Much distress and privation had been caused by the collapse of the embroidery and sewed muslin trade in the north of Ireland. The young women who in the mid-1850s earned respectable wages at embroiderers in the Coleraine area had turned to other branches of work[10]. The making of shirts and the manufacture of sewed muslin were still being carried on extensively in the county. Mr W.G. Self was an

---

6. *Coleraine Chronicle*, 25 February 1860.
7. John N. Murphy, *Ireland industrial, political, and social*, London 1870, p. 383.
8. *The Ulster Magazine and Monthly Review of Science and Literature*, vol. I, January 1860, p. 43.
9. *Coleraine Chronicle*,, 17 May 1862 and 11 June 1864.
10. Ibid., 1 March 1862.

agent working in the shirt trade who provided much work in the area throughout the 1850s[11]. The manufacture of candles, leather and soaps was also extensive[12]. There was still a brisk trade in Irish linen. The Belfast Linen Trade Circular reported in April 1861 that in 1859 twenty-eight factories were operating with 3,125 looms in use[13]. The number of looms in operation greatly increased after May 1859, even though the unsettled state of Europe had had an impact on demand. The American market absorbed over 45 per cent of the total exports of linen goods in 1859. Two years later thirty-five factories (with 4,609 looms) were fully operational. The Baptist Edward Gribbon pioneered the manufacturing of linen in Coleraine, employing many people from the area in his mill[14].

As far as the rural economy was concerned every crop turned out much better than had been expected earlier in the year. At the beginning of September 1859 it was reported: 'We have no complaints about the yield or the quality of the potato crop, and cereals, though light in some places, promised generally a good yield of grain. Turnips, owing to the recent rain, are outstripping in growth the anticipations of all.'[15] In Londonderry and Antrim there was an increase in acreage under flax in 1859. There were also appreciable improvements in all livestock. In Ulster the number of pigs increased in contrast to other parts of Ireland. The total value of livestock had increased by almost a million pounds over 1858, according to William Donnelly, the Registrar General[16]. There were grounds for optimism.

---

11. *Coleraine Chronicle*, 12 May 1860.
12. *Slater's Royal National Commercial Directory of Ireland*, Manchester–London 1870, pp. 189–94.
13. See the reports on the Irish linen trade in *Coleraine Chronicle*, 7 January 1860 and 11 January 1862.
14. See his obituary in Ibid., 24 July 1875.
15. Ibid., 3 September 1859.
16. *Coleraine Chronicle*, 1 October 1859.

One sign of growing prosperity in the town was the number of people with accounts at the Coleraine Savings Bank. The total balance of those accounts grew from £20,354 (in 1848) to £50,739 (in 1859). In the year of religious revival there had been an increase of nearly £5,000 in savings held by the Coleraine bank – a reflection, the local paper claimed, of the growing material prosperity of the 'hard-working farmers and mechanics of the district'[17]. In other words, and in contrast to the United States, the revival in Coleraine took place at a time of economic recovery and optimism, at least as far as the middle classes were concerned for, of course, not everybody was profiting from the general increase in wealth.

The unequal distribution of wealth was reflected, too, in wage and income levels. The Ulster branch of the National Teachers' Association said that teachers' salaries were not much higher than those earned by common labourers. While the latter might earn £31 a year, a schoolmaster could earn only £20. Only in rare circumstances was a salary of £30 per annum possible[18]. A young man in Edward Gribbon's linen factory, recently baptised and added to the Baptist congregation, was taking home 7 shillings a week[19]. A porter at the Coleraine Academical Institution was employed for 10 shillings per week[20]. In 1862 average wages in Ulster for men working in agriculture were around 9s. 4d. a week; women might hope for 4s., children under sixteen years of age perhaps 3s. 2d.[21]. Ministers of religion had more reasons to be content. Following the revival William Richey's annual stipend was raised to £115 18s. 2d. Rev. Canning of New Row took home a little more (£148 10s. 10d.) while Rev.

---

17. *Coleraine Chronicle*, 14 January 1860.
18. *Londonderry Journal*, 20 July 1859; *Londonderry Sentinel*, 5 July 1859.
19. *Coleraine Chronicle*, 23 February 1861.
20. Ibid., 21 July 1860.
21. Ibid., 14 June 1862.

Macdonnell of Terrace Row had to be content with £87 19s. 4d.[22]. The total cost of Irish Anglican bishops to the taxpayer was a whopping £67,065 a year, a sum the editor of the Chronicle thought was huge when he considered 'the light duties of the bishops'[23]. The Archbishop of Armagh had £14,494 to spend (£506 less than the Archbishop of Canterbury); the Bishop of Derry a meagre £6,000. The Bishop of Cork must have felt discriminated against on receiving his £2,000. All this paled into insignificance, however, when the cost of the royal family to the nation was considered. In 1846 that family was spending £4,850 on wine alone and a further £2,050 on bread[24]. For the year 1861–2 a total of £385,000 was granted to support the royal household[25]. Charles Dickens, a critic of the 1859 revival in the British Isles, was said to have earned £70,000 in the 1850s from his literary works. Bleak House netted him a profit of £30,000 alone. A speaking tour had earned him a further £20,000[26]. One wonders how these pillars of the establishment managed to spend all this cash swishing around the country at a time when the capitalist machine was generating not only vast fortunes but also indescribable misery. Eternity will reveal whether the 'good things in life' were used selflessly or not.

There were signs of prosperity in Coleraine, too, though not on the scale just described. Throughout the 1850s there was a steady increase in the numbers of Protestants marrying in Ulster, which contrasted with a decrease in the provinces of Leinster, Munster and Connaught[27]. There were 2,136 more marriages in the quarter ending in July 1859 compared with the equivalent quarter in 1858. In fact, the

---

22. *Coleraine Chronicle*, 12 May 1860.
23. Ibid., 22 September 1860 and 25 October 1862.
24. Ibid., 4 July 1847.
25. Ibid., 16 March 1861.
26. Ibid., 27 October 1855, 11 February 1860 and 30 March 1861.
27. Ibid. 5 March 1859.

number of marriages had exceeded the number taking place in any quarter in any of the preceding twelve years. This was clear proof, the Registrar General said, that the country was prospering. The figures suggest growing optimism and confidence. In the first six months of 1859 there were 7,531 more marriages in the whole of Ireland than in the same period in 1858. Over the entire year 301 more marriages took place. For marriages in the whole of Ulster the Tenth Report of the Registrar General gave the following figures:

1857	7,105
1858	6,220
1859	6,532

The figures for the towns were as follows:

	L'derry	Coleraine	Belfast	Lisburn	Ballymena
1857	722	258	821	426	502
1858	626	214	752	361	436
1859	614	228	856	441	440

We record these figures here for some scholars have argued that marriages were being delayed to a later date and that the tensions thereby created were turned to religious objects, resulting in the revival. For economic reasons young women were thus being forced to seek a heavenly bridegroom as men hesitated in posing the question. In fact, overall, more marriages were taking place at an earlier age than had been the case[28]. The increasing numbers of couples marrying in and around Coleraine was an expression of optimism about the future.

---

28. *Coleraine Chronicle*, 1 and 8 September 1860.

LOCAL ISSUES

If one is to take letters to editors seriously there were, throughout the 1850s, three particular problems that angered ratepayers of Coleraine more than anything else. First, the unsanitary state of the streets and pavements was described by one observer as 'more like dung hills than anything else'[29]. Coleraine had become a byword for filthy streets, air filled with an appalling stench. In May 1860 there was a call for a new dog tax to help deal with the nuisance of stray dogs and dog dirt[30]. The town commissioners were repeatedly called upon to do something about the stench caused by blocked sewers and the town's slaughterhouses. Secondly, there had appeared gangs of 'ill-mannered' and 'idle' young men who hung about the main street corners in town. They were often reported to be obstructing footpaths and making indecent remarks at people passing by. Here, too, the commissioners were asked why they were not doing more to rid the streets of the young people who were making Coleraine a 'byword and a disgrace'.[31] Sentences of up to a week's imprisonment were handed down to the youths.[32] Thirdly, 'one of the most disgusting and annoying nuisances in existence', as the Chronicle put it, caused ratepayers' blood pressure to rise. The police were called upon to stamp out what middle-class letter-writers to the Chronicle referred to as 'pernicious begging' and which today is still being attacked by some well-heeled politicians as 'aggressive' begging. 'Pertinacious begging' carried out by 'professional beggars' simply disturbed the peace of mind of the good people of Coleraine who could not even enjoy a day's shopping without being accosted by children in rags.

---

29. *Coleraine Chronicle*, 4 December 1852.
30. Ibid., 12 May 1860.
31. Ibid., 17 June 1854.
32. Ibid., 2 June 1855.

Apart from these three central concerns of the middle classes the local paper made mention of a range of matters of a more popular nature. The *Coleraine Chronicle* carried in the period the kind of story quite familiar to early twenty-first century readers of tabloid newspapers. Death was omnipresent. The paper reported stories about children being mutilated by pigs[33] or rats,[34] fathers being shot by their sons,[35] people dying after swallowing false teeth,[36] boxers dying during prize fights,[37] and reports on mysterious diseases called the 'black sickness' which was causing paralysis in livestock and killing cattle and pigs.[38] One poor individual is said to have died from the 'ravenous eating of biscuits',[39] a contemporary form of suicide by chocolate. In the nineteenth century death was not far from people's minds.

The era saw a revolution in the means of transport, which facilitated a lot of the movement between towns and countries during the revival. On 12 August 1839 the Ulster Railway had been opened.[40] In 1855 the Ballymena, Coleraine and Portrush Railway was opened, the first train leaving on 7 November.[41] The trains, however, ran on the Sabbath and this remained a bone of contention. 'It is melancholy to think of the numbers within the pale of the Presbyterian Church who, either openly or covertly, are abetting the running of trains upon the Sabbath,' reported the Coleraine

33. *Coleraine Chronicle*, 24 September 1853.

34. Ibid., 2 December 1853.

35. Ibid., 4 September 1847.

36. Ibid., 8 June 1861.

37. Ibid., 7 July 1860. Jimmy Reid, a boxer known to those who knew him well as 'The Rat', received a knock-out blow during the last round of a fight in Glasgow from which he never recovered.

38. Ibid., 18 August 1860. Before dying the animals were seen to 'go about moping for days, disinclined to eat their food'. See also the *Belfast News-Letter*, 1 September 1852.

39. *Coleraine Chronicle*, 30 March 1861.

40. Ibid., 14 August 1852.

41. Ibid., 10 November 1855.

Presbytery. 'Under the shadow of this monstrous abuse, or-dinary forms of Sabbath desecration seem quite innocent in the eyes of the ignorant and unthinking, and are engaged in almost without compunction.'[42] At the synod of Ballymena and Coleraine Rev. Orr similarly denounced the writings of Charles Dickens for the 'melancholy picture' the writer was sure to draw of the Sabbath. Dickens exemplified for the synodalists a literary trend which was antagonistic towards a proper observance of the Lord's Day. At the same time they had to admit that there were not a few Christians who could not be happy if they did not have their fresh bread rolls and morning paper first thing on Monday morning and so they, too, had to bear responsibility for encouraging bakers and printers to desecrate the Sabbath.[43] These battles are, of course, still being fought by those who wish to keep Sunday special.

Whatever may be said about Sunday travel, the trains nevertheless facilitated the movement of people, preachers included. Another technological advance, the telegraph, equally facilitated communication of religious news. The laying of telegraph cables under the Atlantic meant that news of the American revival arrived in Ulster within hours of the events, whereas it once took as many as twenty-five days for people in London to know what was happening in, say, India.[44] Scientific progress was an important factor in the spread of the revival.

Various forms of crime were making the headlines. Rev. James O'Hara of St. Patrick's Church received a five-shillings fine from Charles Stewart in 1848 – it had been levied on

---

42. The Report of the Coleraine Presbytery for 1856–7 makes mention of the 'growing familiarity with Sabbath desecration, especially by means of railway travelling'. William Richey, *Connor and Coleraine; or, Scenes and Sketches of the last Ulster Awakening*, vol. I, Belfast 1870, p. 125f.
43. Ibid., 2 May 1857.
44. Ibid., 10 April 1858.

Stewart for 'furious driving' of his car in the bounds of the parish.[45] Apparently, the rector had the right to keep the money. On a more sombre note, 1,960 men were sentenced to terms of imprisonment for assaulting women between 1855 and 1860 – in one third of all cases their own wives (reported on 23 June 1860). Fireworks were in the news at the start of 1858. A fatal explosion occurred at Sheffield in a factory producing 'bangers'. Three dead bodies were found in the ruins.[46] Other lives were being put in danger by young hooligans throwing rocks off railway bridges. In 1858 there had been a 'diabolical attempt' by some 'evil disposed persons' to derail a railway train passing at full speed under a bridge near Ballinagh.[47] Other people were taking their own lives. One domestic servant in Rugby had committed suicide after reading *Tom Brown's Schooldays*.[48] Speeding, domestic violence, accidents with fireworks, throwing bricks and stones at vehicles, and suicide are nothing new.

MEDICAL ADVANCES

It was an age of medical advances and discoveries. The *Chronicle* drew attention to the theory of a doctor that certain diseases could be related to a substance called ozone (9 September 1854). The first operations were conducted under hypnosis in the 1840s. A limb was amputated from Mary Ann Lakin while she was under the influence of 'mesmerism'.[49] In Bushmills a large tumour was removed from the back of a man who was kept under the influence of chloroform. No pain whatsoever was felt, according to the report.[50] A surgeon at Cannock conducted an operation in

---

45. William Richey, *Connor and Coleraine; or, Scenes and Sketches of the last Ulster Awakening,* 21 October 1848.
46. *Londonderry Sentinel,* 12 February 1858.
47. *Londonderry Sentinel,* 5 February 1858.
48. Ibid.
49. *Coleraine Chronicle,* 31 August 1844.
50. Ibid., 6 September 1856.

1857 which involved a blood transfusion. A husband's blood was used to save his wife's life.[51] In 1848, in Ahoghill, Dr Weir used chloroform in an operation to remove a woman's breast affected with cancer. The paper reported that, on awakening, the woman could hardly believe her breast had been removed – 'till it was shown her on a plate'.[52] While excelling in surgical skill the doctor clearly lacked a degree of sensitivity.

Abroad, the Crimean War had been fought between 1854 and 1856, and the Lady with the Lamp pressed hard for reforms in nursing care and health provision. To spread her opinions on reform, Nightingale published two books in 1859: *Notes on Hospitals* and *Notes on Nursing*. In addition to these, her 'Suggestions for Thought to Searchers after Religious Truths' (1859) argued strongly for the removal of restrictions which prevented women having careers. Most women, however, lived lives remote from such thoughts.

A related issue was smoking and its effects. 'Street smoking' was nowhere so 'disgustingly prevalent' in Ireland as in Coleraine, noted one letter-writer[53]. It was, in his view, a detestable practice. Many fashionable people gave themselves over ostentatiously to the habit of whiffing the pipe in public. 'Is smoking an advance in civilisation?' wondered the *English Churchman*. 'We are rapidly becoming a nation of smokers,' a critic claimed. He asked whether 'non-smokers have the right and liberty to enjoy the air which God has given them, uncontaminated by tobacco smoke'. Surely people were aware, he said, that smoking caused 'carcinomatous ulceration' and other health problems.[54] In response to public protests the Belfast and Northern Counties Railway Company had been forced to introduce carriages specially

---

51. *Coleraine Chronicle*, 25 September 1857.
52. Ibid., 23 September 1848.
53. Ibid., 19 May, 26 May and 2 June 1855.
54. Ibid., 11 October 1856.

for passengers who wished to smoke and enjoy 'their weed' without the risk of the forty-shilling penalty for infringement of their rules. In this way the company hoped to minimise the risk of people 'roasting' themselves and their fellow passengers by setting fire accidentally to carriages.[55] This was an issue for churchgoers, too. Hugh Small spoke on the issue of smoking at the Ballymoney Sabbath School Union meeting on 28 July 1851. Apparently, some smokers present at the meeting did not appreciate his comments.[56]

As well as fines for smoking in certain places, money issues were never far from the minds of the Victorians. Fears of a new 'decimal coinage' being introduced were being voiced in July 1853.[57] In February 1862 there was an article on lotteries and the question was asked whether they were justifiable for religious and benevolent objects.[58] The National Teachers' Association meeting in Londonderry in August 1860 resolved to continue its campaign for a living wage. 'Nothing less than £50 per annum is sufficient,' the conference declared. The teachers were particularly worried about the looming pension crisis.[59]

LOCAL POLITICS

In the political realm there was much that called for, but did not receive, closer inspection by journalists. The historian K.T. Hoppen reports that Coleraine was one of the 'leading contenders in the corruption stakes' in the middle of the nineteenth century.[60] Flann Campbell, too, describes Coleraine as a truly 'rotten' borough – as rotten and as notorious as Old Sarum in Wiltshire.[61] The 1832 election seems to have been the occasion of the 'grossest corruption

---

55. *Coleraine Chronicle*, 4 August 1860.
56. Ibid., 2 August 1851.
57. Ibid., 23 July 1853.
58. Ibid., 1 March 1862.
59. Ibid., 1 August 1860.
60. K.T. Hoppen, *Elections, Politics and Society in Ireland 1832–1885*, Oxford 1984, p. 77.
61. Flann Campbell, *The Dissenting Voice. Protestant Democracy in Ulster from Plantation to Partition*, Belfast 1991, 157f, p. 290f.

ever practiced before an election' in the prim little borough.
Votes were openly bought and sold. A Mr Clarke wrote in
the *Chronicle* that a single vote could be sold for between £50
and £500. Many thousands of pounds were spent on bribing
the electorate.[62] In 1859 there were in fact only 274 men in
Coleraine who had the right to vote. A majority had to be
won over by hook or by crook – or by whiskey. Fortunately
and symbolically, the polling booth was at Mehan's spirit
store in Bridge Street.[63] The dreadful moral state of politics
had not a little to do with the sitting MP for Coleraine,
Dr Boyd. He was a rather undisciplined member of First
Presbyterian Church in Coleraine. His face was 'blotched by
indulgence in drinking'[64] and he milked the political system
for all it was worth. His power was based on the fact that
he owned more than half the property in the borough.[65] In
a letter to Lord Naas in 1852 Boyd reported that he had
received sixty-two begging letters within a ten-day period
asking him to arrange for all kinds of job appointments,
from 'livings in the Church down to the tidewaitership'.[66]
According to Lord Eglinton, Viceroy in 1858–9, the
Presbyterian wire-puller made 'endless demands' which
were handled at the highest levels of British society.[67] This
was a reputation the Earl of Derby, Prime Minister in 1852
and 1858, was well aware of.[68] The *Chronicle* described him as
'a gentleman holding strong Conservative opinions' whose
influence among the electors was so great that 'no man
could under ordinary circumstances successfully contest
with him the representation of Coleraine.'[69] Boyd held the

---

62. *Coleraine Chronicle*, 8 December 1855.
63. Ibid., 14 May 1859.
64. T.H. Mullin, *Coleraine in Modern Times*, Belfast 1979, p. 8.
65. *Coleraine Chronicle*, 11 January 1862.
66. K.T. Hoppen, *Elections, Politics and Society in Ireland 1832–1885*, p. 77.
67. Ibid. p. 303.
68. Ibid.
69. *Coleraine Chronicle*, 17 March 1857.

seat from 1842 to 1862. In 1852 he agreed to step down to endorse the candidature of his fellow Freemason, Lord Naas, thus guaranteeing the latter's election.[70] Otherwise, Boyd was a man who liked the taste and privileges of power. But he was not the only corrupting influence in Coleraine. An anonymous writer to the *Chronicle* in 1854 thought it a 'singular coincidence' that everyone employed in or around the Coleraine Post Office had the surname McCandless. Surely, he wrote, this was 'without parallel in any other post-office in Ireland'.[71] Indeed, Coleraine was a prim little borough full of corruption.

Many of the issues highlighted in this chapter are still very topical. Human interest stories have been with us for many generations and will always be able to sell newspapers. There is nothing new under the sun, claims the proverb. In many ways the concerns of people in 1859 differed little from those which plague people in our own day. This should not surprise anyone. The human condition, and predicament, in its most essential aspect remains unchanged. Societal change is only superficial. The human heart remains desperately wicked and selfish. While the social factors impinging upon the human drama evolve over time, the essence of that drama is timeless. The Bible gives expression, of course, to this truth and, for that reason too, ever remains relevant and authoritative. In every generation there are some who turn to those Scriptures seeking the solution to society's woes. The revival gave expression to a thirst for God and a longing for God to reveal His character and power in a situation perceived to be grave. Initially, the movement was not about adding numbers to congregations, but about Him and His glory. The primary goal was a revived church; the secondary effect a rekindled love for those outside the

---

70. B.M. Walker (ed.), *Parliamentary Election Results in Ireland 1801–1922*, Dublin 1978, 76.82.89.
71. *Coleraine Chronicle*, 29 July 1854.

bounds of the Christian church. This was the case in the mid-1850s in the USA and throughout much of Britain and Ireland.

Kells, the epicentre of the 1859 revival in Ulster, had 231 inhabitants, Connor 242, Ahoghill 508.[72] It is worth bearing these numbers in mind when one reads of monster meetings taking place in various towns in the north which encompassed many thousands of attentive listeners. Coleraine had a population of 5,631 according to the census of 1861. Of these 1,524 were Anglicans, 1,455 Catholics, 2,178 Presbyterians, 202 Methodists, 127 Baptists, 113 Independents (Congregationalists) and 29 belonged to other religious groupings.[73] In other words, about 40 per cent of the population was Presbyterian and a quarter was Catholic. In 1859 these people received a visit from Almighty God and the whole of society was impacted.

72. *The Census of Ireland. Part IV: Reports*, Dublin 1863; R. Wynne's *Business Directory of Belfast, etc. 1865–1866*, p. 277.
73. McComb's *Presbyterian Almanack and Christian Remembrancer 1862*, p. 72.

Chapter 2: The Religious Context

In his book on Ulster Presbyterianism Peter Brooke claims the 1859 revival was a 'planned event', planned by ministers who felt their communities and congregations were slipping out of their grasp. Kirk sessions would or could no longer enforce discipline at a time when many members' lives were being unsettled as the rurally-based cottage industry was making room for factory production. Revivalism, in his view, was a 'human technique' to restore ministerial influence in a changing society.[1] In this perspective the 1859 revival was a 'cathartic purging of the emotions' of the Presbyterian community, resulting in numerous conversion experiences which, he argues, had never been part of the Scottish Presbyterian tradition.

REVIVALISM AND PRESBYTERIANISM

In fact Presbyterianism did have a revivalist tradition. Within the church there had always flowed a stream of religious enthusiasm for the things of God. There had always been ministers and lay people who expected great things from God in their own generation and undertook great things for God. In fact, the first important incident occurring in the history of the Presbyterian Church in Ulster, seventeen years before the first presbytery was set up at Carrickfergus, was the Six

---

1.   Peter Brooke, *Ulster Presbyterianism. The Historical Perspective 1610–1970*, New York 1987, pp. 191–2.

Mile Water revival in Antrim in 1625. In that year a wave of excitement spread along the Six Mile Water – the very district which spawned the 1859 revival. Indeed, Robert Allen refers to this area as 'the cradle of Irish Presbyterianism'.[2] There were numerous similarities between the two revivals which at least one observer of the later revival emphasised.[3] An historian of early Irish Presbyterianism, Rev. Andrew Stewart of Donegore, stated in this period that 'multitudes were brought to understand their way and to cry out, Men and brethren, what shall we do to be saved?' One description of a meeting in Antrim in 1625 might have been used with equal validity to the events of 1859 in Coleraine: 'I have seen them [converts] myself stricken into a swoon with the word; yea, a dozen in one day carried out of doors as dead, so marvellous was the power of God smiting their hearts for sin, condemning and killing. And of these were none of the weaker sex or spirit, but indeed some of the boldest spirits, who formerly feared not with their swords to put a whole market-town in a fray.'[4] The 1625 revival was, initially, the product of the fire-and-brimstone preaching of Rev. James Glendinning, who became incumbent at Oldstone in that year. He preached to them nothing but the law and hundreds asked: 'What must we do to be saved?' Now here arose a problem, for Glendinning did not apparently know what the answer to that question was.[5] The instrument chosen to begin the work of revival in 1625 was, according to Stewart's record, a man 'who would never have been chosen by a wise assembly of ministers', for he was 'little better than distracted; yea, afterwards, did actually become so'. Critics of the 1859 revival would also draw attention to the

---

2. W.D. Baillie, *The Six Mile Water Revival of 1625* [Presbyterian Historical Society], Belfast 1976, p. 24.
3. Dr Weir of Islington, quoted in R.M. Sibbett, *The Revival in Ulster or the Life Story of a Worker*, Belfast 1909, p. 26.
4. J.S. Reid, *History of the Presbyterian Church in Ireland*, i , Belfast 1867, p. 108.
5. W.D. Baillie, *The Six Mile Water Revival of 1625*, p. 9.

supposed cases of madness resulting from religious fervour. Robert Blair describes Glendinning as a very eccentric man holding rather odd opinions. In the end he ran away 'to see the seven churches of Asia'.[6] Whether this meant he went completely mad or just went on an extended holiday to Turkey remains unclear. In 1859 the key men and women in the revival were not hand-picked by a General Assembly or a Methodist Conference; in all likelihood, the revivalist preachers would have been rejected as unworthy. When in 1834 Reid published the first volume of his monumental *History of the Presbyterian Church in Ireland*, he hoped to refocus ministers' minds on an authentic Irish Presbyterian tradition of revival. The original sermon upon which the book was based was an exposition of Revelation 2:5: 'Remember therefore from whence thou art fallen' (KJV). Reid believed something was missing from the churches of his day – an important tradition had been forgotten.

Ulster Scots have also played notable roles in the many revivals that have visited the United States. In her doctoral dissertation on Scots-Irish piety, which, significantly, was titled *Triumph of the Laity*, Marilyn J. Westerkamp has explained how the eighteenth-century Great Awakening in the mid-Atlantic colonies of north America had its roots in Scots-Irish revivalism. This awakening was, she says, 'but one development in a long-standing revivalist tradition' amongst Ulster people.[7] While revivalism may have shocked some university-trained ministers of religion there was nothing in that tradition which would have inherently shocked simple country folk.

SOCIAL CONTROL

A second issue Peter Brooke raises is the loss of social influence experienced by Presbyterian ministers. As far as Col-

---

6.   W.D. Baillie, Ibid. p. 10.
7.   Marilyn J. Westerkamp, *Triumph of the Laity*. New York: Oxford 1988.

eraine is concerned there is in fact some evidence for this trend. Numerous sermons against the evils of drink and Sabbath desecration do not seem to have had a deep impact on the behavioural patterns of more than a handful of town dwellers. In its 1855 report on the state of religion, a committee reported to the Synod of Ballymena and Coleraine that family worship was much neglected and 'profaneness, Sabbath desecration by railway travelling and other forms, intemperance and other kindred vices [...] prevail to a lamentable extent'.[8] The report also drew attention to 'a large outlying population' unreached by the gospel. Saturday markets and fairs were also reducing attendance at the meeting houses and chapels on Sundays, said Rev. Canning of New Row Presbyterian Church, Coleraine. Manual labourers were simply worn-out after six days of work. Those who attended markets and fairs were not uncommonly suffering from a hangover at the normal time of worship. A response was called for. The Protestant ministers in the town had been fighting an uphill struggle ever since the famine to counteract what they saw as twin evils. In December 1848 twenty-five ministers from the town and district, representing all denominations, had signed a petition addressed to the chairman of the Town Commissioners, calling for a public meeting to discuss the question of moving the market day to a Friday in the hope of bringing about 'the proper observance of the Lord's Day'.[9] It was clear from the letters pages in the *Chronicle* that the business community – strongly Presbyterian itself, and with an eye on profit margins – was opposed to any change. One shopkeeper warned the Commissioners 'not to be guided solely or in part by the pious prating of a few clergymen'.[10] When the public meeting did eventually take place, not half of the ministers

---

8.   *Coleraine Chronicle*, 19 May 1855.
9.   Ibid., 16 December 1848.
10. Ibid., 23 December 1848.

who had signed the petition turned up to discuss it. The *Chronicle* noted, however, that hundreds of 'the very lowest of the population' densely packed the Court House and of these about one third was drunk, and half the rest 'seemed in the horrors after the debauch of the double Sabbath they had enjoyed on Sunday and Christmas Day'. The meeting, not surprisingly, was just 'one scene of shouting and yell-ing' from beginning to end. Worse, many participants had gone prepared to 'pelt the clergy' off the benches they were sitting on. None of the ministers could handle 'the savage yells of a drunken mob'. A counter-petition was signed by 155 of the most influential citizens in town including, natu-rally, Dr Boyd. In spite of repeated attempts throughout the 1850s – on 21 May 1856 a huge public meeting was actu-ally held in Second Presbyterian Church to discuss the is-sue of Sabbath observance and temperance – the Protestant ministers could not even persuade their own parishioners that the business done at markets on Saturdays was of less importance than the business done at the meeting house on the Sabbath.

Not only in the economic sphere, but also in the cultural arena attempts were made to impose restrictions and con-trols on human behaviour. In 1855 theatrical performances staged at the Town Hall came under evangelical scrutiny, highlighting in the process the limits of their influence. Once again democratic means were employed to make their position known. A petition was signed by all three Presby-terian ministers, two Methodist ministers, the rector of the Parish church, the two most influential Baptists in the town and a host of respectable elders – sixty-eight signatures in all. Their spokesman was the Rev. William Richey of First Presbyterian. The petitioners expressed their opposition to the 'immoral tendency' and 'pernicious influence' of certain artistic productions on the minds and morals of the young. Richey blamed the decline and fall of Athens on its love for the stage and called for a ban on theatres in the province. He took particular offence at the fact that females sometimes dressed up as men, playing male parts. Such gender-changing behaviour, being 'abominable in the sight of the Lord', had to stop. Also offensive were the so-called tableaux vivants – pictures revealing, for example, Adam's first sight of Eve.[11] In spite of active lobbying, the petition was rejected by the Town Commissioners – admittedly, by a small majority. What the campaign showed was all kinds of opposition to political action by Christians which was geared to shaping the cultural life of the town. There seemed to be a widespread feeling that politics, economics and culture were not the realms for which ministers of religion carried responsibility.

EVANGELICALISM

Apart from a clear recognition that all was not well in Protestant Ulster certain important changes had taken place within the fold of Presbyterianism, which in some ways prepared congregations for the revival of 1859. Of first importance was the campaign led by Henry Cooke against liberal, 'Arian' theological trends within the Synod of Ulster and the Belfast Academical Institution. It was in Coleraine in June 1825 that Cooke had declared his intentions: 'We must put down Arianism or Arianism will put us down.' The controversy came to a climax in 1827 with the evangelicals and fundamentalists winning the day. At the 1828 Cookstown Synod ninety-nine ministers and forty elders voted in favour of excluding all candidates for the ministry who held Arian or other unsound opinions.[12] Forty ministers and seventeen elders voted against the motion. This theological struggle for influence was symptomatic of what has been called the 'evangelical revival' within Irish Presbyterianism. It went

---

11. *Coleraine Chronicle*, 12 May 1855.
12. Thomas Hamilton, *History of the Irish Presbyterian Church*, Edinburgh 1887, chapter 16.

hand in hand with a growing interest in the idea of missions. In 1812 several leading ministers had denounced the idea of converting the heathen as 'absurd and visionary'.[13] This negative stance towards active conversionist behaviour was seriously undermined by the growing strength of evangelicalism and, once the 292 congregations of the Synod of Ulster, and the 141 Secession congregations, were united by the Act of Union on 10 July 1840, there was a surge of evangelistic and moral reform movements. Almost the first act of the united body was the establishment of a Foreign Mission Board and the appointment of two missionaries to India.[14] There followed the Jewish Mission (1842), the Colonial Mission (1846) and the Continental Mission (1856). But evangelistic, conversionist endeavours, rooted in and built upon a biblical hermeneutic, did not come into existence in 1840. Way back in 1710 the General Fund had been set up to finance the preaching of the gospel in Irish to the Irish-speaking population in the south of Ireland. In 1798 the Evangelical Society was formed to support itinerant preaching throughout the north of the island. The Seceders had organised a Home Mission in 1818 which set up preaching stations in areas where Presbyterianism had not yet taken root. Eight years later, the Synod of Ulster followed suit, establishing the Home Missionary Society and, in 1830, the Presbyterian Missionary Society. Within a thirty-year period mission and evangelism had moved from the sidelines to centre-stage. This development was clearly of crucial importance for the growth of popular revivalism.

Worthy of mention in this context are the close links between Ireland and Scotland. Robert Murray McCheyne of Dundee had facilitated the establishment of a mission to the Jews. The disruption within the Church of Scotland

---

13. Thomas Hamilton, Ibid., p. 147.
14. Thomas Hamilton, Ibid., p. 168.

and the setting up of a Free Church of Scotland was followed closely by Irish Presbyterians. The simultaneous revivals at Kilsyth and Dundee, and elsewhere in Scotland, 'told powerfully and most beneficially upon the ministers and people of Ulster', according to Rev. William Richey of First Coleraine.[15]

OPEN-AIR PREACHING

Long before the Evangelical Society called for a system of itinerant preaching in 1798, Ulster had been exposed to such missionary enthusiasm. The Moravian missions attracted a lot of attention in Coleraine. There was, in fact, a Coleraine Auxiliary to the London Association for Moravian Missions. Its president was the rector of the parish church of St. Patrick's, James O'Hara, and its secretary, William Richey. In 1853 it remitted £19 8s 8d to London, of which £10 was used to support a Moravian school in Jamaica (which was, incidentally, called the Coleraine School).[16] The Moravians, or United Brethren, trace the origin of their work in Ireland to an ex-Methodist called John Cennick, who in the middle of the eighteenth century began to preach to crowds in fields. Numbers at these meetings grew to as many as three thousand by 1746. Through open-air preaching he and others established congregations all around Lough Neagh and, in 1765, erected a church on the lands of Ballykennedy that became the centre of the settlement they would rename Gracehill. Apart from teaching people the doctrines of Scripture they are said to have taught the people of that district many practical skills such as the most advanced methods of storing potatoes.[17] The

---

15. William Richey, *Connor and Coleraine; or Scenes and Sketches of the last Ulster Awakening*, volume I, Belfast 1870, p. 96. See also *Narratives of Revivals of Religion in Scotland, Ireland and Wales*, Glasgow 1839 [Reprint Belfast 1989].

16. *Coleraine Chronicle*, 24 December 1853.

17. *Coleraine Chronicle*, 11 February 1854.

Gracehill Moravian Academy for Young Gentlemen celebrated its fiftieth anniversary in 1855.[18]

Baptists were also itinerating over the fields of Ireland. John West had arrived in the country in 1811 to minister to a small congregation in Waterford.[19] A start had been made. Two full-time evangelists were ordained on 30 May 1813 and appointed to work under the auspices of the Baptist Itinerant Society in the Dublin area. Isaac McCarthy, a fluent Irish speaker, travelled 20,000 miles in his first four years of working for the Baptist Irish Society.[20] Under his preaching some Baptist churches experienced revival. Between 1804 and 1846 thirty-eight churches were formed in Ireland. Around Coleraine there were five additional preaching stations in Spittlehill, Knowhead, Crossgare, Articlave and Ballymoney.[21] Apart from the Moravians, the Baptists also contributed to the movement to evangelise Ireland.

Even more important than the work of the Moravians and the Baptists in spreading interest in open-air evangelism was the Methodist revival in the late eighteenth century. Here, too, itinerant preachers were the key to growth. The first society of Methodists in Ireland seems to have been formed in Dublin in August 1847.[22] 'Revivalism' was their trademark. Crookshank, the historian of Irish Methodism, can name over seventy revivals in Methodist circuits which took place between 1820 and 1858. By 1858 there were nearly 19,500 Wesleyan Methodists and over 9,000 Primitive Methodists in Ireland. The latter group, in particular, attracted much popular and working-class appeal, not least because straight-talking laymen often led their

---

18. Ibid., 4 August 1855.
19. D.P. Kingdon, *Baptist Evangelism in 19th Century Ireland*, Baptist Union 1965, p. 9.
20. Ibid., pp. 12–13.
21. *The Baptist Irish Society – Its Origin, History and Claims*, n.p. 1845, p. 21.
22. *Ordnance Survey of the County of Londonderry*, volume I, Dublin 1837, p. 73f.; *A Brief Account of the Origin and Progress of Methodism… By a Methodist in Colerain* [sic], Belfast 1827.

groups. The impact, moreover, of Methodism on members of the Church of Ireland cannot be overestimated. It helped nurture biblically vibrant groups within the establishment.

The first Methodist to preach on the streets of Coleraine was probably John Price in 1772. Two years later a Methodist society was formed. The father of Methodism, John Wesley, visited and preached in Coleraine on a number of occasions between 1778 and 1789 and he once said that Coleraine Methodists were a society just after his own heart – 'in spirit, in carriage and even in dress'.[23] Rev. Adam Averell, too, spoke of the town's 'most warm-hearted, loving, deeply devoted society'. Everything in Coleraine, he said, 'wears the semblance of primitive Christianity'.[24] In September 1854 the group moved to their current premises and after Robert G. Cather took charge of the Coleraine circuit in 1856 the congregation grew steadily.[25] The Methodist general missionary, Robert Hewitt, spent a week in Coleraine in 1857 labouring in connection with the Methodist-inspired and Methodist-directed town mission. This had been set up to reach the 'mass of people living in ignorance and sin'. At the first two meetings twenty people were converted.[26] These evangelistic services were held in rented accommodation in Killowen, in Brook Street, in Stone Row and Long Commons and attracted up to one hundred people every evening.[27] Hewitt laboured in Coleraine during the whole revival period. Between 1855 and 1860 he travelled

---

23. Nehemiah Curnoch (ed.), *The Journal of the Rev. John Wesley A.M.*, London n.d., vol. vi, p. 195f.; vol. vii, pp. 88, 286, 504; *A History of Methodism in Coleraine, from its introduction till about the year 1820; with notices of many of the early Methodists, and numerous extracts from the MMS. Journals of John Galt, Esq., late of Coleraine*, Coleraine 1870; C.H. Crookshank, *History of Methodism in Ireland*, volume iii, London 1888, p. 460.
24. Alexander Stewart and George Rivington, *Memoir of the Life and Labours of the Rev. Adam Averell*, Dublin 1848, p. 117.
25. C.H. Crookshank, History of Methodism in Ireland, volume iii, p. 478.
26. C.H. Crookshank, Ibid., volume iii , p. 490.
27. C.H. Crookshank, Ibid., volume iii, p. 478.

16,000 miles around Ulster, visiting 1,237 places, where he preached 1,724 times at 1,552 meetings. He distributed 23,155 books and tracts which had cost nearly £19 in total. He claimed thousands had been converted as a result of these endeavours.[28]

Hewitt had the full support of the minister at Coleraine. Rev. Cather was keen to hold so-called 'field meetings' – on Dunmull Hill, for example – for those who had become alienated from the churches. At one such meeting in 1857 over 1,400 people listened to the Word of God being preached.[29] There was clearly considerable demand for meetings where people did not need to dress up, but were free to wear whatever clothes they wished. But the preachers did not wait for people to come to them. The Town Missionary, John Mills, carried out a house-to-house visitation amongst the poorest of the poor. Four hundred and thirty families were visited in the first year of the Town Mission (from February 1857 to February 1858), and he had prolonged talks with 1,184 adults and 700 juveniles during this time. Two hundred and thirty of these families had no church connections whatsoever.[30] Mr Mills talked in his first annual report of several remarkably interesting conversions, including the conversions of five prostitutes.[31] In Coleraine at that time there was complex of streets and lanes in Killowen, known to local residents as Cabul, where every second house was a brothel. There were also brothels in Shambles Lane, which is rather interesting given that the street today is known as Abbey Street, not too far away from two churches. Mr Mills reached out to these women and, at the same time, helped mobilise his fellow Methodists to deal with the causes of the vice. The Methodist Society set up a 'ragged school' in

28. *The Irish Evangelist*, June 1860, pp. 70–1.
29. C.H. Crookshank, *History of Methodism in Ireland*, volume iii, p. 490. See also *Coleraine Chronicle*, 31 July 1858 and 7 August 1858.
30. *Coleraine Chronicle*, 13 March 1858.
31. Ibid., 2 January 1858.

1857, for example, to rescue children from the corrupting influences of their environment. Within a year 110 children were being provided with a rudimentary education, free meals (2,802 meals were dished up in the first year) and free clothes.[32] Rev. Cather put his motto into action: 'A house-going priest made a church-going people.' If people did not go to church, then he and his fellow church members had to go out to the people. It is perhaps therefore significant that it was a Methodist evangelist, William Graham Campbell, stationed at Antrim, who seems to have been instrumental in the conversion, in the autumn of 1857, of James McQuilkin, the man reputed to have been the first convert of the Ulster revival.[33] The very same evangelist preached to a large crowd in the Diamond of Coleraine on 7 June 1856, exactly three years before the first revival meeting in the town.[34] All this work done by zealous Methodists helped prepare the way for revival, and the field meetings were the precursors of the 1859 revival meetings.

Class Divisions

The impact of the itinerant Moravian, Baptist and Method-ist preachers did not fail to impress Presbyterians at a time when there was a growing realization that large sections of the Ulster population had little or no exposure to the Word of God. At a meeting of the Belfast Town Mission in 1859 the Rev. Robert Knox claimed there were 20,000 Protes-tants in that town alone – which boasted a total population of nearly 98,000[35] – who never attended a house of wor-ship.[36] This was no less the case in Coleraine. The report on

---

32. *Coleraine Chronicle*, 13 March 1858.
33. I.R.K. Paisley, *The 'Fifty Nine' Revival*, Belfast 1981, p. 14f; Jack Henry, *A Door That Opened. Rev. John Galway McVicker and the Founding of Bal-lymena Baptist Church*, Ballymena 1989, p. 18; Alfred R. Scott, *The Ulster Revival of 1859*, p. 52.
34. *Coleraine Chronicle*, 14 June 1856.
35. *Coleraine Chronicle*, 29 April 1854.
36. Ibid., 26 November 1859.

the state of religion presented to the Coleraine Presbytery in May 1853 noted that 'the small farmers, and generally the humbler classes of Presbyterians, were frequently unable to procure decent apparel, considered by them as indispensable for attending public ordinances; they were unable to contribute to congregational funds, and, from a feeling of false delicacy, forsook the house of worship.'[37] Doubtless many of these 'humbler classes' had been made at one time or another to feel that certain clothes and a certain degree of cleanliness were in fact deemed necessary to mingle with the respectable tenant farmers and shopkeepers who made up the main body of Presbyterian churchgoers. In 1859 the trustees of New Row Presbyterian Church were made up of six merchants, two doctors, one builder, one woollen draper, one grocer, one shoemaker and two 'gentlemen', one of whom was a bank manager.[38] The newly appointed trustees in 1861 comprised seven merchants, two Justices of the Peace, one farmer and one bookkeeper. Such people would have had very little social contact with the labouring classes except in their role, perhaps, as employer or magistrate.

Class divisions were still very real. The census of 1841 tells us that 17.5 per cent of the population of Coleraine were completely illiterate (a lower percentage than in Ballymena or Belfast), which would have presumably caused problems or at least embarrassment when hymns were sung.[39] The editor of the *Coleraine Chronicle* expressed his shock at learning in March 1859 that, even in the Presbyterian province of Ulster, more than half the women and nearly a third of the men could not append their signatures to the marriage deeds, but were forced to draw the sign of the cross instead.[40] What use would such people have for Bibles

---

37. Ibid., 28 May 1853.
38. 'Record of the Appointment and Names of Trustees of New Row,' 5 March 1861. PRONI M/C IP/31, Vol. VII.
39. *The Census of Ireland for the Year 1841*, Dublin 1843, xxxiii.
40. *Coleraine Chronicle*, 5 March 1859.

and hymn-books? How could these multitudes be reached if they were too ashamed (or if their fellow Presbyterians put them to shame) to turn up at the meeting house in ragged clothes? If they were free from the obligations of work on one day of the week, would they really want to mingle with their employers and landlords?

The disparity between the comfortable middle classes and the deprivation of the toiling working classes was plain for all to see. Industrialisation was polarising society. Increasingly, those working in the sweat of their brows found they had neither time nor energy nor even a desire to walk to meeting houses and chapels on a Sunday. One section of the baptised reverted to heathen practices while another section watched in bewilderment or indifference. Rev. William Richey produced a tract entitled *Home Heathenism: A Plea for the Perishing*, which called upon Christians to 'search out and endeavour to alleviate and remove the abounding misery and vice of a careless world'. The *Banner of Ulster* called it an appeal to the church to 'awake from its lethargy'. The churches did not seem to be in a fit spiritual state to deal with the immense challenge of modernity.

PRESBYTERIAN RESPONSE

A committee of twelve Presbyterians, convened by Rev. J. Johnston of Tullylish (near Banbridge), set out in 1851 to remedy this situation. They encouraged ministers to go out in pairs and, having chosen a place near the centre of a town, to hold a discourse of 'a solemn and awakening character'. Ministers were advised to choose an hour in the evening that would be 'most convenient for the working classes'.[41] The committee recognised this was a work 'alien to the natural disposition of even Ministers' (*sic!*).[42] There

---

41. *Second Annual Report of Special efforts by Presbyterian Ministers to propagate the Gospel in the North of Ireland, in 1852, by means of Open-Air Preaching*, Newry 1853, p. 23.
42. Ibid, p. 5.

were only eight volunteers in 1851, but by 1857 sixty-three ministers of the gospel were involved in this outreach to the unwashed and unsaved.[43] By 1859 well over 100,000 people would have heard one of these 'awakening' discourses.

Rev. Johnston himself, the initiator of the movement, preached to about two hundred people in a destitute locality in Coleraine in 1852, supported by the Revds Richey and Canning, of First and Second Presbyterian respectively. It became a regular feature of church life in the summer months. The Synod of Ballymena and Coleraine reported in 1857 that eleven ministers within the synod had engaged in this evangelistic work; 16,000 people had heard addresses at fifty-eight open-air meetings.[44] In 1854 Rev. Canning preached on a number of Sunday evenings in Long Commons, while his colleague Richey delivered sermons at the corner of New Row to what the *Chronicle* describes as a 'numerous and deeply attentive audience'.[45] Two years later Richey was reported preaching at Downhill and in Derry; in August 1858 various spots in Coleraine became his pulpit.[46] At Ahoghill, which was to become a centre of the revival just a few years later, open-air activity began on 20 June 1854. Rev. Adams created considerable excitement in the village of 508 inhabitants and distributed a lot of tracts at the end of the meeting.[47] The *Chronicle* quotes one person, whom it calls one of the 'most destitute class', as saying after the meeting: 'Thank God the minister has made it plain to poor ignorant creatures' like himself.

The very novelty of Presbyterian ministers standing on street corners, often in a poor part of town, preaching the message of salvation seems to have been enough to draw large crowds. Whether they turned up to listen or for

---

43. Myrtle Hill, 'Ulster Awakened', in *Journal of Ecclesiastical History*, p. 41 (1990), No. 3 (July), p. 445.
44. *Coleraine Chronicle*, 23 May 1857.
45. Ibid., 9 September 1854.
46. Ibid., 26 July 1856 and 21 August 1858.
47. Ibid., 24 June 1854.

the entertainment value is difficult to ascertain. Crucially, however, interest in religious topics was generated.

LAY PREACHING

Equally novel, and still more controversial, were public talks by laymen. The debate on the role of laymen in church life was being carried on throughout England, Scotland and Ireland at this time. In Scotland the Haldane brothers had pioneered lay preaching in modern times and, in 1856, John Brownlow North (1810–75), son of the rector of Alverstoke, Hampshire, and grand-nephew of Prime Minister Lord North, continued the tradition.[48] Rev. Dr Cooke, the leader of evangelical Presbyterians in Ulster at the time, claimed that Brownlow North was 'one of the best theologians', whose preaching of Christ for Christ's sake led many to open their hearts to the gospel.[49] Thousands crowded to hear him preach from pulpits in all the main Protestant denominations in the period under consideration. In 1856 he was working in the north-east of Scotland[50]. 'Lay preachers are again at work', noted the *Chronicle*, 'and the ranks of the wealthy and the noble are again harnessed to stir up the very depths of our Christian sympathies and prepare the way for better times.'[51] In 1859, at the General Assemblies of the Free Church of Scotland and the Presbyterian Church in Ireland, Brownlow North was given the right hand of fellowship and formally sanctioned to preach the gospel.[52] He shared a platform in Portstewart in August 1859 with Dr Cooke, Rev. Henry Grattan Guinness and

---

48. Brownlow North's desire to preach in Ireland had not a little to do with the fact that he was married to Grace Anne Coffey, daughter of Rev. Thomas Coffey of Galway.

49. K. Moody-Stuart, *Brownlow North. His life and work*, London 1961, p. 117.

50. Kenneth S. Jeffrey, *When the Lord Walked the Land. The 1858–62 Revival in the North East of Scotland*, Carlisle 2002, pp. 53, 56f.

51. *Coleraine Chronicle*, 29 August 1857.

52. *Coleraine Chronicle*, 4 June and 2 July 1859; *Londonderry Sentinel*, 15 July 1859.

William Moore, a local landowner-preacher.[53] On the Dunmull Hill near Portrush he rubbed shoulders on 14 August
with two other laymen, Messrs McQuilkin and Meneely of
Connor fame. An 'immense congregation' of between seven
and eight thousand people gathered on the hill that was celebrated as a place of worship in 1859.[54] Of this latter meeting Rev. Jonathan Simpson (Portrush) wrote that it was 'the
noblest meeting ever seen in the neighbourhood; the very
sight was grand, apart from its bearings upon eternity.'[55]
So many people were 'stricken' that day that 'the people in
the neighbouring houses never got to bed the entire night'.
Simpson added: 'It were worth living ten thousand ages in
obscurity and reproach to be permitted to creep forth at the
expiration of that time, and engage in the glorious work of
the last six months of 1859.'[56] It was his view that the lay
preaching of Brownlow North had contributed immeasur-
ably to the revival movement. During his two-month stay in
Ireland from the end of June to the end of August, Brownlow North delivered about fifty addresses to crowds numbered in their thousands.[57] Some of these addresses – on
the parable of the rich man and Lazarus (Luke 16: 19-31)
– were published by the Banner of Truth Trust in 1960.[58]

Directly and indirectly Brownlow North excited interest
for evangelism and prayer for revival. One Scottish woman
who was visiting friends in Limavady in the summer of 1859
had heard Brownlow North preach in Rev. George Steen's
meeting-house. Initially she had mocked the revival but
was mightily impressed by North's message. In a letter to
Brownlow North dated 17 August, 1859, Steen related that

53. *Londonderry Sentinel*, 12 August 1859.
54. *Coleraine Chronicle*, 13 August and 20 August 1859.
55. K. Moody-Stuart, *Brownlow North*, p. 148.
56. Ibid., p. 149.
57. Ibid., pp. 146–53.
58. Brownlow North, *The Rich Man and Lazarus*, London 1960.

this woman was now 'praying most anxiously for Scotland, that the Lord may make it like the north of Ireland'.[59]

Yet another Scottish layman who helped galvanise support for the movement was John McCombie, editor and proprietor of the *Coleraine Chronicle* – the leading regional newspaper in terms of copies sold weekly. The paper experienced a 'most unexpected increase' in subscriptions once the revival had begun in Coleraine. One thousand two hundred copies were being sold weekly in October 1859. This represented a 25 per cent increase since the beginning of 1857.[60] McCombie was a native of Ross-shire – the scene of a revival in the eighteenth century.[61] He was a member of the Free Church of Scotland, the most pro-revival of denominations in Scotland.[62]

In the Coleraine area two laymen in particular made the headlines. William Moore of Moorefort gave 'lectures' throughout the decade in the Carryreagh schoolhouse, which was built on his own property. These talks were very popular and proved, the *Chronicle* supposed, that the days were over when it would have been considered an infringement on pastoral duty if a layman 'had had the boldness or temerity to speak publicly or lecture on religious matters'.[63] Weekly lectures or sermons were held on a Sunday evening and Moore was zealous in instilling into the minds of the rising generation 'the inestimable truths contained in the Bible'.[64] The lectures seemed 'exactly suited to awaken slumbering Christians'.[65] Moore's status as a landlord and magistrate gave him considerable influence over a wide audience. The crowds that turned up to hear Moore reminded ob-

---

59. K. Moody-Stuart, *Brownlow North*, p. 152.

60. *Coleraine Chronicle*, 17 September and 5 November 1859.

61. Steve Bruce, 'Social change and collective behaviour: the revival in eighteenth-century Ross-shire,' *The British Journal of Sociology*, vol. xxxiv, Nr. 4, pp. 554–72.

62. *Coleraine Chronicle*, 18 September 1852.

63. Ibid., 3 December 1853 and 3 March 1855.

64. *Coleraine Chronicle*, 15 October 1853.

65. Ibid., 3 March 1855.

servers of the Methodist George Whitefield and his meetings in the previous century.[66]

In June 1856 William Moore opened his home at Moore-fort to a certain Mr Charles H. Mackintosh, who had been preaching in the Diamond and the Town Hall in Coleraine.[67] The two men preached on the streets of Tubbermore (as the name was spelt at that time) and at a fair in the town in May 1858. A correspondent of the *Chronicle* called them 'devoted servants of God [who] esteem it a privilege to travel from town to town preaching to their fellow men'. The messages were 'powerful exhibitions of the gospel plan of salvation'.[68] The work of these two men in Coleraine is significant because Mackintosh was to become one of the chief men of the Brethren in Coleraine.[69] By August 1857 at the latest a Brethren's Room at 4, Church Street was being used for outreach. This lay-led movement originated in Dublin and not the town of Plymouth, which was to be for ever linked in the popular mind with the Brethren. The gifted and, in part, wealthy individuals who steered the movement in its early days contributed much to revival preparations and were one of the groups that most benefited from the movement of 1859. In 1830 John Parnell, later to become Lord Congleton, rented a cabinet-maker's room in Aungier Street in Dublin to meet with other brethren around the Word. Through the influence of the ex-Anglican vicar John N. Darby the ideas of the Brethren spread to many other towns in Ireland and Britain.[70] One of those towns was Bristol, where the Prussian-born George Müller organised an assembly in the 1830s and founded his world-famous orphan house. Müller was already reasonably well-known in

66. Ibid., 24 December 1853.
67. Ibid., 14 June 1856.
68. Ibid., 15 May 1858.
69. Ibid., 24 February 1862.
70. *The Principles of Christians called 'Open Brethren'*, London and New York 1913, pp. 87–95.

Ulster by 1859 and needs to be mentioned for at least one reason. The above-mentioned twenty-five-year-old James McQuilkin was reading a book entitled George Müller's *Life and Labours in Bristol* when he came under conviction of sin in 1856. The link is described in Müller's autobiography. McQuilkin learned much about the importance and the power of prayer through his readings so that in the spring of 1857 he began to pray for a prayer partner. He resolved to do this in spite of the persistent opposition of his wife.[71] His prayer was soon answered. One day Jeremiah Meneely knocked on McQuilkin's door and thus began in September 1857 a prayer meeting in Tannybrake schoolhouse near Kells which many Christians see as the real powerhouse behind the 1859 revival.[72] Inspired by the real-life stories of George Müller, these two young men took the advice of Rev. J. H. Moore of Connor and did 'something for God'.

The Methodist and Brethren influences upon McQuilkin have already been highlighted, but there was also a Baptist woman, a Mrs Colville from Gateshead – sent out by the Baptist Missionary Society in 1856 – who profoundly shaped his thinking. Listening in to a conversation she was having with another woman had moved his mind to what were for him new Scriptural truths.[73] Nonconformist, dissenting views were to propel him into active evangelistic work. When at the end of 1859 he moved to Kenilworth in England it was to minister in a Baptist chapel. Before dying at the very young age of thirty, in 1862, he had become instrumental in fanning the flames of revival in Warwick and Leamington.[74] William Richey of First Coleraine wrote of him: 'Few individuals were more self-sacrificing or more successful in winning souls to the Saviour than the

---

71. William Richey, *Connor and Coleraine*, p. 110.
72. A.R. Scott, *The Ulster Revival of 1859* [mid-Antrim Historical Group], p. 52; Jack Henry, *A Door that Opened*, p. 18.
73. *Coleraine Chronicle*, 17 July 1859.
74. Jack Henry, *A Door That Opened*, pp. 17, 47.

large-hearted, prayerful, earnest and humble-minded James McQuilkin.' Without such Christians it would seem that revival is unlikely to impact a whole community. He, too, was a man synods would have overlooked. A friend described him as 'a poor, young man, with a wife and two children [...] a lapper of cloth in one of the mills near Connor'.[75]

It is clear that figures within the Brethren helped to mobilise lay people and gather believers together around the Bible. Brethren views of ministry, church government and baptism were gaining ground in Ireland long before the Ulster revival began. The country districts of the province seem to have been particularly susceptible to Brethren influences. Initially, the other dissenting denominations were unsure about how to deal with Brethren preachers. In May 1857 the Synod of Ballymena and Coleraine actually debated the question whether a 'Plymouth Brother' or 'Darbyite' – as they were then termed – should be allowed to use a Presbyterian pulpit to spread their views. Rev. Rentoul of Ballymoney deprecated the 'growing practice' adopted by some of his Presbyterian colleagues of preaching in other Protestant churches, but Rev. Macdonnell of Third Presbyterian, Coleraine, could see no harm in opening up the pulpit to other gifted preachers. For his part, he said if a Catholic priest asked him to address his congregation in the chapel, he, Macdonnell, would 'feel very proud of the permission' and avail himself of it.[76] Presbyterians were, however, divided on this issue, and remained so. At the May 1861 synod of Ballymena and Coleraine there was another debate on the best response to Brethren activities, but, again, no clear agreement could be reached on the matter.[77]

The Congregational minister in Coleraine, Rev. John Kydd, could not tolerate such lack of clarity. He attacked the Brethren in a pamphlet produced in 1857, which led to

---

75. William Richey, *Connor and Coleraine*, p. 110; *Coleraine Chronicle*, 16 July 1859.
76. *Coleraine Chronicle*, 23 May 1857.

a published reply refuting the charges being levelled against them. Perhaps the Congregationalist felt under threat from Brethren proselytisers. For many years after the revival tracts full of arguments for and against Brethren doctrines came off the presses in Ireland. Most were hostile in tone.

Nevertheless, during the course of the revival itself, and for many years afterwards, Christians felt drawn to Brethren assemblies. Jeremiah Meneely, McQuilkin's prayer partner, helped to establish assemblies in the north of Ireland and in Scotland too.[78] The revival atmosphere softened doctrinaire positions. There is one classic example of crossing denominational barriers. Meneely baptised the Reformed Presbyterian minister in Cullybackey, John Galway McVicker, in the River Maine in September 1859. Later he would help found the Baptist church in Ballymena (1860). Two years later he threw in his lot with the Brethren, helping to found an assembly in the same town. McVicker went on to become a renowned Bible teacher in Brethren circles all over the United Kingdom.[79]

In an age of reform, and a society that was becoming progressively more democratic, Brethren views on the acceptability of lay ministries and lay preaching found fertile ground. Indeed, even critics accepted that the revival suggested that God approved of the instrumentality of laymen. The Rev. S. J. Moore of Ballymena emphasised, at the General Assembly of the Presbyterian Church in June 1859, that the work of awakening sinners to their deplorable state had been carried out chiefly by the converts themselves. 'Were ministers multiplied fifty-fold', he said on that occasion, 'they could not have carried on the work, however diligent they might be.'[80]

---

77.   Ibid., 25 May 1861.
78.   F. Roy Coad, *A History of the Brethren Movement*, Exeter 1968, p. 170.
79.   F. Roy Coad, Ibid., p. 170; Jack Henry, *A Door That Opened*, passim.
80.   *Coleraine Chronicle*, 2 July 1859.

EVANGELICALS UNITED

While Brethrenism may have polarised opinion, the decade was characterised by attempts to institutionalise Christian unity. The growing willingness to exchange pulpits was a symptom of this change. Since the early 1840s a movement aimed at bringing together those of sound evangelical opinions had gained strength in Britain. In October 1845 this culminated in a conference on Christian unity which was held in Liverpool. Presbyterians in Coleraine clearly followed these developments closely. Rev. Canning of Second Presbyterian was present at this conference, as were Rev. Magill of Third Presbyterian (Terrace Row) and Rev. Jonathan Simpson of Portrush.[81] A spirit of unity was exhibited by the 217 ministers and laymen representing twenty-one different Protestant denominations[82]. Soon branches were formed in most of the important towns throughout the United Kingdom.[83] The first public meeting in Ireland of the new body, the Evangelical Alliance, was held on 24 February 1846 in the Primitive Methodist Chapel in South Great George's Street, Dublin. Christians representing a number of denominations, though most were Presbyterians and Baptists, had organised a meeting on 22 October 1845, in the Baptist chapel at Tobermore, to promote a closer union of evangelicals. The Baptist minister in Coleraine, W.S. Eccles, was there as a representative of the Irish Baptist Union, and one of the three anonymous letters that appeared in the *Chronicle* in December 1845 and January 1846, calling for the Liverpool resolutions to be put into practice in Coleraine, was no doubt his.[84] A 'preacher of the gospel' said that an evangelical alliance in Coleraine would 'prove the falsity of the assertion of the enemy that Protestant-

---

81. Ibid., 1 October 1859, 20 December 1845 and 21 April 1860.
82. C.H. Crookshank, *History of Methodism in Ireland*, vol. iii, p. 365.
83. C.H. Crookshank, Ibid., p. 366.
84. *Coleraine Chronicle*, 20 December 1845, 27 December 1845 and 3 January 1846.

ism is division'.[85] An Episcopalian admonished his fellow townspeople: 'Let it not be said of the followers of Christ in Coleraine that they are afraid to meet on the same platform.'[86] Theological principles drew evangelicals together while confessional biases still pulled them apart.

The first minister to break through the walls of anonymity and fear by proclaiming himself publicly in favour of a 'union of prayer' was Rev. Magill of Third Presbyterian (Terrace Row).[87] Discussions began amongst the clergy and three weeks later Rev. H.J. Heathcote, of the Congregationalist Independent Church, outlined the principles of a 'union of Christians' in an open letter to the *Chronicle*.[88] It should be remembered that these moves were taking place before the official founding conference of the Evangelical Alliance (19 August–2 September 1846) in the Masonic setting and atmosphere of Freemasons Hall, Great Queen Street, London, the building rented for the purpose.[89] Little seems to have come of these promising beginnings in the Bann-side town. In November 1848 the Baptist Church formally broke off all fraternal ties with the Congregational Church after the latter had admitted a woman to fellowship who was still under the discipline and censure of their church.[90] Accusations of sheep-stealing filled the town. In 1853–4 there seems to have been tension between the minister of First Presbyterian and the rector of Killowen Parish church. The *Chronicle* published an exchange of letters and described the fight as a 'gladiatorial exhibition' featuring a 'tough, pugnacious' Presbyterian.[91] It is unclear which side landed the final punch.

---

85. Ibid., 27 December 1845.
86. Ibid., 3 January 1846.
87. Ibid., 3 January 1846.
88. Ibid., 24 January 1846.
89. Ibid., 12 September 1846.
90. *Minutes of the Congregational Church 1844–1850*, p. 36ff.
91. *Coleraine Chronicle*, 14 January 1854 and 21 January 1854.

To counteract this bitterness 'united meetings for prayer' were held. The first took place in 1853, but the only people who took the time to make a show of unity were the Presbyterian ministers in the town.[92] It was here that the Evangelical Alliance came into its own. In April 1855 the organisation's travelling secretary, Rev. Charles Jackson, gave a lecture in the Town Hall on the principles and development of the Alliance. Apart from the three Presbyterian ministers only the Methodist Church was represented[93]. At the meeting, the Methodist minister, Tobias, pointed out that only a few individuals had ever had a vision for cross-denominational unity and co-operation. And of the original founding members of the Coleraine branch only three had retained membership. Clearly there was still a great deal of work to be done if Christians were to form a united front. Rev. William Richey claimed that several of the initial teething problems had actually been resolved, though his Presbyterian colleague, Canning, remained 'rather chary' of commencing anything of such a nature in Coleraine. Yet, he added, Protestants had 'a common Enemy' and nothing should be placed in the way of joint prayer and fellowship meetings.[94] Richey gave a number of lectures before the Coleraine branch of the Evangelical Alliance which were serialised in the *Chronicle* and also appeared as a tract.[95] The local paper actually reported quite extensively on Alliance conferences in Scotland and England and helped galvanise support for the movement.[96] Issues such as Sabbath observance, temperance and mission drew ministerial backing from all denominational backgrounds. Throughout the 1850s ministers, for example, shared platforms at local support meetings of the various missionary societies. The idea of an allied attack on societal

---

92. Ibid., 19 March 1853.
93. Ibid., 28 April 1855.
94. Ibid., 28 April 1855.
95. *Coleraine Chronicle*, 3 May 1856, 10 May 1856 and 17 May 1856.
96. Ibid., 6 September 1856, 20 June 1857 and 14 April 1860.

disruption took on practical forms. Contacts intensified in the years leading up to the revival of 1859.

Work was to be tied to worship. At the same time as Presbyterian ministers in Coleraine were pushing the idea of evangelical union, prayer meetings conducted by church elders and other lay people were on the increase within the bounds of six presbyteries making up the Coleraine and Ballymena synod.[97] To accompany the drive for more prayer in the town a systematic distribution of devotional tracts was decided upon. Adverts for this material appeared in the pages of the *Chronicle*.[98] This Christian literature had a focus on 'unions of prayer' to support the home missionary effort. Furthermore, there seemed to be a lot of biblical support for such co-operation and alliances. The idea of cross-denominational prayer meetings, first proposed in 1846, became a central feature of the religious state of affairs on the north coast of Ireland.

Fruit of this evangelical co-operation in Coleraine can be detected. In November 1853, the Coleraine Auxiliary of the Edinburgh Bible Society was established to provide cheap Bibles (9 pence) and New Testaments (3 pence) to those who could read or had a desire to learn to read. A depot was opened in Meeting House Street. A systematic distribution of tracts was conducted by the Young Men's Christian Associations linked to all the Presbyterian churches in town.

Secondly, the young Christian men began to draw together for fellowship. Each Presbyterian congregation seems to have organised its own YMCA. In 1858 New Row had such an organisation under the presidency of its minister, Canning, which became particularly active and numerically strong.[99] The Wesleyan Methodists formed their own YMCA in January 1859 which experienced vibrant growth during the

---

97. Ibid., 19 May 1855.
98. Ibid., 10 December 1853.
99. *Coleraine Chronicle*, 1 May 1858 and 28 May 1858.

revival: from just a handful of members there were soon twenty-eight young men zealous in evangelism.[100] In addition to these denominational structures, a Coleraine Young Men's Christian Association was established in 1852, with Joseph Cuthbert (First Presbyterian) and Henry Gribben (Baptist) as co-secretaries.[101] This inter-confessional YMCA had put the idea of evangelical unity and cooperation into practice for years prior to the revival.

Thirdly, the Academical Institution was established on Christian lines. The clergymen of all the Protestant churches in town were on the managing committee (formed on 6 June 1857) and clergymen conducted religious exercises when the school was opened on 1 May 1860.[102] The school was opened and closed each day with prayer and the reading of a portion of Scripture.[103] It was resolved that the basis of the school 'from which, in future, there shall be no departure', was to reflect the progress and strength of the movement towards 'Christian union' in Coleraine. 'All members of the Committee of Management, all Trustees, and all Teachers in the Institution [are] to be persons holding the principles set forth in the outline of Christian truth adopted by "The Evangelical Alliance".'[104]

Praying together, having fellowship with one another, sharing platforms, cooperating in the distribution of the Scriptures as well as in moral reform campaigns and educational projects – from an organisational point of view, at the very least, these joint ventures were a prerequisite of the revival meetings in 1859. The link was emphasised by Rev. Canning of Second Presbyterian at the Belfast Conference of the Evangelical Alliance in September 1859, where he said:

---

100. The Irish Evangelist, March 1860, p. 46.
101. *Coleraine Chronicle*, 4 February 1854.
102. Ibid., 5 May 1860.
103. Ibid., 31 January 1800.
104. *Coleraine Chronicle*, 14 May 1853; William Richey, *Connor and Coleraine*, p. 126.

> I find myself in the midst of ministers and members of all Evangelical Churches on this platform, praising and praying for the prosperity and for the peace of God's spiritual Jerusalem; and yet such a scene, blessed be God! I witness every morning in the town where I labour. Such a scene may be witnessed every morning in the week, at half past nine o'clock, in the Town Hall of Coleraine. [...] there has been a meeting of an evangelical alliance every morning for more than two months past. Some 500 people meet there [...] high and low, rich and poor kneel side by side in prayer and most earnestly drink in the brief word of instruction and exhortation addressed to them.[105]

The Coleraine Auxiliary of the Evangelical Alliance was a product of the growing strength of evangelicalism within all the churches. Its first chairman was the layman William Moore, a nomination symbolic of the increasing respect enjoyed by this Bible teacher. In 1858 the Methodist Rev. Robert G. Cather, Rev. William Richey and the Killowen rector Rev. William W. Sillito were members. The lay members included timber and general merchants, Hugh and Thomas Bellas; John Canning, a teacher at the Irish Society Male School and actuary at the Savings Bank; town commissioner Dr William Cavin M.D.; the surgeon and apothecary Dr Clarke; Mr A. Clarke; the magistrate and chairman of the Poor Law Union Workhouse, John Cromie; another town commissioner, Alexander Cuthbert, who was a tanner by profession; grain merchant and insurance agent John Huey; Dr J. Jasper Macaldin, M.D., FRCSI; Mr Joseph MacCarter, a tanner; the Methodist woollen and linen draper, Mr Archibald McIlwaine; William MacLaughlin of Portstewart, a deacon of the Congregational Church; town commissioner John Matthews, another woollen and linen draper; the magistrate William Moore, who seems to have also owned a flour store; Andrew Orr, a magistrate and vice-chairman

---

105. Ibid., 24 September 1859 and 1 October 1859.

of the Poor Law Union Workhouse; James Thompson, the keeper of the bridewell and yet another woollen and linen draper; the registrar of marriages and clerk of the market, William Young; and , as if to emphasise the gender inequality, a Mrs Williams, probably the widow of James Williams, a hardware merchant.[106] Hugh Bellas, Cavin, Mathews and Huey were trustees of New Row Presbyterian Church.[107] Most members of the Alliance were, then, well-known businessmen; all of them were pillars of the community. Seven of the twenty-two members reappear as signatories in the commemorative Bible used during the revival prayer meetings and kept by the Borough Council to this day.

The Alliance embodied not only a desire for greater fellowship amongst believers, but also the recognition that efforts to reach the masses of people alienated from Christianity should be co-ordinated. The open-air preaching and the tract distribution campaign gave expression to the missionary and evangelistic impulse that had reignited Christians over the previous half-century. That impulse brought evangelicals together. To mention just one example from the days of revival: On Sunday, 16 October 1859 the rector of a large Anglican parish in the south of England, who was spending a few days in Coleraine, was asked to conduct the service in New Row Presbyterian Church. He received a warm welcome which surprised a correspondent, since Church of England ministers did 'not usually fraternise very cordially with Dissenters'. The rector said he felt honoured to serve a Presbyterian congregation and hoped the example would further break down barriers in the town 'which never should exist' anyway.[108]

---

106. Evangelical Alliance. *British Organisation. Report presented to the Eleventh Annual Conference, held in London, November, 1857*, London 1858, 'Appendix: List of Members and Subscribers,' p. 10.

107. In addition, Thomas Bellas was newly appointed a trustee in 1861. *Session Minutes 1850–1870 New Row Presbyterian Church* (MIC 1P/31, PRONI).

108. *Coleraine Chronicle*, 22 October 1859.

There were, then, a number of factors of great importance for the reception and spread of the revival message in Coleraine. There were strongly evangelical ministers meeting together and learning to pray together in the spirit of the Evangelical Alliance. Bibles and tracts were being circulated systematically. Society was perceived to be in moral decline and politicians reflected that corruption. It was widely believed, in church circles at least, that only a revival of religious affections brought about by a divine visitation could truly counteract these nefarious trends in society.

Chapter 3: Revival Comes to Coleraine

The nature and characteristics of revivals would have been familiar to the Presbyterian and other evangelical ministers labouring in Coleraine in 1859. Certainly, the revivals in Cambuslang (1742), Kilsyth (1742 and 1839) and Dundee (1840) were known in the province.[1] There are a number of references to talks being given on the subject. Rev. Rentoul of Garvagh spoke on 'Revivals' of religion with special reference to Sabbath schools, prayer meetings and temperance. The subject, he believed, was gathering momentum in Christian circles.[2] Rev. A Lowry of the presbytery of Munster spoke on 'Revivals' at the half-yearly meeting of the presbytery on 1 May in Waterford.[3] Rev. John Wilson spoke on 'Revivals' at the ordination service for Rev. William Irvine in Dungiven.[4] The Congregationalist Rev. Thomas Pullar preached on 20 July in his Coleraine church on the subject 'What prevents the revival of religion in Ireland?' The *Chronicle* said the topic demanded 'the earnest attention of the Christian public'.[5] Rev. J. Alfred Canning of Coleraine spoke on 'Revivals' at a soirée in the Wesleyan

1. William Richey, *Connor and Coleraine*, 96; *Restoration in the Church. Reports of Revivals 1625–1839* [Reprint 1980].
2. *Coleraine Chronicle*, 9 November 1844.
3. Ibid., 11 May 1850.
4. Ibid., 26 April 1851.
5. Ibid., 19 July 1851.

chapel in Portrush on 30 December 1851.[6] Rev. John Simpson of Toberkeith addressed a 'social meeting' at Roseyards, near Dervock, on 'Revivals in Religion, and the means of promoting them'.[7] On 21 to 23 June 1858 Rev. Robert Sewell (Londonderry) spoke on 'Revivals' at the half-yearly meeting of the Northern Association of Congregationalist ministers and churches at Straid.[8] Prayer meetings for revival were held in Great George's Street Presbyterian Church for months prior to any revival meeting in Belfast.[9] Rev. John Hall (Dublin) lectured on 'Revivals of the 18th Century' on 25 February 1859 in First Presbyterian Derry. The meeting was held under the auspices of the Young Men's Mutual Improvement Association associated with the church.[10] The attendance was 'unusually large', a local newspaper reported. It is clear that the subject of revival was in the air and being discussed in Christian circles on the Causeway Coast throughout the 1850s.

A meeting in Coleraine under the auspices of the Continental Society in October 1855 heard Rev. Georges Fisch (Lyons, France) speak on 'extensive revivals of religion' in the south of France, 'principally through the efforts of the Evangelical Alliance'.[11] Richey notes in passing that religious events in Sweden too had created much interest in the province.[12] Certainly, to date, little attention has been given to movements on the continent of Europe as being a possible contributory factor to the expectant hope of revival in Britain and Ireland.

---

6. Ibid., 3 January 1852.
7. Ibid., 4 March 1854.
8. Ibid., 3 July 1858.
9. *Londonderry Sentinel*, 1 October 1858.
10. *Londonderry Journal*, 23 February 1859 and 2 March 1859; *Londonderry Sentinel*, 25 February and 4 March 1859.
11. *Coleraine Chronicle*, 13 October 1855.
12. William Richey, *Connor and Coleraine*, p. 113.

REVIVAL IN THE USA

More than anything else, however, news of the revival in America in 1857–8 encouraged Nonconformist ministers to think through the issue of spiritual awakening. The *Chronicle* first reported in April 1858 on a 'great religious revival' in the United States. Christians located the origin of the movement in a daily lunch-hour prayer meeting in the Dutch Reformed Church in Fulton Street, New York, started by a man called Jeremiah Lamphier in September 1857.[13] This, of course, was the very same month in which the prayer meeting began in Kells.[14] There sprang up 'union prayer meetings' in other places which were attended by members of all denominations. This was the model later adopted in Ulster. Nobody was allowed to speak for longer than five minutes. Ministers voluntarily adopted forms not part of their own particular denominational tradition: Episcopal clergymen engaged in extempore prayer and exhortation, Presbyterians sang hymns, laymen presided over meetings and seemed to direct the movement.[15] The work of evangelism itself was mainly carried on by lay people; well-known evangelists of the time, such as Charles Finney, played insignificant roles. The revival, which affected chiefly the business classes, became known as the 'businessmen's revival' or the 'laymen's revival'. As many as 50,000 conversions were said to have taken place in a single week.

News of these developments in America was communicated to Ulster through the letters of newspaper

---

13. Lamphier was appointed lay missionary in the city of New York on 1 July 1857. *The Revival Movement in Ireland. An Impartial History of the Revival Movement from its Commencement to the Present Time.* Belfast: George Phillips and C. Aitchison 1859, p. 4.

14. A.R. Scott, *The Ulster Revival of 1859*, p. 53; *Coleraine Chronicle*, 10 April 1858.

15. William McLaughlin, *Revivals, Awakenings and Reform*, Chicago and London 1978, p. 141; *Coleraine Chronicle*, 1 May 1858.

correspondents and expatriates.[16] Interest was created and the hope of a similar movement in Ulster was excited by such reports. Two Scottish laymen who had witnessed revival meetings in America visited their relatives[17] near Connor in the spring of 1858 and the two gave a number of talks in the area on the subject. Crowded meetings in Connor were convened. These two men were themselves astonished and deeply impressed by the progress of the prayer movement in the Connor and Kells area. They brought this news with them from Connor to Coleraine, where they had been booked for a talk on the state of religion in America. Their account of the movement in Connor created, according to Rev. William Richey, 'a sensation scarcely less profound than that excited by their narratives of the American Revival'.[18] The Synod of Ballymena and Coleraine, meeting in May 1858, noted improved attendances at worship services and the 'happy results' of open-air preaching in the district. The report of the Committee on the State of Religion recommended that 'measures should be taken to promote a revival of religion' in Presbyterian congregations. Ministers were encouraged to bring before their congregations the subject of revival on the second Sunday in June, 1858.[19]

HENRY GRATTAN GUINNESS

Shortly afterwards Rev. Richey of First Presbyterian in Coleraine announced that the Rev. Henry Grattan Guinness (1835–1910) would preach in New Market Place on June 9.

---

16. William Richey, *Connor and Coleraine*, 107, 113. Richey notes in passing that religious events in Sweden, as well as the USA, had created much interest.

17. The surnames of the two Scots were Grant and Macfarlane. The former was the nephew of Peter Drummond of Stirling, the other the son of a Scottish minister. Both lived in the USA and both were connected with George H. Stuart of Philadelphia, a man whose Christian work was known throughout Ulster at the time. William Richey, Ibid., p. 107.

18. Ibid.

19. *Coleraine Chronicle*, 22 May 1858.

Guinness was a tireless evangelist and was instrumental in establishing a number of different missionary organisations.[20] In 1858 he delivered nine discourses in Dublin, Ballymoney and Sligo as well as Coleraine.[21] In the Victoria Market in Derry he referred to the revivals in progress and expressed his own hope that 'there would be a revival here too'. In March he spoke to 'immense crowds' described as being 'more thick and dense than we have ever witnessed' in Coleraine. Two thousand people attended each of the services organised for him – a very large percentage of each congregation having to stand the whole time. 'The common people received him gladly,' an observer noted. In a letter to the *Chronicle* Richey wrote:

> Let us hope that many of your readers will unite in asking for a special blessing on the proposed visit. The intelligence from the Western world, for some time past, may well rouse the churches of Christ in our own land, and put them upon pleading with the 'Hearer of Prayer' for a season of Revival.

Richey wished to bring home to many the reality of God's power to stir up a lethargic church. 'Oh, what a revival God could grant us', Rev. Richey wrote, 'by the gracious movement of His blessed Spirit.'[22] Prayer was offered for a year prior to the outpouring of that Spirit. The preaching of the evangelist Grattan Guinness proved to be particularly

---

20. Guinness was born in what was then called Kingstown, near Dublin. An uncle on his father's side was associated with the legendary black stout. His mother was the widow of a soldier by the name of d'Esterre who died following a duel with Daniel O'Connell in 1815. Guinness had once been a Congregationalist. He was baptised by the Brethren leader Lord Congleton in Somerset Street Baptist church in Bath. *Londonderry Sentinel*, 12 February 1858; *Coleraine Chronicle*, 13 October 1860; T.C. Luby, *The Life and Times of Daniel O'Connell*, Glasgow and London 1918, pp. 437–46.

21. *Londonderry Sentinel*, 11 June 1858; *Coleraine Chronicle*, 20 and 27 February, 20 March, 29 May, 5 June, 12 June and 10 July 1858.

22. *Coleraine Chronicle*, 5 June 1858.

successful. Thousands of eager listeners from all evangelical backgrounds were present at these meetings in Coleraine. Richey handed out two thousand tracts at the end of just *one* of them.[23] Demand for devotional literature was increasing. Guinness's own sermons were selling like hotcakes in one of the main bookshops in town.[24]

The other denominations were also preparing for revival. As has already been noted, Rev. Robert Sewell of Londonderry preached on the subject at the half-yearly meeting of the Northern Association of Congregationalist ministers in June 1858.[25] The Wesleyan Methodists notified the public that a 'mass meeting, as they express it in America', would be held on Dunmull Hill, about three miles from Coleraine, on 1 August 1858, and invited Christians of all denominational attachments to attend.[26] On the following Sunday, 8 August, a so-called field meeting took place on the lawn of Jackson Hall, at which the Methodist ministers, R.G. Cather and W. Crooke, as well as the Congregationalist minister, John Kydd, gave addresses.[27] August 1858 was the month the great Baptist preacher Charles Spurgeon preached to crowds of thousands in Belfast[28] and William Richey was preaching to large crowds at various places in Coleraine.[29]

Throughout the autumn of 1858 meetings were held on the Dunmull Hill. The *Chronicle* added its journalistic weight to the campaign: 'While the season is favourable, ministers should preach to the poor in the fields, in the streets and in the lanes that through their instrumentality many may be saved.'[30] A united prayer meeting was set up in Ballymoney

---

23. *Coleraine Chronicle*, 12 June 1858.
24. Ibid., 26 June 1858 and 1 January 1859.
25. Ibid., 3 July 1858.
26. Ibid., 31 August 1858.
27. Ibid., 7 August 1858.
28. Ibid., 14 August 1858.
29. Ibid., 21 August 1858.
30. *Coleraine Chronicle*, 4 September 1858.

in November 1858 following a meeting in the town hall, at which William Getty, vice-president of the Young Men's Christian Association, provided a gathering of 300 with a detailed account of the American revival.[31] Rev. Prof. Gibson and Rev. William McClure (Londonderry) had returned that month from a most encouraging four-month visit to the scenes of revival in the USA.[32] They passed on the word that a major revival was in the offing. Back in Coleraine Rev. McClure gave a talk in New Row Presbyterian Church on 'America – Impressions of its churches and people' on 28 November.[33]

KELLS, CONNOR AND AHOGHILL

News of the awakening in Kells and Connor was brought to the attention of the General Assembly meeting in Londonderry in 1858.[34] On 17 May 1859 the Synod of Ballymena and Coleraine, meeting in Cookstown, listened to the reports of the Presbyteries of Ahoghill and Ballymena on the state of religion within their bounds. The protocol of the meeting records 'a most extraordinary Religious Awakening & Revival [...] remarkably similar in character to that witnessed in the early "plantation" of Presbyterianism in Ulster, in 1625, along the Six Mile Water at Oldstone'.[35] The Synod noted that the 'extraordinary outpouring of the Holy Spirit' was producing 'convictions so deep and pungent as to prostrate to the dust strong men as well as females, youths and even children'. Rev. Canning of New Row called for a published record of the revival; Rev. Macdonnell of

---

31. Ibid., 4 September 1858.
32. Ibid., 27 November 1858. In his book *Pentecost: or, the Work of God in Philadelphia A.D. 1858*, Belfast 1858, William Gibson points out that the 2,000-member Young Men's Christian Association in Philadelphia was a prime instrument in advancing the work of revival.
33. *Coleraine Chronicle*, 11 December 1858.
34. J.S. Reid, *History of the Presbyterian Church in Ireland*, p. 509. Rev. J.H. Moore, minister at Connor, reported on the movement.
35. *Minutes of the Synod of Ballymena and Coleraine*, Cookstown 1859, p. 191.

Terrace Row urged all ministers and elders to give 'serious consideration' to 'this remarkable revival of religion'. Interestingly, the prostrations – similar to, but not identical with, what today is referred to as 'being slain in the Spirit' – did not arrest attention or even cause comment. They were simply accepted as an outworking of deep conviction of sin or, in other cases, of being overpowered by the sense of God's presence. Synod members were not so much interested in how people were falling to the ground, but rather in how they were living when they got back to their feet. The evidence of changed lives seemed to them compelling.

As yet no revival meetings as such had taken place in Coleraine, but the wave of revivalist enthusiasm had been advancing for some time towards the town. The prayer meeting in Kells had been multiplying since its inception in September 1857. James McQuilkin was instrumental in the conversion of Robert Carlisle, Jeremiah Meneely and John Wallace[36] that same month.

It was these four men – a lapper of cloth, a blacksmith's assistant, a butcher and a stonebreaker – who mobilised more people than any other movement in Ulster during the whole of the nineteenth century. The wave of revival coming out of the prayer meetings in Kells and Connor would finally reached Coleraine.

In January 1858 a child in one of the Sunday school classes was 'so overpowered by the Spirit', said a co-worker, 'that its body was prostrated and it suffered greatly in consequence'.[37] The prayer group leaders were astonished; this was the first time they had ever seen or heard of such manifestations. By May 1858 about sixteen others had been converted and added to the fellowship meeting. By February 1859 the Kells prayer meeting numbered about fifty young men.[38]

---

36. Wallace was, like McQuilkin, a poor, uneducated working-class Irishman. A.R. Scott, *The Ulster Revival of 1859*, p. 52.
37. *Coleraine Chronicle*, 16 July 1859.

Rev. Moore of Connor had still not even heard of the existence of this meeting of converted young men, but he began to assist them in the summer of 1858. On 9 December 1858 Samuel Campbell, a young worker in a linen factory belonging to James Ross of Kells, was physically prostrated at one of their meetings, receiving an inward assurance that his sins had been forgiven.[39] Campbell, described at the time as a very wild and reckless youth,[40] was the means whereby revival came to Ahoghill. His family was resident there. Within weeks his brother John, also a linen worker, his sister and finally his mother made professions of faith.[41] The Campbells began to talk to their neighbours about their new beliefs and started a prayer meeting in Ahoghill.[42]

John Campbell organised a meeting in Second Ahoghill – Frederick Buick's meeting house – to give his testimony. A second meeting to be held in Ballymontna schoolhouse, near Ahoghill, at which McQuilkin, Meneely, Wallace and Carlisle were due to speak, attracted so many people that the venue had to be changed. This second meeting took place in Second Ahoghill on 2 February 1859. Of this eventful meeting George Müller wrote: 'Some believed, some mocked, and others thought there was a great deal of presumption in these young converts.'[43] Another meeting followed on 16 February, of which Müller wrote: '[A]nd now the Spirit of God began to work, and to work mightily.'[44]

While Müller saw the 16 February meeting as the real turning point in the revival movement, Professor Finlay Holmes points to the 14 March meeting in First Ahoghill as the key date. The church, which was capable of seating

38. A.R. Scott, *The Ulster Revival of 1859*, p. 60.
39. A.R. Scott, Ibid. p. 57.
40. *Coleraine Chronicle*, 16 July 1859.
41. A.R. Scott, *The Ulster Revival of 1859*, p. 58.
42. *Coleraine Chronicle*, 16 July 1859.
43. *Autobiography of George Müller*, London and Bristol 1905, p. 449.
44. Ibid. p. 449.

1,200 people, was far too small for the three thousand who turned up to hear Rev. Adams speak on revivals and to listen to the testimonies of the converts from Connor. Adams, however, keen on delivering his discourse, did not permit the young men to speak. One of them, James Bankhead, a local farmer, resisted attempts to restrain and silence him and, according to the *Ballymena Observer* (26 March 1859) declared 'a revelation had been committed to him and that he spoke by command of a power superior to any ministerial authority'. Adams's attempts to shut him up caused a great commotion, particularly in the galleries, which he then asked to be cleared, fearing they might even collapse.[45] Outside the church building, Jeremiah Meneely, James Bankhead and others addressed the crowd. The *Observer* reported that the speakers proclaimed pardon to all sinners, 'inviting them to come forward and receive the Spirit of adoption [...] and bidding the people receive the Holy Ghost'. Large numbers were moved, the paper says, by 'the fervency and apostolic language' of the converts. As they preached, many in the crowd fell to their knees in prayer. By 7 April about two hundred individuals had professed a new-found faith in Christ.[46] Although the *Ballymena Observer* titled the report 'Extraordinary Religious Excitement in Ahoghill', this meeting actually took place in chilling rain and the streets on which people were kneeling and praying were covered with mud. This was not a cosy room with comfortable chairs and soft music playing in the background. Nothing on that day could have naturally produced excitement.

After 14 March the revival movement progressed steadily northwards. Within six weeks roughly four thousand

45. A.R. Scott, *The Ulster Revival of 1859*, 61; R.F.G. Holmes, 'The 1859 Revival Reconsidered,' introduction to John T. Carson, *God's River in Spate* [Presbyterian Historical Society Reprint 1994], ix.

46. A.R. Scott, *The Ulster Revival of 1859*, p. 61.

converts could be counted.[47] First Ahoghill itself saw 700 individuals experiencing renewal by November 1859; about one hundred of these had experienced either physical prostration, convulsions or a trance-like state during the revival months, according to the minister in charge.

Rev. Adams himself began to preach revival sermons in Portglenone on 27 March and in Straid on 29 March.[48] Other ministers soon took up the subject, but it was the converts themselves who attracted most attention. A layman brought McQuilkin, Meneely, Campbell and other members of the Kells prayer group to speak at Grange Corner. After addresses from Meneely and McQuilkin, Campbell read out Isaiah 55: 6–7 and as he spoke dozens of people seemed to be thrown to the ground. The meeting went on till daybreak. Rev. Hall Stewart, the Presbyterian minister at that place, met the Kells leaders to discuss the phenomena. All were perplexed, yet none could deny that many had truly been converted.[49] These so-called 'physical manifestations' would continue to perplex observers throughout the year. Many tracts were written for and against tolerating the emotional aspects of revivalism. Coleraine, more than most towns, was the place of publication of many of these tracts.

On 5 and 11 April 1859 McQuilkin and other Kells men held meetings in First and Third Presbyterian Churches in Ballymena, at which several people were convicted of their sin.[50] By 25 May the *Belfast News-Letter* could report that there was not a single street in Ballymena itself where people had not been converted. In early May the revival began in Broughshane and Cullybackey.

---

47 A R Scott, Ibid. p. 62.

48. Ibid. p. 63.

49. Ibid. p. 63.

50. *Autobiography of George Müller*, p. 449; A.R. Scott, *The Ulster Revival of 1859*, p. 65.

BELFAST

McQuilkin and Meneely went to preach in Belfast on 28 May and held meetings in five different Presbyterian meeting houses.[51] In two days of meetings in the Donegall Place Methodist Church two hundred people had gone forward to the penitents' form at the front of the church, according to the *News-Letter* (11 June 1859). Converts from Ahoghill held meetings in Great George's Street Presbyterian Church on 27 and 29 May. The meeting house in Great George's Street was where the southern Irish revivalist Thomas Toye ministered. Congregational prayer meetings for revival had been going on there since 17 April 1858.[52] As long ago as 1833, in the wake of the revivals in the United States, Toye had called upon Irish Presbyterians to seek and plead for 'such an effusion of the influence of the Holy Spirit as shall lead on those who believe in Jesus Christ, and are regenerated by divine grace to much higher attainments in spiritual religion, and shall at the same time greatly augment the number of the righteous'. Through the prayer of faith and the preaching of the gospel in Clonakilty, County Cork, he had helped pioneer such a revival in that very year.[53] Toye provides a personal link between the revival fervour of the 1830s, which impacted Belfast to some degree, and that of 1859–60.

BALLYMONEY

Of the pastors in Ballymoney it was the Methodist minister, William Crooke Jr., who first went to Ahoghill to form a judgment of the movement's character. He returned to his church with some of the converts and began to organise meetings in the town at which they

---

51. A.R. Scott, *The Ulster Revival of 1859*, p .82.
52. *Brief Memorials of the late Rev. Thomas Toye, Belfast, by His Widow*, Belfast 1873, p. 72. On Toye's revivalist activities in Ulster and Scotland see pp. 70–106.
53. *The Orthodox Presbyterian*, No. XLIV, May 1833, p. 282f. Toye came from Clonakilty in County Cork.

could give their testimonies. One such meeting, held on 6 June, was, in Rev. Park's words, an exhibition of divine sovereignty in the conversion of people. As a man was praying for the Holy Spirit's power to be manifested in the gathering, some fifteen people, mainly young girls this time, were simultaneously 'stricken' and prostrated on the ground.[54] Regular open-air meetings were held in a field at Milltown over the next few months, to build on this interest.[55]

Mr George Carter of Coleraine wrote a letter on revival, dated 31 May, to the *Londonderry Sentinel*.[56] He had attended a meeting in Ballymoney on 30 May after seeing a placard advertising the event. The meeting was addressed by converts from Rasharkin and a short address was given by Rev. Crooke. There were, he said, about thirty cases of people apparently in great mental agony following the talks. The revival was 'baffling alike the minister and the priest'. Here is his letter:

> Sir—As meetings for the revival of religion are now being held in so many parts of the north of Ireland, and as they are daily increasing in magnitude and importance, I thought a few facts connected with the affair might prove interesting to some of your readers. On seeing a placard announcing a meeting of this kind to be held in Ballymoney, on Monday 30th. Inst., I resolved to attend, in order to satisfy my own mind as to the manner in which it was carried out, and, also, as to the truth of the reports which have from time to time appeared in the Belfast and other newspapers. At the time appointed several hundred persons were assembled in front of a platform, which was erected in a field near to the railway station. The service was conducted by ministers of the Presbyterian and Wesleyan denominations, and commenced in the usual

---

54. A.R. Scott, *The Ulster Revival of 1859*, p. 77.
55. *Coleraine Chronicle*, 4 June 1859.
56. *Londonderry Sentinel*, 3 June 1859.

manner with singing and prayer. A short address was delivered by Rev. Mr Crooke, from the words 'Why will ye die, O house of Israel!' [Ezek. 33: 11]

The converts from Rasharkin then severally addressed the meeting. During the delivery of these addresses, which were remarkable for their *earnestness* [italics in original], several people began to show symptoms of this strange *impression.* [italics in original]. I say strange, and I assure you sir, that it is the most extraordinary religious phenomenon I ever witnessed. About thirty cases occurred, many of which I attended, and in each case closely observed the conduct of the individual affected. What is very strange in the matter is that every case was accompanied by the same symptoms, viz.: 1st. A deep sense of sinfulness. 2nd. Entire physical prostration, accompanied by very acute pains in the chest and forehead, in some cases *rendering medical aid necessary.*—The time they continue in this state varies from ten minutes to several hours. 3d. They commence praying most fervently that God would deliver them from the *torments of hell.* The time they continue in this state varying as in the second case, although generally of shorter duration. 4th. They all at once appear to receive consolation, and to exultingly rejoice in being reconciled to God through Jesus Christ.—From this time a *smile* appears upon their countenance, and they commence reading the Bible and praying with any who may, either from curiosity or otherwise, feel disposed to listen to them. It is thus the 'revival' is spreading from town to town, and from village to village, amongst all classes, and all denominations, irrespective of, and baffling alike the minister and the priest. Forbearing to express any opinion of my own, I leave these few facts to speak for themselves.—

COLERAINE

Clearly, lay people from Coleraine were already attending revival meetings and bringing news back to their home town. The first actual meetings in Coleraine were conducted by laymen in houses and shops. One of them took place on 2 June in a store in North Brook Street which was 'crammed to the door' by people who chiefly belonged, the *Chronicle* claimed, to 'the lower walks of life'.[57] Those forced to stand outside joined in the psalm-singing. Other meetings took place in Killowen. The Methodist minister in Ballymoney, Rev. William Crook, Jr., was the man who arranged for an open-air meeting to take place on 7 June on the Fair Hill in Coleraine, just at the back of the First Presbyterian meeting house and immediately adjoining what had once been the site of the Abbey of Coleraine.[58] The ministers of Second and Third Presbyterian seem to have arranged a similar meeting for the very same day, but on the other side of the river. Discussions were held. One of the first signs that the work of the Evangelical Alliance was bearing fruit was the result of these discussions. The Presbyterian ministers decided to cancel their meeting and join the Methodist-organised gathering on the Fair Hill. That was rather unusual in that Methodism had long been regarded by Presbyterians as an object of scorn and reproach because of the specific Methodist doctrine of assurance of salvation. Such a belief and such an experience were to be at the heart of the Ulster revival. Old hostilities gave way before the new spirit of cooperation.

Agreement was reached, then, just to hold the one meeting on the Fair Hill. Rev. Richey of First Presbyterian had been touring the north of Ireland in the month of May and arrived back in town just as the meeting was commencing.[59] We are fortunate to possess accounts of that momentous meeting, the announced object of which was to allow one or two

---

57. *Coleraine Chronicle*, 4 June 1859.
58. C.H. Crookshank, *The History of Methodism in Ireland*, vol. iii, p. 507; William Richey, *Connor and Coleraine*, p. 128.

converts from Ballymoney to speak about their experiences.[60] On a simple platform in the middle of the green were seated the ministers of various evangelical denominations. Richey noted that the platform was just yards away from the spot where Henry Cooke had given a keynote speech that led to the ejection of the 'blighting Arian heresy' from the Synod of Ulster.[61] Shortly after 7 p.m. about 4,000 people were surrounding the platform. By 8 p.m. this number had grown to about 6,000. A clergyman gave out a psalm. Singing began. A second minister said a prayer; a third expounded a short portion of Scripture. Then permission was given to anyone to address the meeting for a few minutes. Rev. Canning described the two converts who spoke on this occasion: one was a young man, the other somewhat older. Both were clearly of 'the humbler class' of workers. He says their addresses were short, focusing on their own personal 'awakening' and ending with an earnest appeal to the consciences of sinners.[62] Richey goes on to describe one of those who spoke as 'a tall and somewhat toil-worn looking man [...] about fifty years of age, strong, gaunt, and staid-looking, and to all appearances one of the most unlikely persons to be carried away by excitement'. Before sharing his testimony he asked everyone to sing with him Psalm 66, reading out verses 16 to 20. As the sound of singing died away he related his experience the previous evening at Portrush, where he had listened to reports of revival in other parts of Ulster. As he listened, he said, 'there fell upon his spirit an indescribable spirit of awe'. He was made to feel the 'holiness of God' and his own unfitness to meet Him. Full of 'fear of wrath' and burdened by a sense of guilt, he went home but was unable to sleep. Not having the courage to tell his wife about what he was feeling,

---

59. William Richey, *Connor and Coleraine*, p. 128.
60. I.R.K. Paisley, *The Fifty Nine Revival*, p. 91.
61. William Richey, *Connor and Coleraine*, p. 129.
62. William Richey, Ibid. p. 129.

he got up, went to his barn, closed the door behind him and poured out his heart to God. There he received a revelation of divine mercy and received the assurance that his sins had been forgiven.[63] Other speakers followed. Richey relates that as one of the converts was speaking cries of distress could be heard. Around the individuals concerned 'groups were gradually formed'; spontaneous prayer was offered for them. As the crowd was now much larger, Rev. Canning of New Row suggested the crowd be divided up into four groups to ensure everyone would be able to hear the testimonies. Each group was under the charge of a minister of religion.[64] Canning, noting the growing excitement and emotion, decided to calm things down by deliberately reading a short address from a script in the most unemotional way possible. This lasted for six or seven minutes. Yet he was struck by the intensity, anxiety and earnestness with which people listened to his remarks and, as he came to a close, a strong man fell to the ground 'as if smitten with a severe blow'. Within another five minutes there were thirty individuals lying prostrate in the market square of Coleraine. The first man who had fallen to the ground was still conscious, but 'as helpless as a child'. The man uttered a cry of terror, saying he could see hell before the eyes of his heart and, at the same time, was horrifyingly aware of the seriousness of his own sin. This stoutly built man continued to cry and scream for some time until Canning calmed him by reading out some verses of Scripture. Instantly, the minister said, the man's eyes were opened and his entire countenance changed for the better. The screaming stopped. Within another five minutes he was back on his feet again. From that day on, Canning later

---

63.   William Richey, Ibid. p. 130. For a short report on the Portrush meeting, see Jonathan Simpson, *Annals of My Life, Labours and Travels*, Belfast 1895, pp. 137–8. Rev. Simpson reports that several people aged between 9 and 70 were prostrated that evening under conviction of sin. About thirty were visited that evening with 'deep impressions of eternal things'.
64.   *Coleraine Chronicle*, 20 August 1859.

reported, the man had completely changed, 'walking in the fear of the Lord and the comfort of the Holy Ghost'.[65] The *Chronicle* had already been won over to revivalism. It reported that 'nothing at all approaching to it in absorbing interest has ever before visited our country'.[66]

SPIRITUAL MANIFESTATIONS

Much of the debate surrounding the 'Toronto Blessing' in the 1990s was reminiscent of the battles of 1859 in Ulster. The physical phenomena, new in the experience at least of all the protagonists, had to be explained somehow. It was natural for ministers and laymen alike to seek explanations which accorded with their own Biblical or materialist view of life. The revivals in history were studied to find similar phenomena. Jonathan Edwards, perhaps the greatest theologian-pastor America has produced, was found to have discussed the issue in his own day.[67] The *Chronicle* quoted him with delight. The sight of sober Presbyterians of Scottish origin justifying what critics said was mass hysteria caused by overheated and cramped factory conditions must have been an interesting spectacle. Speaking to the Free Church of Scotland Commission on Irish revivals on 17 August 1859, Rev. J. C. Canning expressed his belief that the bodily prostrations and emotional suffering – all of them, without exception – were indeed the outward manifestation of 'deep distress about sin wrought in the soul by the power of the Holy Ghost'. They were genuine physical responses to sudden conversions 'from darkness to light', from sin to a God of mercy. These phenomena did not take place in overheated factories and church buildings, but rather in the cool evening breeze on the top of a hill, yet there have been many historians who have suggested they were expressions

---

65. *Coleraine Chronicle*, 20 August 1859.
66. Ibid., 11 June 1859.
67. See Jonathan Edwards, *On Revival*, Edinburgh, n.d.

of hysteria fed by cramped gatherings – the sort of thing commonly witnessed at rock concerts in our own day. For Canning the odd manifestations served an important purpose, in that they directed public attention to evangelistic services and brought people along who might otherwise not have wished to attend. These phenomena also began to take place during normal Sunday worship services: cases were registered in the New Row and Terrace Row meeting places. On 24 July 1859, for example, a 'very intelligent man' who was 'quite the reverse of excitable' was convicted of his sins during the morning service. He was not prostrated, but 'in an agony of mind remained fervent in prayer for a long time'.[68] There is no suggestion that on these occasions the ministers wished to stamp out what some considered inappropriate emotionalism. The response of leaders was always to take time to pray for the individuals concerned.

REVIVAL MEETINGS

On the evening of 8 June 1859 another vast crowd assembled in the market place to hear the gospel being preached. Not fewer than 150 people 'were stricken down by the power of God'.[69] Most of the clergymen had been up the previous night ministering to people seeking peace with God. The *Chronicle* noted on 11 June that there was 'not a street, nor a lane in the whole town but can number three or four of these who have been enlightened'. The Wednesday evening meeting saw strong men and young women as well as children being carried off the hill. And as prayer was being offered for an outpouring of the Holy Spirit, a flash of light lit up the sky for a few seconds bringing the whole crowd to its knees.[70] Numerous people were physically prostrated,

---

68. John Weir, *The Ulster Awakening; Its Origin, Progress, and Fruit. With notes of a tour of personal observation and inquiry,* London 1860, p. 73.
69. I.R.K. Paisley, *The Fifty Nine Revival*, p. 92.
70. The editor of the *Chronicle* wondered whether the phenomenon could be ascribed simply to natural causes.

including a number of compositors working in the *Chronicle* offices.[71] Business in town was partially suspended during that first week of revival.

On 9 June 1859 nearly 100 people, 'agonised in mind through conviction of sin and entirely prostrate in body', were carried into the new Town Hall where a 'band of comforters' prayed and talked with them into the early hours of the morning.[72] About thirty individuals were converted that evening in the new building. The hall was thus inaugurated 'by one of the most glorious celebrations that could possibly be imagined'.[73]

The same day saw what the *Chronicle* called 'the most remarkable instance of the Divine power that has yet marked this spiritual and practical religious revival',[74] when the pupils attending the Irish Society School, not too far from the Fair Hill, were each and all 'simultaneously prostrated' by the convicting power of the Holy Spirit.[75] Lessons were cancelled. The united prayers and cries of the children reached the adjoining streets. Neighbours entered the building, but at once fell to their knees and joined in the cry for mercy. Soon every room in the school was filled with people seeking God. The clergymen were called and spent the day in the school.[76] It was not until 11 p.m. that the school premises could be locked up for the night. One of the boys converted that day became an officer in the Methodist Church.[77] The boys at the Irish Society School came from the poorest families in Coleraine so they were provided with Bibles and Testaments, which were paid for by the town's main distiller, James Moore.[78]

---

71. This led to difficulties in getting the next day's paper published and delivered on time.
72. William Richey, *Connor and Coleraine*, p. 131; *Coleraine Chronicle*, 18 June 1859.
73. *Coleraine Chronicle*, 18 June 1859.
74. Ibid., 11 June 1859.
75. Ibid., 11 June 1859 and 3 September 1859.
76. William Arthur, *The Revival in Ballymena and Coleraine*, London 1859, pp. 11–13.
77. C.H. Crookshank, *The History of Methodism in Ireland*, vol. iii, p. 508.

A similar incident involving a young child took place in a small house in a very run-down part of Coleraine. Rev. Weir of London, who observed the scene, later wrote about the occurrence. An eight-year-old boy had led three others – all members of different families – to Christ; one of these converts was a soldier in the 59th Regiment, who, after spending the previous evening scoffing at the revival, was knocked 'prostrate at the feet of Jesus' by the lad's simple testimony.[79]

Before the first week of revival was over one prostitute had been, in Canning's words, 'thoroughly changed by the Spirit of God'[80] – the first of a number to be converted. A Ladies' Committee was formed in Coleraine to raise funds and take practical steps to reintegrate these women into society.[81] Benjamin Scott, chamberlain of the City of London, claimed that prostitution was totally banished from the town during the months of revival.[82] Some returned to their parents. Half the women entered asylums. Some were sent to the so-called Belfast Penitentiary, which took in prostitutes from Carrickfergus, Ballymena, Lurgan, Armagh, Monaghan, Coleraine, Derry and other places. The numbers of former prostitutes in these refuges doubled during the revival.[83]

On 25 June 1859 the *Chronicle* remarked that the cases of conversion were not so numerous nor was the excitement nearly as intense as at first.[84] But there was still no end of

---

78. An unnamed Scotsman similarly donated half a guinea to be spent on Bibles for the poor of Coleraine. These were distributed by the Town Missionary, Mr Topping. *Coleraine Chronicle*, 3 September 1859.

79. John Weir, *The Ulster Awakening: its origins, progress and fruit*, London 1860, p. 73f.

80. *Coleraine Chronicle*, 20 August 1859.

81. Ibid., 18 June 1859.

82. Benjamin Scott, *The Revival in Ulster: Its Moral and Social Results*, London 1859, pp. 41–2.

83. *Coleraine Chronicle*, 3 September 1859.

84. Ibid., 25 June 1859.

poetry and new songs. Open-air meetings took place every evening, still attended by thousands. The Town Hall was kept open all night, until 5 a.m. – and even then people did not always want to leave.

In the second week of the revival the united prayer meeting began in the Town Hall. Held daily at the time set aside for breakfast for workers and labourers – initially at 9.30 a.m., but shifted in November to 10.25 a.m. to accommodate them – it was the focal point and power-house of the movement for spiritual change. The meetings lasted a mere thirty minutes and were presided over by one of the evangelical ministers in town. A committee representing all the different evangelical denominations managed the practical details of the meetings. The usual format was, first, the singing of a psalm, followed by a Scripture reading, then a time of open prayer. At each meeting notes were passed to the presiding minister asking for specific prayer for particular individuals or situations or requesting thanksgiving for answered prayer.[85]

This was essentially the format of the prayer meetings in the American revival of 1857–8. The first united prayer meetings in Coleraine seem to have been set up in the summer of 1858, shortly after news of the revival in America broke. It met initially in a private house, and then moved to the Infant School building as numbers grew, then to the Baptist chapel in Meeting House Street. The idea of adopting the 'American plan', as the *Chronicle* termed it, had been suggested by one of the ministers in town and was acquiesced in by almost all the Protestant clergymen. The one difference was that in Coleraine a clergyman always chaired the meeting, while in the United States laymen controlled matters.[86] Rev. Weir of London has provided an account of what he experienced at such a meeting:

---

85. William Richey, *Connor and Coleraine*, pp. 164–5; *Coleraine Chronicle*, 25 June 1859.
86. *Coleraine Chronicle*, 18 June 1859.

Next morning, at half-past nine o'clock, was held the daily half-hour meeting for united prayer, in the New Town-hall of Coleraine. Here the Spirit of God had displayed His marvellous power at the opening of the movement, and here this morning was gathered an assembly, of all ranks and ages, including an ex-M.P., strangers from a distance, and many of the labouring classes and the very poor of the town, who had been brought to Christ. There knelt beside me an aged man, evidently poor, with patched clothing, and with worn and rugged face. Oh with what fervour and importunity, yet in subdued undertones, did he back the petitions offered up by the successive suppliants! Here – as he rose up, I grasped his hand – I felt was one of those 'secret ones', who in Ireland have long been waiting for and expecting the blessing which now gladdens their hearts, and who continue to wrestle for blessings greater still. [87]

It is not difficult to see that prayer was a major feature of the 1859 revival in Coleraine as it has been the central feature of all revivals that have periodically occurred since the day of Pentecost. Alongside the central prayer meeting were numerous other prayer meetings which sprang up during the first week of revival. In the town centre as well as in the country areas surrounding Coleraine – Damhead, Ballindreen, Loughan, Articlave, Crossgar – all boasted of well-attended prayer meetings in homes. The young men in Coleraine set up a number of men's prayer meetings in different parts of the town, some of which took place every morning of the week. Prayer was offered for the young men who, once a week, distributed tracts and Christian periodicals to anyone interested.[88] Then there were congregational prayer meetings in the various places of worship. Initially these were geared to accommodating people who refused to go home after the evening meetings. Such meetings also

---

87. John Weir, *The Ulster Awakening*, p. 112.
88. William Richey, *Connor and Coleraine*, pp. 166–7.

served the practical aim of nipping any proselytising tendencies in the bud.[89]

'Fellowship meetings' also formed spontaneously, encompassing people who lived close to one another or worked with one another. These were able to build upon foundations laid during the previous decade. The fellowship groups established during the revival met during the lunch breaks. One such meeting was led by a woman who gathered around her some of the factory workers in Killowen, mostly young women, and together they prayed and read sections of the Bible.[90] District prayer meetings also sprang up here and there. There were still about fifteen operating five years after the revival. Finally, there were rooms where *ad hoc* prayer meetings took place. A weekly meeting had been organised, for example, by Thomas McWilliam in Portstewart before the revival started. He fitted and furnished a room rented at his own expense which could seat a hundred people. In November 1860 McWilliam was presented with several pounds' worth of books and a gold watch, by a number of laymen together with Rev. Jonathan Simpson, 'in grateful acknowledgement of his untiring labours in the cause of Christ' before, during and after the revival.[91] Zealous in the distribution of tracts were the members of the various denominational YMCAs. The group at St. Patrick's, Coleraine, which was formed during the revival, was particularly active.[92] The General Assembly of the Presbyterian Church in Ireland was equally full of praise for its young members. In the autumn of 1859 it encouraged evangelistic efforts and offered support to all those who might wish to train for the ministry[93].

---

89. William Richey, Ibid. p. 165.
90. William Richey, Ibid. p. 166.
91. *Coleraine Chronicle*, 17 November 1860.
92. Ibid., 22 October 1859 and 17 March 1860.
93. Ibid., 8 October 1859.

James McQuilkin and his partner in the gospel, Jeremiah Meneely, took converts around the country and preached to huge crowds wherever they went. It was reported by the Moderator of the General Assembly in 1859, Rev. William Gibson, that Ahoghill converts had for some time prior to June 1859 specifically prayed for the Holy Spirit to be poured out over Coleraine.[94] So it was that McQuilkin and Meneely spoke on the Dunmull Hill just outside Coleraine on 14 August.[95] They do not, however, seem to have held any meeting in the town. But they did provide a powerful example to other young men. The *Chronicle* reports that small groups of believers and converts from Coleraine went on evangelistic walks around the area along the north coast of Ireland.

Young men from Coleraine played just as crucial a role in spreading interest in the gospel as did the men at Kells. In the middle of June some of the Coleraine converts, together with more established members of churches, addressed a public meeting at Magilligan, at which some twenty people were prostrated under conviction of sin. The Presbyterian minister taking part in the meeting was delighted and overjoyed at seeing 'the power of God manifested amongst his people'.[96] On 19 June young converts spoke to a large crowd that assembled at Damhead. The content of the addresses is reported upon in the *Chronicle*: '[H]aving told with joy what God had done for them, and the happiness all would feel had they the same blessed assurance, [the earnest young men] entreated them to fly to the only sure Way of Salvation.' Many, the report continued, were 'deeply affected'.[97] Again, some days later, several young men from Coleraine were invited to attend an open-air praise and

---

94. William Gibson, *The Year of Grace*, p. 128.
95. *Coleraine Chronicle*, 13 August 1859 and 20 August 1859.
96. *Coleraine Chronicle*, 25 June 1859.
97. Ibid., 25 June 1859.

prayer meeting in Articlave. There were 1,500 present that evening; about forty people were reported to have been converted before midnight.[98] In Bushmills, too, addresses by young Coleraine men gave great momentum to the work being done in that town.[99]

Throughout July many other meetings were organised for them in Articlave,[100] Portstewart,[101] Castlerock, Maddy-benny, Loughan, Tullans, Ballysally, Coolderry, Wattstown, Farmhill, Ringrash, Drumaquill, the Irish Houses and Dam-head.[102] On 3 July about five hundred people turned up at the schoolhouse in Bohill to listen to converts from Coleraine. As one of the men began to speak a correspondent reported that the Lord 'seemed to pour down His Holy Spirit in large effusion on the people' and that 'in a short time a scene en-sued which will not soon be forgotten by those who had the privilege of witnessing it'.[103] In Ballyleese young work-ing-class men accompanied the Congregationalist minister, John Kydd, to a meeting that took place in torrential rain. Even in such inclement circumstances several people were so deeply impacted by the passionate appeals of the converts that they had to be ministered to by others.[104] In the Presby-terian meeting house at Ballywillan four hundred people lis-tened to spirit-stirring addresses by young Coleraine men; four people had to be physically carried out of the meet-ing.[105] At a meeting at Armoy on 29 July several young men and women cried out for mercy and were led to the session room to receive counsel.[106] They were warned not to confuse

---

98. Ibid., 2 July 1859.
99. Ibid., 9 July 1859.
100. Ibid., 9 July 1859.
101. Ibid., 16 July 1859.
102. Ibid., 16 July 1859.
103. Ibid., 9 July 1859.
104. *Coleraine Chronicle*, 9 July 1859.
105. Ibid., 23 July 1859.
106. Ibid., 13 August 1859.

physical manifestations with conversion, but to rest solely on the 'Word of prophecy' for their security. The speakers from Coleraine were persuaded to return again to Armoy to hold a follow-up meeting. In August Moss-side was the venue of meetings;[107] in September Coleraine converts were evangelising Ballycastle.[108]

Most of these young men had enjoyed little education and possessed few rhetorical skills, yet they were willing and available to do the work of evangelism. An extract of one such address by a young Coleraine man at an open-air meeting was reprinted in the *Glasgow Guardian* [109]:

> Dear friends, I was a great sinner, but Christ has been a great Saviour to me. Thanks be to God, He has brought me from darkness to light, and from the power of Satan unto God. If there be an unconverted soul before me, I would just ask you to seek Christ this night. Let it not pass without finding him. Oh, let it not pass without finding Christ to be precious to your souls, for oh! He is lovely, altogether lovely to them that find Him. Ah, what is hindering you from finding Him this night? What is hindering you? Is it not your unbelief? Will you not believe Christ's word? He says, 'Come unto me, all ye that labour and are heavy laden, and I will give you rest. Take my yoke upon you, and learn of me, for I am meek and lowly, and ye shall find rest to your souls. For my yoke is easy, and my burden is light.' Ah, yes, the burden of Jesus Christ is easily borne; ah, yes, it is easily borne, dear friends, besides the burden of sin. Ah, yes, some of us here felt the burden of sin, and we know the change now, God be thanked. I would just ask you this night to seek Him who can take away that burden of sin, who can enlighten your minds, and bring you from Satan's bondage, and set you free. Is there any one here this night who would refuse

107. Ibid., 6 August 1859.
108. Ibid., 10 September 1859.
109. Quoted by John Weir, *The Ulster Awakening*, p. 71f.

Christ's offer? Ah, I think not. Surely I do not look upon one who would say, I refuse Christ; Christ is all and in all to them that believe. I would ask you to come while it is day, for the night comes when none can work. Work now, come now. Do not wait till to-morrow; perhaps to-morrow will be too late. The devil's time is to-morrow; he told me to-morrow; and he is telling many here that you are too young to come to Christ, that you are [*sic*] time enough yet. But, ah, friends, heed not the devil. Seek Christ, seek Christ this night; seek him, for He is precious, He is precious. Oh, my friends, how long will you be slaves to sin? How long? Oh, think for a moment what it is to be under Satan's power. Will you not turn? 'Turn ye, turn ye,' says the Lord, 'why will ye die?' Will you choose to die, and go down to destruction, rather than seek God, and go to happiness? There are two classes of people here, the believers and the unbelievers. Ah, think of this, think of this. There are one of two places we must go to, just the two places; there is no third place. And there are but two roads. Which of the two will you choose? Will you take the broad road that leadeth to destruction, or will you choose the narrow road which leads to everlasting life? Will you choose to go to destruction, or to heaven? Which, which? You have your choice this night; now which will you choose? Ah, think for a moment, dear friends, is there any of us would choose that road that leads to destruction, any of us that would take hell for our portion? Oh, think of that, my dear friends; be warned this night, and flee from the wrath to come. Oh, the wrath of God, the wrath of God abiding on you, morning, noon, and night, in your lying down and in your rising up. Picture to yourselves, any of you that have a master; picture to yourselves that he should be angry with you, and his wrath abide upon you day and night. Would you find happiness? I am sure you would not. But, ah, what is the wrath of man to the wrath of God? Oh, think of this, my dear friends, and flee from the wrath to come. Oh, seek Christ, seek Christ now, for now is the accepted time, and now is the day of salvation.

It was the same old Christ-centred message, not an entertaining speech spiked with jocular asides, such as is all too common today. But the words were only part of the message. The journalist who captured the speech described the convert's whole bearing:

> [T]he power of the address [..] owed so much of its effect to the intense earnestness of the speaker. There could not have been a finer specimen of natural eloquence – the eloquence of the heart – than were afforded by this young disciple of Christ. There was no enthusiasm, no shrieking or vociferating, but melting appeals addressed with the tenderest affection to fellow-sinners. The speaker appeared as if he could not bear to part with his hearers until he had prevailed on them to come to the Saviour, who had done such great things for him. He saw so clearly, and felt so powerfully that there were peace, joy, and salvation in none but Christ, that he seemed as if he could not believe that his hearers would hesitate to take Him for all their salvation, and all their desire, when he was freely offered to them.

Here was a convert who felt with every fibre of his being that everything was at stake and yet a way out of a catastrophic situation had been provided. The preaching was not with enticing words of wisdom, but a demonstration of the power and zeal of the Holy Spirit. The message was simple, but effective, because the speaker believed every word he was saying. And a good number of those who heard him that evening did, too.

THANKSGIVING SERVICE

Given the background of the main beneficiaries of the revival in Coleraine it was again natural that a group of working-class men should request that a day be set aside by the town's Board of Commissioners as a Day of Thanksgiving for 'the mercies He has showered on the people of Coleraine'.[110] The group

---

110. *Coleraine Chronicle*, 12 November 1859.

sought the use of the Town Hall for the purpose of a time of special worship. Dr Macaldin, an elder at First Presbyterian who was also chairman of the general committee of the daily union prayer meeting, brought their request before the board. The General Assembly of the Presbyterian Church had chosen a Tuesday for this purpose. It was unanimously agreed that the proposal be adopted in Coleraine. On the evening of the third Tuesday in November, the 15th, a united worship service was held. The committee requested the public of Coleraine to stop all secular employments on that day and to ensure that 'the working classes more especially share in that privilege'.[111] Thanks were to be offered for the outpouring of the Holy Spirit which had occurred 'to an almost unparalleled extent'. Dr Macaldin said the people of Coleraine had been experiencing the literal fulfilment of Zechariah 12:10 during the previous months: 'And I will pour upon the house of David, and the inhabitants of Jerusalem, a spirit of grace and of supplications: and they shall look upon me.' As a result of the Spirit's work the whole community had enjoyed moral, spiritual and social blessings. With one or two exceptions the shopkeepers in town followed these recommendations and closed their places of business.[112] The Town Hall was 'crammed to suffocation' by over 1,500 people in the evening – almost as many people stood outside, but were eventually led away to the New Row Presbyterian meeting house for an inter-denominational service conducted by Episcopal, Presbyterian and Methodist ministers.[113]

In this context mention must be made of the expensive Bible and Book of Psalms which was bought with voluntary contributions from those who felt grateful to God for what had happened in Coleraine. They were to be a 'memorial of

---

111. Ibid., 12 November 1859.
112. *Coleraine Chronicle*, 19 November 1859.
113. From 4 p.m. to 5 p.m. the various denominational YMCAs also came together to hold their own meeting—'*the* meeting of the day', to quote the *Chronicle.*

the most gracious and wide-spread Religious Awakening which commenced upon the Evening of the Seventh of June' in 1859 'at an open-air meeting for prayer & preaching of the Gospel held on "the Fair Hill" of Coleraine, where many, "with strong crying and tears" were led to exclaim "What must we do to be saved?" and where many more throughout the night, and during the period which has since elapsed, were led by the Spirit of God to embrace an offered Saviour, and to find peace and joy in believing.'[114]

The copy of the Bible was, moreover, declared to be a memorial of the first opening of the Town Hall of Coleraine where, in the evening of 9 June, nearly one hundred persons 'agonised in mind, through conviction of Sin, and entirely prostrate in body, were borne into that building to obtain shelter during the night, and to receive consolation from the instructions and prayers of Christian ministers and Christian people'.

Thirdly, the Bible gave testimony to the 'blessed spirit of Union and brotherly love' which had been 'one fruit of God's wondrous work in Coleraine, and which has found its express [*sic*] and its witness' in the daily union prayer meeting in the Town Hall. 'Filled with adoring gratitude to Almighty God for the gift of the Holy Spirit, by whom many hundreds of souls have been brought to the Saviour' the signatories, ministers and laymen alike, wished the Bible to be kept in the custody of the town councillors 'as a token of our gratitude to God for the times of refreshing with which he has been pleased to visit Coleraine' and as a witness to coming generations of 'how good and how pleasant it is for brethren to dwell together in unity'.

The idea of purchasing the volumes, which are still kept by the Town Council, came from Rev. Canning of New Row.[115] A collection was made there, for this purpose, on Sunday 24 July. Canning dedicated the books for the use of the daily union prayer meeting on 10 October 1859. Rev.

---

114. *Coleraine Chronicle*, 15 October 1859.
115. John Weir, *The Ulster Awakening*, p. 73.

O'Hara, who chaired the meeting that day, was the first to use them in the service of God. The inscription was executed by Hugh Knox and was signed on 6 October by all the ministers labouring in Coleraine at the time, as well as by the members of the Committee of Management. The chairman of this rather *ad hoc* committee was Dr Macaldin.[116] Apart from Macaldin the other lay signatories were the editor of the *Chronicle*, John McCombie, a member of the Free Church of Scotland; James Nelson, the Scripture Reader and Baptist evangelist; the Town Commissioner Alexander Cuthbert, a tanner by profession and an elder at First Presbyterian;[117] the merchants John Young (a deacon in the Baptist Church[118]), John Horner and John Mathews; the surgeon Andrew C. Clarke; the registrar of marriages William Young; the keeper of the bridewell James Thompson, who, along with Mathews, was a vice-president of New Row Young Men's Christian Association[119]; Thomas Nevin, a member of the kirk session at Terrace Row Presbyterian and, later, secretary of the committee of the Coleraine Bible and Colportage Society[120]; the builder Thomas Boyd,[121] who was an elder at New Row Presbyterian, as was Mathews; property owner Samuel White, honorary secretary of the New Row Presbyterian Young Men's Christian Asso-

---

116. Macaldin later moved to London. *Coleraine Chronicle*, 17 and 25 May 1862.
117. Cuthbert died at the age of 68 in May 1860. The obituary made special mention of his 'indefatigable labours' during 'the recent remarkable revival of religion' in which he had overworked himself. 'Almost his last words were breathed in prayer for an abundant outpouring of the Holy Spirit upon the Church and the world.' *Coleraine Chronicle*, 12 May 1860.
118. Coleraine Baptist Church. Record Book from 1860.
119. *Coleraine Chronicle*, 18 October 1862.
120. Ibid., 1 May 1869.
121. It was Thomas Boyd who did the building extension work at Terrace Row, made necessary by the increased attendances following the revival. *Coleraine Chronicle*, 9 February 1861. He was presented with a new Bible by friends on 30 January 1862 for having 'affectionately and consistently taught and exemplified the truth that is in Jesus'. He taught Sabbath school and Bible classes in his home and led a district prayer meeting. Ibid., 1 February 1862.

ciation;[122] and the Congregationalist John Kirkpatrick.[123] Many rubbed shoulders at the various talks and lectures given throughout the year as well as at religious meetings. Horner, Thompson and Young were, for example, all associated with the Coleraine Young Men's Christian Association.[124] At meetings of the Edinburgh Bible Society auxiliary in Coleraine Horner, Mathews, Young, Macaldin and Cuthbert could be found gathered together.[125]

The list of signatures was recognised at the time as being very incomplete. Abraham J.H. Moody of Magilligan and Coleraine, a Town Commissioner and grocer, was nominated and elected a member of the committee of First Presbyterian Church at the end of November 1858. In June 1861 he was ordained an elder of that church by the laying on of hands by members of the presbytery. In an autobiographical memoir he claims he too played his part in meetings in *all* the places of worship in the town.[126] Though his name did not appear amongst those of the committee in charge of the united prayer meetings, he said, he was nevertheless a contributor to the cost of purchasing the Bible used and to the cost of renting the rooms. He referred to the months of June and July in particular as being a 'remarkable period of awakening sinners and causing them to fly to Jesus, sinners struck down and laid prostrate upon the earth calling out for mercy'. These bodily

---

122. Ibid., 27 October 1860. In March 1861 White was presented with a gift from his Sabbath school class in 'affectionate and grateful acknowledgement of his indefatigable labours' over the previous eight years, Ibid., 9 March 1861. He cooperated with the Brethren leader Charles Mackintosh in the distribution of tracts, Ibid., 18 August 1860. He was also vice-chairman of the Coleraine Literary and Scientific Association, Ibid., 25 November 1854.
123. Kirkpatrick moved from Armagh to Coleraine in 1856 and was admitted to fellowship at the Independent chapel. Coleraine Congregational Church. Minute Book 1854–1877, p. 58.
124. *Coleraine Chronicle*, 4 February 1852.
125. Ibid., 4 March 1854.
126. 'Autobiographical Memoir of Abraham J.H. Moody, 1809–1899,' pp. 20–2 (T2901/4/1, PRONI).

reactions to the preaching and testimonies, which had occurred in many people, he says, at the beginning of June, were, by the end of July, a 'more rare occurrence'. The usual spiritual measures of awakening people continued, however, without intermission. There had been prayer meetings night and day, non-stop preaching – 'it is a blessed period … a soul-sanctifying period and causing all to think of their future state … a time of reviving grace'. It was no doubt with reference to Christians such as Moody that the *Chronicle* suggested that the names of those 'many most earnest men [...] who were thought worthy to conduct services in connection with the Revival' be added to the memorial.[127] The proposal does not seem to have been acted upon. No representative of the Brethren signed the Bible although they remained very active in preaching the Word in the open air throughout 1859 and 1860.[128] The rector of the Parish Church in Killowen, William Sillito, was an evangelical and generally supportive (theoretically) of the revival, yet he did not sign it. He had actually missed many, if not all, of the revival meetings, spending the months between Easter and December at Portstewart, where he said he was recuperating from 'a severe attack of influenza'.[129]

Not all those named on the memorial Bible were in a position to devote their summer to the revival. William Richey, the minister of First Presbyterian, though a signer of the memorial, had in fact spent much of the summer in Harrogate. He had become seriously ill at the end of June. The *Chronicle* certainly felt that Richey had played a key role in the early days of the revival for it stated, in an editorial in July 1859, that 'were he taken away we feel it would be impossible to supply his place'.[130] The pastor of First Presbyterian was able, however, to return

---

127. *Coleraine Chronicle*, 15 October 1859.
128. Ibid., 18 August 1860.
129. William W. Sillito, *An Address on the Religious Revival, and Matters Connected Therewith, to the Parishioners of Killowen, especially those who worship in the Parish Church*, Coleraine 1859, p. 5.
130. *Coleraine Chronicle*, 2 July 1859.

to Coleraine at the end of September.[131] His place had been temporarily filled by Rev. James McKee, a missionary in India with the London Missionary Society.[132] It was not long after his return to Ireland that Rev. Richey handed in his resignation on health grounds.[133] He sailed off to the warmer climes of Australia, where he died.[134]

At the 1860 General Assembly of the Presbyterian Church in Ireland Rev. Robert Knox expressed his concern that Presbyterians did not fall into the habit of simply commemorating the extraordinary year of 1859. They had to avoid the dangers of lethargy and nostalgia. He called upon his fellow pastors to 'look for the continuation of the work of the Spirit in the present year and pray for it'.[135] Each generation, he believed, had a responsibility to listen to the Spirit of God.

131. Ibid., 2 July 1859, 9 July 1859 and 10 September 1859.
132. Ibid., 7 April 1860. McKee returned to India in 1860.
133. Ibid., 7 July 1860.
134. Julia E. Mullin, *The Presbytery of Coleraine*, Belfast 1979, p. 53f.
135. *Coleraine Chronicle*, 7 July 1860.

Chapter 4: Reactions to the Revival

People are generally afraid of religious experience they do not know. This not uncommonly leads to rationalisations of that fear which exhibit themselves in cleverly fashioned critiques and explanations. Sigmund Freud and Karl Marx sought to explain the nature of religious belief and practice in different ways, the former by appealing to unresolved psychological and relational conflicts, the latter by an analysis of societal relations which made such belief necessary for the victims of economic exploitation. Both have had enormous influence over the minds of men and women in the twentieth century. Interestingly, rather than looking objectively and through the lens of Scripture at expressions of spirituality, Christians revert to the use of similar tactics during periods of revival.

Fear is a bad teacher. Those familiar with the account of the outpouring of the Holy Spirit on the Day of Pentecost know of religious, Pharisaic reactions to the invasion of human activity by that divine person: those touched by and filled by the Holy Spirit were mocked as drunkards and madmen. They were perceived by the religious establishment as rebels who had taken leave of their senses and lost all self-control. That story has often been repeated through history. Jonathan Edwards was eventually voted out of his church in Northampton after he changed its policy on communion. Some members had objected to the manner in which revival had been brought to his congregation. Visionaries will always suffer at the hands of those who are content with the status quo, but should be encouraged to know that history generally applauds their actions and vision and passes over in silence those critics of particular methods and effects. Ulster in 1859 was no exception to this spiritual law.

MEDIA BIAS

The nineteenth century was no different from our own in that the media were intent on discrediting religious phenomena. Articles appeared in the *Times* of London, the *Lancet*, the *Edinburgh Medical Journal*, the *Dublin Quarterly Journal of Medical Science*, the *Journal of Medical Science* and the *Medical Times*, in which the learned tried to explain how and why ignorant men and women were succumbing to an epidemic of religious hysteria and fanaticism, causing insanity in some and depraved minds in others. Some medical authorities claimed the revival fed on the instability of underfed, malnourished females. Others said it was solely a result of the excitable Irish temperament. The visions and trances, paralysis, periods of deafness and dumbness, which were all recorded as taking place during the revival, were put down to nervous temperaments. Some believed there was a virus at work in the population. Ulster's four district lunatic asylums admitted sixty-seven cases in the year to 31 March 1860 with 'religion' listed as the cause of the mental illness, and it was assumed at the time that these people had become unstable as a result of the revival. The *Times* voiced the prevailing theological views held by ministers in the Church of England, namely that revivalists were in error in believing that instantaneous conversions took place. In this view, religion which freed itself from ministerial control became of necessity emotional and unbalanced. The *Times*, however, played down the religious factor, not wishing to give support to the growing secularist movement, and noted the general increase of insanity in nineteenth-century society. This media bombardment, highly selective in its choice of facts to report, was resisted by a good number of medical authorities who were themselves supportive of the revival.

The main press organ in Ulster offering resistance to the revival was *The Weekly Northern Whig*. It was the voice of theological liberalism.[1] It wrote in June of the 'Extravagances of the "Revival" Movement at Coleraine'.[2] The report had been supplied by a clergyman. It read as follows:

> The work commenced here on last Tuesday evening, by an open-air gathering, at which some of an organised band, which travels the country for this purpose, joined about a dozen clergymen in preaching, singing and yelling. Some of the organisers were manifestly idiotic, and all were grossly ignorant of the simplest principles of Christianity. Since then, things have become daily worse and wor[s]e. Business may be said to be at an end; and, from morning till night, but much more from night till morning, clergymen, bad characters, and fast commercial travellers, who can find nothing else to do, and wish to be able to tell a good story for the rest of their lives, give the tone to hundreds of persons who roam the streets or roam from house to house yelling, screaming and blaspheming. Respectable and educated young women contend with notorious bad characters for the privilege of kissing and embracing well-known profligates on the public streets. Numbers of girls from the country have come into town and remained at the above occupation. Anyone who seems to be in his right senses is threatened and reviled by the maniacs; and a gentleman who endeavoured to stay the torrent ran the risk of being drowned. The clergy engaged in the movement relate the conversions of Unitarians, and the rabble does the same office for Roman Catholics. A young woman stands up in the assembly, and calls on some one to whom she takes a fancy

---

1. Finlay Holmes, *Our Irish Presbyterian Heritage*, Belfast 1992, p. 108.
2. *The Weekly Northern Whig*, 4 June 1859.

to advance and kiss her. They climb up trees in order to meet the Saviour. They chase the devil for hours about the house until they get him finally into a corner, when they choke him. Bands of seven or eight, male and female, parade the streets and kiss at every street corner. Then come the revelations. Every one, of course, sees Christ, but their view is oftener bent on the infernal regions. ... The same seer saw a deceased corpulent person, put to a strange use. The old Devil was cutting him up in pieces and feeding the young ones with him! Whenever they favour us with a view of Heaven, it is found quite filled with orange lodges in session. Now, sir, these are not stupid attempts at jokes, but the fundamental points of the new religion, preached and circulated. When anyone 'takes it', the *sisters and brothers* [italics in the original] run and cover the party with Bibles, and then all commence to howl and yell fearfully. One case was probably intractable (Mrs. ------), and they beat her severely about the head with Bibles. No one who knows anything of either history or human nature can feel any surprise at this sort of thing. The 'revivalists', like many other bodies, are made up of knaves and fools. Want of religious principle and general ignorance prepares them for 'it'; the heat of the weather keeps it up; profligates and pickpockets find their account in it; many join it in the expectation of being supported while it lasts; expectation keeps people's minds constantly on the stretch; the howls of the 'organisers' would drive even sensible people mad; whatever power mesmerism has comes into play, and the end of all is a delusion which only requires the inspiration of some ill-disposed ruffian to produce mischief. Such things have happened before, and the present times shew that we are not a whit worse or better than the Fratricelli, the Beguins, the Munster Anabaptists, and the others who, at different times, have brought disgrace on religion, as well as shame on human nature. It is not surprising, as a wind-up to these things, to find that several persons have gone to lunatic asylums, and others are under restraint in their own houses.

Another article in the same issue of the paper attacked 'the religious commotion known as Revivalism'. In an attempt to garner support for the radically sceptical rejection of the revival, the *Northern Whig* quoted from a speech by the influential Presbyterian, Dr Henry Cooke, given in May Street meeting house. The talk was commented upon as follows: 'So far as we have been able to ascertain, the distinguished presbyter steered a cautious course in dealing with the new-fangled "awakening".' Whilst Cooke's statement that the 'manifestations', in certain cases at least, had been followed by apparent reformation of character, and his readiness to regard the work as something supernatural, from which good would arise, were grudgingly noted in passing, Cooke, the paper emphasised, had given no encouragement to 'the rage amongst the thoughtless and the idle, for running after conversions' nor to the disposition to 'work up the excitement upon the "keep the trade" going principle exhibited by fanatical agitators.'

The first, extremely critical article in the *Northern Whig* drew a swift response from an 'observer' of the revival in Coleraine, claiming the report was 'a tissue of falsehoods' and 'a combination of lies, such as only your contemptible and little-minded "clerical" correspondent could compose or imagine'.[3] The editor of the *Chronicle* said the County Derry clergyman's remarks were 'totally devoid of the least particle of truth'.

SCOTTISH RESPONSES

During the second half of 1859 there was a large influx of religious pilgrims from Scotland and England and further afield. From Scotland came large numbers of clergymen and laymen representing the Free Church.[4] They took back news of what was happening in Ulster. Many also took issues of

---

3.   Northern Whig 25 June 1859; *Coleraine Chronicle*, 18 June 1859.
4.   *Coleraine Chronicle*, 25 June 1859.

the *Chronicle* back home with them. Its reports were read out at meetings in London, for example. Nine ministers and laymen from across the water addressed meetings in Coleraine in the last week of June 1859.[5] In the second week of July nine names of clergymen are recorded, fourteen in the third week and twelve in the fourth week, together with 'hosts of laymen'.[6] Eighteen ministers from Britain were in Coleraine in the second week of August, thirty-three in the final week. Twenty-one names are recorded in the first week of September, seventeen in the third week – including a Rev. Dr Lachlin Taylor, who had come all the way from Toronto to witness events.[7] The actual number of clergymen and laymen who came to Coleraine is almost certainly higher than the 226 names recorded on the pages of the local newspaper. Given the population of the town at the time (5,500) the number of visitors is high, reflecting the great interest excited by news reports. Clergy thronged to the town, said the *Chronicle*, as if Coleraine had become the centre of the glorious work of reviving the church.[8] It talked of the 'migration season of our Scotch brethren'.[9] 'This city of our habitation has become the head quarters, as it were, to which and from which earnest men from all parts of the United Kingdom come and go for and with tidings of what God the Lord is doing for His people.'[10]

This rather lofty view of a small town in the north of Ireland was a reflection of the wholehearted support the editor of the *Chronicle* gave to the revival movement. Its reporting was partial, not to say biased. This encouraged a paper like the *Glasgow Herald* to claim the *Chronicle's* editor had been 'clearly knocked out of his Irish mind by the agitation of the

5. *Coleraine Chronicle*, 2 July 1859.
6. Ibid., 30 July 1859.
7. Ibid., 24 September 1859.
8. Ibid., 6 August 1859 and 13 August 1859.
9. Ibid., 23 July 1859.
10. Ibid., 6 August 1859.

times'.[11] In spite of such warnings there was a lot going on in Coleraine which attracted hundreds of onlookers from over the Irish Sea. How can one explain the fact that even a small, regional newspaper like the *Huron Signal* reported that the people of Coleraine were an awful illustration of 'social depravity' as they engaged in 'the most shocking, lamentable and disgusting extravaganza' which had ever 'deluded a portion of the human race'. 'The most terrible of all human maladies, fanatical outrage, has broken out in Ireland,' it wrote. 'The violent insanities of Coleraine and all similar yelling extravaganzas can result only from false and unworthy and absurd notions of the Supreme intelligence.' Moreover, 'Would any sane, intelligent man offer the Coleraine worship to an infinite and eternal Being? Certainly not.'[12] For some Canadians, at least, the madness breaking out in Coleraine was an insult to the Supreme Power of the Universe. One man's revival is another man's 'insane ravings'.

For liberal Presbyterians in Ulster there was much said and done during the revival which they perceived to be offensive. Class prejudices, denominational traditions and loyalties, views on race and racial characteristics or sexual stereotypes – these and many other factors led people in 1859 to resist the powerful religious movement for change. Many of the arguments used in our own day to decry phenomena such as the 'Toronto blessing' can be found in the histories of revivals. Rev. Dr Reichel of the Assembly's College spoke in Malone Street, Belfast, in March 1861, on the revival and said it had been a 'miserable caricature which disgraced not only our religion but our common sense'.[13] There were in fact a number of features of the revival which met with widespread disapproval. Some Presbyterians took issue with the theology of assurance which became a leading motif of

---

11. *Coleraine Chronicle*, 2 July 1859.
12. Ibid., 13 August 1859.
13. Ibid., 30 March 1861.

the testimonies. The unusual and, some said, supernatural manifestations caused confusion and consternation among clerical elites.

Much of the criticism, however, had to do with matters of style and decorum. Like the Kells men, the converts, including those in Coleraine, spoke the common language of the people. There was no flowery rhetoric here, no sermons read off scripts. What they could do, they did do: provide enthusiastic accounts of their own experience. This was not appreciated by everyone. Rev. John Williams, a Baptist minister in Glasgow, wrote that he felt 'disgusted' at the 'ignorance, stupidity and superstition' of what he called 'the speaking converts'. 'Several good men of Coleraine', he claimed, felt similarly disgusted. He says one convert talked for a long time 'in an incoherent manner' about a vision of a black man and a white man he had received while under conviction of sin. Williams was left with the impression that the convert had found peace, not by faith in the atoning work of Christ, but by seeing the white man wrenching him, the convert, out of the hands of the black man.[14] On another note, it is likely that Williams was also angered by the fact that converts had been allowed to preach in Coleraine, while he, an educated and ordained minister, had not been given the opportunity.

For rational intellectuals, especially well-paid ones, there is always a lot to bemoan about revivals. Criticism of the words, accents and rhetorical style of these largely un-educated people entered the letters pages of the *Chronicle*. The Congregationalist minister in Coleraine had no such class prejudices. According to Rev. Kydd the awakening in the town was chiefly among the working classes, many of whom had neither decent clothes nor decent language.[15] It

---

14. *Coleraine Chronicle*, 6 August 1859.
15. James W. Massie, *Revivals in Ireland. Facts, Documents and Correspondence*, London 1859, p. 9.

was natural and clear to him that working-class people were drawn to men like McQuilkin and Meneely to hear 'plain, uneducated men speak fluently [...] the great truths of the Gospel'.[16] Though generally respectable in appearance, the converts from Ballymoney who brought their message to Coleraine all spoke English without elegance and with broad County Antrim accents.[17]

The use of a regional accent and ineloquent language had, two years previously, led to a barrage of criticism in British newspapers of Charles Spurgeon, who spoke with a cockney accent. 'His whole speech or turn of thought savours of Cheapside and the Bank,' wrote one critic. The Baptist preacher liked to use what the *Edinburgh Witness* called 'vulgarities' and 'figures of speech borrowed from the shop and street, which unknown before in the pulpit, attracted public notice much on the same principle as the stage clown competed for it with Whitfield at Bartholomew Fair'. Many of Spurgeon's colloquialisms were said to 'border on profaneness', yet they gave his sermons a certain homely tone 'or rather twang' which seemed to be the 'true secret of his success' with the masses.[18] Similarly, it seems most probable that the simple message of the working-class men (most of the converts who spoke at meetings were men) had a great appeal. A certain Mr W. Craig, who had close links with the society at Connor that financially supported the converts on their speaking tours (six evangelists were employed by this society at £10 per annum) wrote in a letter to the Coleraine paper: 'These missionaries speak the common language of the people, and God is acknowledging their labours wherever they go.'[19] The *Chronicle*'s defence of the language of

---

16. *Coleraine Chronicle*, 2 July 1859.
17. *Londonderry Guardian*, 14 June 1859.
18. *Londonderry Sentinel*, 4 September 1859.
19. *Coleraine Chronicle*, 16 July 1859. Craig notes in passing that Mrs Conville, the Baptist missionary who had unwittingly contributed to McQuilkin's conversion, had returned to London.

the converts, and of McQuilkin and Meneely in particular, was not ill-founded. The language of the market place was, after all, the language Luther deliberately selected when translating the Hebrew and Greek testaments into German. The rest, as they say, is history.

FEMALE PREACHERS

One particular feature of the revival which caused raised eyebrows was the presence of female preachers on platforms (though usually not in pulpits) who were granted permission to speak on religious matters in the province.[20] Reference has already been made in our introduction to the addresses delivered by Miss McKinney of Omagh. In all likelihood McKinney was a Primitive Methodist or simply a woman who had received a direct calling from God. The American Methodist, Mrs Phoebe Palmer, spoke at a number of meetings in the Coleraine town and district.[21] Many people went forward as penitents to the communion rails of Donegall Square Methodist Church in Belfast, when she and her husband addressed those assembled.[22] There were two female converts from Rasharkin who were members of a group of converts travelling around the region, preaching the gospel to any who would listen. They addressed a meeting in a Methodist church in Derry, giving their testimonies, exhorting listeners to 'pray heartily to God for His Holy Spirit and the pardon of their sins' and offering spiritual assistance to those who were prostrated under conviction of sin.[23] In Portrush, too, women were

---

20. On the role of women in the revival see Janice Holmes, 'The "World Turned Upside Down": Women in the Ulster Revival of 1859,' in Janice Holmes and Diane Urquhart (eds.), *Coming into the Light: The Work, Politics and Religion of Women in Ulster 1840–1940*, Belfast 1994, pp. 126–53.
21. Phoebe Palmer, *Four Years in the Old World*, Toronto 1866, pp. 45–83; *Coleraine Chronicle*, 6 August 1859. The Palmers joined Rev. George Vance for Sunday services at the Methodist chapel in Coleraine on 31 July 1859.
22. *Coleraine Chronicle*, 23 July 1859.
23. *Londonderry Guardian*. 14 June 1859.

actively involved in the pastoral care of converts. Jonathan Simpson, who had no housekeeper at the time, received the voluntary help of the Misses Harley, who had come over specially from Glasgow to do what they could. Their visit was described as being 'providential' for 'Christian ladies are the best counsellors'.[24] Some clergymen reacted to the excitement by allowing uneducated teenage girls to address their congregations from the pulpit.[25] The significant contributions of these women to the revival in Ulster do not seem to have caused much public controversy at the time. Privately, some male clergymen at least must have wondered about the theology of 'female preaching'. It was only fifteen years after the revival, when a Mrs Leadbeater preached in Coleraine and other places, a furious letter battle was unleashed in the local press in the north of Ireland.[26]

Other women came to local prominence at the time and enjoyed a few seconds of fame. Some fell in trances, lost control of their bodies, went deaf, dumb and blind for certain periods of time. Some claimed to have received divine markings on their bodies from the Lord. There were notorious cases of women claiming whole Bible verses had been tattooed by the Holy Spirit on to their bodies. Often these cases of stigmata turned out to be impostures. The most celebrated case was that of a Belfast woman who had a fiery cross and 'Jeasus' [*sic!*] imprinted on one breast and 'Christ' on the other.[27] Not a few Presbyterian ministers bought train tickets for Belfast to check the evidence. She was subsequently 'inspected by several' of them in the 'squalor

24. Ibid., 5 July 1859.

25. W.T. Latimer, *History of the Irish Presbyterians*, Belfast 1893, p. 220.

26. *Coleraine Chronicle*, 1874 (29 August, 26 September, 17 October, 24 October, 31 October, 14 November, 21 November, 28 November, 5 December, 12 December, 26 December).

27. A.R. Scott, *The Ulster Revival of 1859*, p. 128; W.S. Armour, *Armour of Ballymoney*, London 1934, p. 5.

of her abode'.[28] Clearly, such incidents helped to disqualify revivalism in the eyes of those inclined to generalise.

PRESBYTERIAN OPPOSITION

The historian of Irish Presbyterianism, W.T. Latimer, noted that while three-quarters of Presbyterian ministers were actually involved in the revival, about 10 per cent offered some opposition.[29] Two such critics were the Presbyterian ministers Isaac Nelson (Belfast) and William Hamilton (Edenderry), who attacked the revival as a movement Presbyterians should have opposed on theological grounds. Nelson's book on the subject *The Year of Delusion: A Review of 'The Year of Grace'* (Belfast 1860–2) was critical of most features of the revival: 'violent conversion', the American influences, lay preaching, the supernatural elements. Nelson, a supporter of the Evangelical Alliance, was said to be the only minister in Belfast hostile to the movement. Hamilton was minister at Edenderry, County Tyrone, from 1840 to 1872. His *Inquiry into the Scriptural Character of the Revival of 1859* (Belfast 1866), which was reprinted a few years ago and distributed by the Ballymena-based Covenant Reformed Fellowship, agreed with most of the points Nelson had highlighted. He added that the prostrations were 'Satan's work'.[30] Isaac Nelson could not have accepted such a judgment, as he thought all belief in the Devil and demons was 'absurd'.[31]

This was not the view of some of the practitioners of revival. A friend of James McQuilkin, in an article for the *Chronicle* in July 1859, drew attention to this aspect of revival that most contemporaries shied away from. He noted in the Kells and Connor neighbourhood that there were a number of people of whom he writes: 'I cannot look upon them

---

28. *Coleraine Chronicle*, 17 September 1859.
29. W.T. Latimer, *History of the Irish Presbyterians*, Belfast 1893, p. 219.
30. William Hamilton, *An Inquiry into the Scriptural Character of the Revival of 1859*, Belfast 1866, pp. 250–1.
31. Isaac Nelson, *The Year of Delusion: A Review of 'The Year of Grace'*, Belfast 1860–62, pp. 38, 56.

without shuddering. … They seem to answer the description of those given in the New Testament as possessed of devils.' He said that 'this is also God's mysterious work' though he could 'not fathom it'.

CATHOLIC OPPOSITION

Others saw the whole movement as devilish. As there was much reporting on individual Catholics being 'saved' by Protestants it was inevitable that the representatives of the Roman Catholic Church would make some response to the revival movement. The *Chronicle* encouraged proselytism. When six Catholics in Malin renounced communion with their church and became Presbyterians, its editor expressed his hope that 'many other Romanists may be led to follow their good example'.[32] One Catholic who was physically prostrated at a revival meeting was David Creswell of Moneymore. On getting back to his feet he found to his amazement that he had been healed of his terrible stammer.[33] On 17 September 1859 it was reported that a Catholic woman in Lisburn had become affected by revivalist fervour. Two Protestant clergymen had gone to see her at the request of neighbours. Shortly afterwards, it was reported, she had been 'carried away in a covered car by a Roman Catholic priest'.[34] In Limavady it was claimed priests were preventing Catholics from attending revival meetings. Alternative evening meetings were arranged in the chapel there. On 14 August 1859 a young Catholic woman was 'struck' during one of these meetings.[35] The doors were immediately shut to prevent her screaming being heard by those outside. Another Catholic woman was stricken in her own home. A correspondent recorded that her father began to pray for the Blessed Virgin to

32. *Coleraine Chronicle*, 20 August 1859.
33. William Gibson, *The Year of Grace* [Reprint, Belfast 1989], pp. 208–10.
34. *Coleraine Chronicle*, 17 September 1859.
35. Ibid., 27 August 1859.

come and banish the evil spirit from his daughter, to which the girl cried: 'None but Jesus – none but Jesus'. The interpretation from the reporter read: 'Thank God, Rome is daily losing her power over the deluded people in this place.' The revival was seen, then, by some at least, as a divine blessing upon the Protestant people of Ulster at a time when Catholicism was becoming increasingly self-assertive and confident. 'Roman Catholics have burned their prayer books, and become Protestants, in spite of the virtues of holy water and wine,' mocked an editorial in the *Chronicle*.[36] Elsewhere the editor noted that a Catholic prayer, printed on a leaf of paper, was circulating in the town which promised to keep them secure from the enemies of Christ.[37] One Catholic cleric was said to be selling a kind of healing plaster on the streets of Coleraine. It was to be applied to the body of a person whose mind had become 'diseased' by the revival. Only 8d. was given in change out of a half crown for the plasters which had been applied to two women. The two 'specially blessed' young women had since had their minds 'enlightened by the light which is certainly not in that church'.[38] In response to such journalism, the parish priest in Coleraine, Alex Macmullen, complained in a letter dated 26 July 1859 about the local newspaper's tendency to 'cherish aimless animosity' against Catholics. The existence of such prayers and plasters was denied by Macmullen.[39] For the editor of the *Chronicle* this was all just 'Popish hostility' to the movement of the Spirit.[40] 'If, as certain Roman Catholic parties allege, the movement be a work of Satan, then Satan is manifestly "divided against himself", for in every case the result is conversion to a life of piety and earnest cooperation with others

---

36. *Coleraine Chronicle*, 4 June 1859.
37. Ibid., 23 July 1859 and 30 July 1859.
38. Ibid., 30 July 1859.
39. Ibid., 30 July 1859.
40. Ibid., 23 July 1859.

for the promotion of God's glory and the extension of the Redeemer's kingdom.'[41]

For Dr Paul Cullen, the Roman Catholic Bishop of Armagh who was later made a Cardinal, the revival was 'diabolical' in nature.[42] Cullen had helped reform the Irish Catholic Church and he spearheaded a devotional revolution in the country in the middle of the nineteenth century.[43] Many Catholics no doubt followed the bishop's directions, and for obvious reasons. A Belfast paper reported on 28 May 1859: 'The Roman Catholics [..] maintain that it [the revival] is a mania whose origin must be laid to the charge of Satan; but this opinion is probably a little influenced by the fact that any Roman Catholics who have come under its influence have ceased to hold communion with the Church of Rome, and have become Bible Christians.'[44] The parish priest in Portrush, Rev. McCann, also spoke of the revival's 'diabolical influence' which was leading to hallucinations and suicide. The 'religious madness', he claimed, was 'one of the most monstrous delusions' that had yet blighted Ireland.[45]

The editor of the *Chronicle*, who, admittedly, was not impartial, rejected these accusations out of hand. As far as he was concerned the revival was 'in no way denominational or sectarian' since members of all denominations had been similarly affected. In one editorial he quotes the American theologian Jonathan Edwards to back up his argument. McCombie emphasised, 'A work is not to be judged of by any effects on the bodies of men, such as tears, trembling, groans, loud outcries, agony of body, or the failing of bodily strength.' Only a changed life and a holy character marked especially by selfless love were proof that a work of God had been done.

---

41. *Coleraine Chronicle*, 28 May 1859.
42. .E. R. Norman, *The Catholic Church and Ireland in the Age of Rebellion 1859–1873*, London 1965, p. 32.
43. Emmet Larkin, "The Devotional Revolution in Ireland, 1850–75", in *The American Historical Review*, Vol. 77, Nr. 3, June 1972, pp. 625–652.
44. *Belfast Weekly News* 28 May 1859.
45. *Coleraine Chronicle*, 30 July 1859.

McCombie warned scoffers not to blaspheme the Holy Spirit by referring to the revival as 'the work of the devil'.[46]

CATHOLIC SUPPORT

While Catholic leaders such as Bishop Cullen and Bishop Flannery of Killaloe[47] opposed the revival as a devilish movement, prominent and less prominent laymen saw the movement in a completely different light. One Dublin paper which remained sceptical, nevertheless suggested a practical test be applied to the revival: could it deal with sectarianism – the 'evil spirit of party'? Would it lead to the abandonment of Orange processions?

This issue will be dealt with in the next chapter in greater depth. Let it suffice here to quote a Catholic judge, whose testimony was published by the *Banner of Ulster*:

> The Right Hon. Chief-Baron Pigott, in sentencing three prisoners last week at the Down Assizes for riot and assault, in connexion with a miserable exhibition of party feeling, took occasion to refer to the religious movement in the North as having extinguished all party animosities, and produced the most wholesome moral results upon the community at large. His lordship spoke in the most favourable terms of the movement, and expressed a hope that it would extend over the whole country, and influence society to its lowest depths. [...] It is altogether a striking and significant testimony to the genuineness of the work, and bears its appropriate lessons of reproof to those Unitarian and Episcopal divines who have shown such an unseemly hostility to the movement.[48]

Less prominent Catholic laymen also held a positive opinion on the revival. Rev. Canning of New Row reported to the Free

---

46. *Coleraine Chronicle*, 18 June 1859.
47. A.R. Scott, *The Ulster Revival of 1859*, p. 176.
48. *Londonderry Standard*, 4 August 1859. This article specifically mentions a sermon by George Salmon, D.D., Fellow of Trinity College Dublin, as an example of the tendency among some Anglican divines to reduce the revival to natural or artificial causes. The sermon was published under the title *Evidences of the Work of the Holy Spirit, being a Discourse preached in Stephen's Church, Dublin, on Sunday July 3, 1859*.

Church Commission on Irish revivals in August that he had overheard a Catholic saying the movement was the work of the devil. To this his friend had replied: 'If that be so, the devil is not nearly so clever as I took him to be; but I never knew the devil to shut up public houses, to make drunkards sober, and to stop profane swearing.' In fact, he could not think of a single result of the revival which had not been beneficial.[49]

ANGLICAN OPPOSITION

Chief Baron Pigott alluded to Anglican opposition to the revival. Dr George Salmon preached on the topic on Sunday July 3, 1859. Published together with an appendix under the title *Evidences of the Work of the Holy Spirit, being a Discourse*, he expressed his view that the whole revival movement was 'from first to last [...] an excitement "artificially" got up, and [...] producing "disease", "hysteria", and other organic derangements of body and mind, in the hope of their eventuation in spiritual good'.[50] For Salmon, and some of his colleagues, dissenting denominations were likely to make more of the revival than the Church of Ireland, because it was not consistent with principles of the latter to permit laymen to speak in religious assemblies.[51] In the north of Ireland the same reservations were initially felt by Anglicans. It was noted that Episcopalians in Derry stood aloof from the Nonconformists who had taken a lead in the movement. After some hesitation some began to conduct their own services in their own churches.[52] The initial aloofness had not a little to do

---

49. *Coleraine Chronicle*, 20 August 1859 and 27 August 1859.
50. *Londonderry Standard*, 4 August 1859.
51. Other denominations were struggling with the same issue. The General Assembly of the established Church of Scotland debated the principle of admitting laymen to the pulpit on 30 May 1859. This debate had been developing since December 1858 when Reginald Radcliffe, a 'gentleman of independent means', had conducted a series of evangelistic and revival meetings in Aberdeen. These had been very well attended and had produced remarkable effects. Dr Paul of Aberdeen Presbytery believed, however, that the law of the Church was being violated by such practices. *Coleraine Chronicle*, 4 June 1859.
52. *Coleraine Chronicle*, 16 July 1859.

with Presbyterian criticism of the Anglican form of government which had been poisoning the air in the city over the previous years.[53] In particular, the two Presbyterians most prominent in the revival in Derry, Denham and McClure, had played a rather unedifying role in the controversy with Anglicanism. Little wonder, then, that Anglican hearts did not immediately warm to Presbyterian advances.

The Archdeacon of Derry, A.W. Edwards, in a letter clarifying his position on the 'powerful influence' of the revival on his parish, expressed his guarded view that not everyone behaving oddly was 'necessarily possessed by the devil'.[54] Not a few Anglican priests were either wholly or partially opposed to the revival.[55] The Lord Bishop of Cork, Cloyne and Ross prohibited his clergy from attending meetings. He was particularly critical of extemporaneous prayer.[56] Archdeacon Stopford and Rev. O.T. Dobbin condemned many of the accompanying 'hysterical' phenomena of the revival.[57] Other rectors of parishes issued words of caution, warning people to beware particularly of the proselytising activities of the various dissenter groups.[58] One Anglican clergyman claimed that the masses were being controlled by 'a kind of animal magnetism.'[59]

53. Alan R. Acheson, *The Evangelicals in the Church of Ireland, 1784–1859* (Ph. D. thesis, Queen's University Belfast, 1967), p. 310.

54. *Coleraine Chronicle,* 10 September 1859.

55. For the impact of the revival on the Church of Ireland see Alan R. Acheson, *The Evangelicals in the Church of Ireland,* 1784–1859, pp. 309–339.

56. *Coleraine Chronicle,* 11 February 1860, p. 4.

57. *Coleraine Chronicle,* 3 September 1859, p. 2.

58. Thomas MacNeece, *Words of Caution and Counsel on the Present Religious Revival, addressed to his parishioners* (Belfast, 1859); Arthur W. Edwards, *A Letter on the Religious Revival, addressed to the parishioners of Dunboe* (Londonderry, 1859); Daniel Mooney, Revivals. *A Sermon: Preached in the Parish Church of Ballymena, on Sunday, the 5th June, 1859* (Armagh-Belfast-Ballymena, 1859); Stephen Gwynn, *The Ulster Revival: A Strictly Natural and Strictly Spiritual Work of God. Being a reply to certain popular opinions, as to its supernatural and physical character* (Coleraine, 1859); William W. Sillito, *An Address on the Religious Revival, and matters connected therewith, to the Parishioners of Killowen, especially those who worship in the Parish Church* (Coleraine, 1859).

59. *Coleraine Chronicle,* 18 June 1859, p. 5.

ANGLICAN SUPPORT

Only late in the summer, and only in a few localities, did Episcopalian ministers begin to conduct their own revival services[60]. Thus, the established church in Ireland played only a minor role in the revival movement of 1859. Only moderate enthusiasm for it could be engendered. There were, however, noteworthy evangelicals who were of the decided opinion that the revival was, at its core, a movement of the Holy Spirit. Alan Acheson and A.R. Scott name nearly three dozen individuals who supported revival meetings.

One such man was the Anglican parish priest in Coleraine, James O'Hara (1801–1893), a solid evangelical.[61] He was related to the Scottish evangelists James and Robert Haldane.[62] In 1840 he was nominated by Rev. Edward Harvey to the curacy of Coleraine, where he remained till Harvey's death in 1848. He was thereupon appointed rector, a position he occupied until 1869. The congregation at St. Patrick's almost trebled during his ministry. The building had to be enlarged twice. He took an active, if moderating, part in the revival of 1859, always discouraging the excesses of emotion, yet always sympathetic to 'those who sought to receive a spiritual blessing' or impart a blessing to others. On the one hand, he had felt it necessary to caution the young and inexperienced members to control their zeal. On the other hand,

60. Ibid., 16 July 1859, 4; James William Massie, *Revivals in Ireland. Facts, Documents, and Correspondence* (London, 1859), p. 59. Cp. Alfred Russell Scott, *The Ulster Revival*, pp. 171–4.

61. On James O'Hara see: *Coleraine Chronicle*, 1 April 1848, 8 April 1848, 15 April 1848, 29 April 1848, 31 December 1859, 3 January 1860, 29 May 1869, 31 March 1900 and 23 June 1900. An obituary which contains much useful information can be found in the issue of the *Chronicle* for 19 August 1893.

62. Alexander Haldane, *The Lives of Robert Haldane of Airthrey, and his brother, James Alexander Haldane, London 1853* [Banner of Truth edition 1990], pp. 306, 356, 630–1, 695. O'Hara reported that Haldane's views on the believers' union with Christ had shown him 'more of the HOLINESS necessarily connected with FAITH than any Commentary that has ever come in my way'.

he established additional catechetical classes, held on a week-ly basis, and organised special services in his church, which were held 'very frequently'.[63] In December 1859 he was pre-sented with a full set of canonicals by the female members of his church. The accompanying address stated: 'Throughout a period of upwards of 17 years and during the Religious Re-vival with which we were lately visited, Mr O'Hara has been a most active and zealous labourer in his Master's vineyard in this Parish.'[64] Parishioners were grateful for their pastor's 'earnest zeal' with which he had endeavoured, from the start of the revival, to promote its 'true benefits'. He spoke himself of 'the blessed effects of the late glorious Revival in Reli-gion among ourselves'. 'This was truly the work of the Holy Spirit,' he said, adding that 1859 had been a 'very mysterious but glorious year', in which he had rejoiced over the abundant support he had received from members of all Protestant con-gregations in the town.

Forty years later it was claimed that O'Hara's labours during the revival were still remembered with pleasure and affection by some townspeople. This is not improbable. Henry A. Gribbon, vice-chairman of the Urban Council in that year, said that Coleraine was 'the only town in Ireland that has continued down to the present year to commemorate the religious revival of 1859', which showed, in his view, that people were still loyal not merely to Queen and country, but to their God and Saviour.

PUBLIC DEBATE ON REVIVAL

Many critics of the revival believed it was, in essence, an outbreak of mass hysteria. The medical journal, the *Lancet*, took this position, for example, in a study of patients in the

---

63. *Coleraine Chronicle*, 10 September 1859.
64. *Coleraine Chronicle*, 31 December 1859 and *Londonderry Sentinel*, 13 January 1860. The address was signed by Elizabeth N. Knox, Lizzie Stott, Elizabeth McFarland and E.J. McNaughten.

Belfast Lunatic Asylum.[65] The author of the study spoke of the 'frantic tone of religious frenzy' peculiar to the revival, of the 'blasphemous ravings' of the initiated, and the 'high degree of rascality amongst the knaves who encourage the evil'. It suggested that the best remedy for such people was a 'free and pitiless drenching with cold water'. The *Banner of Ulster* carried out its own investigation and dished the findings of the *Lancet*. There was not a single case of religious mania or hysteria in the Belfast Lunatic Asylum, the Presbyterian paper claimed.

Alexander Cuthbert, a Coleraine man and Presbyterian doctor working in Londonderry, James C. L. Carson, a Baptist elder and medical practitioner in the town, and James Jasper Macaldin, another doctor and elder at First Presbyterian, all wrote articles and letters in which they accepted that there certainly had been cases of emotional excitement, but denied that these could or should be equated with hysteria. They argued that all revivals had been associated with individual cases of unacceptable emotional behaviour; it would be dishonest to claim, however, that such exceptions discredited the rule of an orderly move of God's Spirit. Clearly, there had been in Coleraine some extraordinary cases of emotional, psychological or spiritual turmoil. This they all accepted. We have already spoken of the very first revival meeting where such manifestations took place. Cases occurred not only outside in the fresh air. In the *Chronicle* on 18 June, 1859, two further cases of conviction are described which took place during a Monday evening meeting held in Second Presbyterian. One woman, having been completely prostrated, was carried into the session room where she was ministered to by the Rev. Canning and others until midnight. At about that time 'peace of conscience was accorded to her'. At a Sunday morning service in Third Presbyterian the

---

65. *Londonderry Sentinel*, 8 July 1859.

pastor, Rev. Joseph Macdonnell, was 'gladdened in heart', the *Chronicle* recorded, to see four of his people carried out from amongst the other worshippers. The four were 'exhibiting that mental emotion and bodily torture which he [the pastor] knew well had then awakened in them the desire to cry "what shall I do to be saved".'[66] Some ministers were bound to consider such unusual occurrences in sober Presbyterian circles as 'extravagances'.

The debate was carried on in the local paper by representatives of the different denominations. The most outspoken controversialist of the time perhaps was Dr J. C. L. Carson. His *Letters on Revival*[67] did much to undermine the 'hysteria theory' of revival. The first two letters to the *Chronicle* were published as a tract and were so favourably received that most of the leading newspapers in Ireland, England and Scotland, but also in Germany, India and the USA, republished them.[68] In the first three weeks some eight thousand copies of the *Letters* were printed to meet the great demand.[69] The tract achieved a worldwide circulation of perhaps half a million copies, Carson believed. He claimed, in one of his letters on the awakening of Ulster, that no other kind of revival could have had the same effects on the inhabitants of Coleraine. The physical expressions of mental distress and conviction of sin were perfectly geared, he believed, to drawing the attention of the masses to the state of their souls. Those who had previously mocked the revival and scoffed at its effects became suddenly quiet on witnessing the impact. He wrote: 'A scene like the one which took place on the night in which the new [town] hall in Coleraine was first filled with these cases, has perhaps never been equalled in the world.' The physical manifestations

---

66. *Coleraine Chronicle*, 18 June 1859.
67. James C.L. Carson, *Three Letters on the Revival in Ireland*, Coleraine 1859.
68. *Coleraine Chronicle*, 8 October 1859.
69. Ibid., 5 November 1859.

had 'put terror into the heart of all who saw them' and the conversion of hardened sinners could not be denied. Carson admitted to his own scepticism and unbelief when he had initially heard of the revival at Ballymena. He had even publicly stated that the revival movement 'would soon be stopped in its progress by the coldness, formality, and narrow-minded bigotry and sectarianism of Coleraine'. On 20 September 1859 he wrote: 'The revival has taken more root in Coleraine than anywhere else, and I believe this has been greatly owing to the fact that the clergy, of different denominations, have allowed the physical manifestations to progress without interruption. [...] They seemed determined to make the best use they could out of what God had sent; and they have had their reward. [….] It might safely be said that more people have been converted in this district during the last four months than during the previous fifty years. Indeed, I am certain this statement is far within the mark.'[70] Further: 'If one half of the inhabitants of Coleraine had been converted in a minute, in the usual way, the other half would not have believed it – they would have laughed at it as a vision.'

The Presbyterian Dr Macaldin, in a letter to the Baptist evangelist Henry Grattan Guinness, emphasised that the 'vast number' of cases he had personally witnessed revealed a true conversion of souls to Christ. He criticised his fellow doctors, 'so-called medical authorities', as he referred to them, for 'writing of things they don't understand' and so creating in the minds of others 'impressions unfavourable to the whole movement'. He admitted, like his Baptist colleague Dr Carson, that he did not understand the physical phenomena; he did not pretend to. But he did accept the fact that God had 'in His wisdom and His love, seen fit to smite down, if it so pleased Him, the stubborn and rebellious heart, whether of man or child'. He believed, moreover, that

70. James C.L. Carson, *Three Letters on the Revival in Ireland*, pp. 12–14.

the Spirit of God '*may* [his italics] make use of' phenomena such as visions, revelations, prophesying, deafness, dumbness and immobility to seriously impress 'a hitherto dead carnal mind with a sense of spiritual things', but he refused to give any prominence to or attach much importance to them.[71] The important issue was whether lives had been radically changed.

Rev. Jackson Smyth was told in June 1859 that one half of the inhabitants of Coleraine had in fact been affected by the revival.[72] This may be true. The problem, of course, is defining the word 'affected'. At the time, one feature of community relations was particularly highlighted. The inscription in the revival Bible notes the 'blessed spirit of brotherly love which has been one fruit of God's wondrous work in Coleraine'. Inter-personal relationships had much improved. The revival gave additional impetus to inter-denominational cooperation. 'It is a pleasant feature of the times', the *Londonderry Sentinel* wrote on 3 June 1859, 'to see evangelical ministers preaching in one another's pulpits.' Such could only happen where trust had been built up and where prejudices and fears had been banished. The very fact that the union prayer meetings continued for years is a testimony to the deep impact on the town's population. The daily prayer meeting in Coleraine continued well into the second half of the 1860s. Over fifteen district prayer meetings were also still functioning in 1865. Equally significant is the fact that annual commemoration and thanksgiving services took place in the town right up into the early years of the twentieth century. Coleraine was the last place in Ireland where such services were held. The revival in Coleraine was not simply a passing emotional experience, but it was that too. The suddenness and unusualness of the revival, which provoked 'the contemptuous ridicule of some

---

71. *Coleraine Chronicle*, 24 September 1859.
72. *Londonderry Guardian*, 14 June 1859.

and the fierce hostility of others', to quote the report on the state of religion to the General Assembly in Dublin in 1859, had been upsetting to what the same report called the 'careless, self-complacent professors of religion' but it had reached the masses and the fruit had been undeniably good. 'It is true that the ordinary operation of the Holy Spirit is slowly progressive, and almost escapes observation. Yet who shall venture to say that it may not also be immediate, public, powerful, and extensive at His Sovereign Will?' Indeed, the history of the Christian church, the report said, taught that the religious life of the community of the people of God as well as of individual believers had been 'forwarded by impulses rather than by continuing progress'.[73]

---

73. *Coleraine Chronicle*, 16 July 1859.

Chapter 5: The Twelfth in 1859

Charles Finney's *Lectures on Revivals*, first published in 1835, were being sold in Coleraine for 2 shillings and 6 pence at S. Eccles during the 1840s.[1] It was one of the three books that were the source of much inspiration for the original 'Kells Four'. Bonar's *Life of McCheyne* and George Müller's *Narrative of the Lord's Dealings* were the other two. These books helped clarify the vision of the young men whose hearts were bent on doing something for God.

THE BIG ISSUE

Charles G. Finney, in one of his lectures on promoting revival, which he wrote while still a minister of the Presbyterian church in America, noted that there are times when, in the providence of God, issues come up for discussion and the church is called by the Spirit to take a stance.[2] In his day Freemasonry, slavery and temperance were those issues. In this regard huge responsibility lay, Finney claimed, on God's ministers to take a lead in repentance and take a stance on enforcing discipline. Ill-will and some alienation would

---

1. *Coleraine Chronicle*, 22 March 1845. On Finney's influence on Ulster see Andrew Holmes, 'The experience and understanding of religious revival in Ulster Presbyterianism, c. 1800–1930', *Irish Historical Studies*, vol. xxxiv, No. 136, November 2005, p. 368f.

2. *Revivals of Religion. Lectures by Charles Grandison Finney with the Author's final Additions and Corrections. Newly revised and edited with Introduction and original notes by William Henry Harding*, London 1913, pp. 336–343.

always be caused by taking a stance, but the long-term view of the matter was all-important.

In his own day William Morgan's exposé of Freemasonry, published in 1826, had led to much discussion between 1826 and 1830. It is reported that 45,000 men repented of their membership of lodges and 2,000 lodges had to be closed down as a result. On the other hand, churches began to exclude lodge members from fellowship and refuse them access to communion until the oath was broken and the sin forsaken. Finney himself renounced his own membership of a Masonic lodge and there was a 'general stampede' of Christians from lodges. The fruit of such widespread repentance was not long in appearing. The 1831 revival began at the centre of the anti-Masonic region and became, Finney records, the 'greatest revival the world had then seen'. The important point was that revival was preceded by renunciation of lodge membership; regalia associated with lodges were generally burned. Finney personally obeyed what he perceived to be the leading of the Holy Spirit and severed his connection with lodges. He was blessed with the knowledge that God then used him to awaken more souls than most other evangelists in the nineteenth century.

ORANGEISM

Many Freemasons would see Orangeism in much the same way that early nineteenth-century Orangemen viewed the Black lodges: an abhorrent, lower-class organisation. Orangeism, though having no formal links with the Masonic Grand Lodge, is nevertheless an outgrowth of Freemasonry. The Orange Order was set up by tenant farmers,[3] most of whom were disgruntled

---

3. It is very difficult to access lodge records. Aiken McClelland published data on the occupational composition of two lodges in Ballynahinch, based on documents dating from 1853. Farmers, labourers and weavers were by far the most typical occupations of Orangemen in that area. Aiken McClelland, 'Occupational Composition of Two Orange Lodges,1853,' in: *Ulster Folklife* 14 (1968), pp. 62–65.

Freemasons who desired a more politically combative secret society to ostensibly defend their own interests.[4] It is therefore not at all surprising that Masonic elements permeate the whole of the Orange system and vocabulary. Indeed, Masonic lodges in Belfast and Londonderry bore the title 'Orange' long before the first Orange lodge was set up. This is even more obviously the case with the 'Magnanimous and Invincible Order of Royal Blackmen's Association' (September 1797), which was reorganised on 14 September 1846 at Portadown. The leading Orangeman, Stewart Blacker, stated, before the House of Commons Select Committee inquiring into the character and tendency of Orange lodges in July and August 1835, that Black lodges had come about from the desire of the 'lower orders' and 'various improper characters who had been expelled from the Orange Institution for misconduct' to have 'something more exciting or alarming in the initiation of members'. Black lodges, he maintained at the inquiry, were spreading a 'mixture of freemasonry with that of the old orange system', a form of 'mummery' rooted in the desire of 'vulgar minds' for 'awful mysteries and ridiculous pageantry'. 'Black' and 'Orange' lodges had a common pedigree. Their public parades, processions and marches, for example, were modelled on and took the lead from Masonic processions in the eighteenth century. Freemasonry was, in fact, of crucial importance not only for the secrecy, oaths and structures of the organisations, but also for the desire to parade their identity and values.[5]

---

4.   On the origins of the Orange Order see Kevin Whelan, 'The Origins of the Orange Order' in *Bullan* 2 (1996), pt 2, pp. 19–37; Peter Gibbon, 'The origins of the Orange Order and the United Irishmen. A study in the sociology of revolution and counter-revolution' in *Economy and Society*, vol. 1, pt 2, (1972) pp. 134–63. Recent studies of the Order include William Brown, *An Army with Banners. The Real Face of Orangeism* (Belfast, 2003) and Ruth Dudley Edwards, *The Faithful Tribe. An Intimate Portrait of the Loyal Institutions* (London, 1999).

5.   *Orangeism in Ireland and throughout the Empire vol. I (1688–1828)* (London, n.d), p. 287; M.W. Dewar, J. Brown, S.E. Long, *Orangeism: A New Historical Appreciation* (Belfast, 1967), p. 105.

In the body politic of Ireland, Orangeism was for much of the nineteenth century an intractable problem for the authorities. A Presbyterian resident of Bushmills wrote in July of the same year to the *Coleraine Chronicle*, complaining about a sleeping disorder related to the phenomenon. He objected to having to listen to the firing of guns and the beating of drums all through the night of the eleventh and twelfth of July. He was offended, moreover, by the slogans being chanted and the songs being sung in his town. 'Kick the Pope', 'Croppies lie down' and 'The Protestant Boys' were that year's favourites while 'God save the Queen' was not once heard. He believed that behind the vulgar banter lay the core evil of 'religious ascendancy'. This he regarded as 'that foul demon of discord, which is both the curse and the ruin of the country'; and, until the members of the established Church 'cease to nurture that monster, Ireland will never be peaceable, contented or happy'.[6] Peace would come when that demon was exorcised. The question governments had grappled with over the previous decades was how to deal a death blow to the annual marching and singing. In the year of revolutions, many dissenters were yearning for redemption from an environment of ritualised hatred and triumphalism. For them the so-called religious core of the Orange Order was, on the contrary, little more than a thin veneer of pseudo-religiosity.[7]

In this chapter, which covers events well beyond the confines of Coleraine, we wish to consider the impact of the 1859 revival on the Orange Institution. In particular, the celebration of the Twelfth during the so-called 1859 revival will be highlighted. General histories of Ulster make fleeting mention of the unusual events of that year.[8] Most studies of

---

6. *Coleraine Chronicle*, 22 July 1848, p. 2.
7. For a discussion of religion and the Orange Order see David A. Roberts, 'The Orange Order in Ireland: a religious institution?' in *British Journal of Sociology* 22 (1971), pp. 269–82.
8. Jonathan Bardon, *A History of Ulster* (Belfast, 2001), p. 344.

the Orange Order pass over this episode in silence, and most studies of the revival fail to consider the impact on the males belonging to the institution. The 1989 edition of William Gibson's *The Year of Grace* devotes just over two pages to this matter. It is significant that Ian R. K. Paisley's *The 'Fifty-Nine' Revival* (1958; reprinted 1981) omits all mention of this subject. Yet the events of that year are fascinating in themselves and can perhaps be instructive. The 1859 revival sheds an interesting light on the relationship between Orangeism and evangelical religion.[9]

NONCONFORMISTS AND ORANGEISM

James Wilson, a Presbyterian farmer in county Tyrone, was himself a member of Caledon Masonic Lodge No. 333 and it was he who established No. 1 Orange Lodge.[10] It was not the Masonic nature of Orangeism that upset most Presbyterians. The modern Masonic system was actually developed by a Presbyterian minister, Dr James Anderson. While Orangeism had Presbyterian members from the beginning, however, they were certainly a tiny minority of the whole.[11] The first Orange lodges, according to the report of a Select Committee set up to investigate the Orange Order in 1835, consisted almost exclusively of members of the Church of England.[12] Any Dissenters who joined the Order seem to have been forced to do so by their Episcopalian landlords.[13]

---

9. David Hempton, Myrtle Hill, *Evangelical Protestantism in Ulster Society 1740–1890*, London and New York: Routledge 1993, pp. 145–160; Myrtle Hill, 'Ulster Awakened: The '59 Revival Reconsidered' in *Journal of Ecclesiastical History 41* (1990), no. 3, pp. 443–62.

10. Hereward Senior, *Orangeism in Ireland and Britain 1795–1836* (London and Toronto, 1966), p. 14; Finlay Holmes, *Presbyterians and Orangeism 1795–1995* (Belfast, 1996), p. 2.

11. Francis Plowden, *The History of Ireland from its Union with Great Britain in January 1801, to October 1810*, vol. 1 (Dublin, 1811), pp. 64–7, 87, 92.

12. *Report of the Select Committee Appointed to Inquire into the Nature, Character, Extent and Tendency of Orange Lodges, Associations or Societies in Ireland* (20 July 1835), p. 36 (Rev. O'Sullivan), p. 258 (Earl of Gosford).

13. W.T. Latimer, *A History of the Irish Presbyterians* (Belfast and Edinburgh, 1893), p. 183.

There were, of course, always exceptions to the rule. For the Twelfth celebrations in Belfast in 1847, for example, the Presbyterian minister of Carryduff, Rev. Browne, offered his services to Orangemen.[14]

Nearly all evangelicals, however, remained wary of what might be termed the spirit of politicised Masonry. For example, when there was an apparent attempt by Orangemen in 1836 to remove King William IV from the British throne and replace him with their own Duke of Cumberland, the plot was given some credence in evangelical circles. The Select Committee blamed corruption in the judiciary, the army and the police service on the machinations of the Orange Order. Few Christians wished to support such a system. There had clearly been enough incriminating evidence to persuade the Grand Lodge, in that year, to dissolve the Order. Only in the 1850s did it begin to revive. The bloody riots of 1857 in Belfast, triggered by the open-air preaching of evangelicals, some of whom sympathised with Orangeism (for example, the Presbyterian Rev. Hugh Hanna, who later joined the Order, and the Church of England clergyman William McIlwaine), give expression to the Order's growing significance over sections of the Protestant poor. In 1859 most Protestants were still loath to join an organisation linked to a domineering Anglicanism and linked repeatedly to outbreaks of violence. Throughout the initial and middle decades of the nineteenth century Presbyterians, and members of other dissenting bodies, were quite simply offended by the social snobbery of Orange leaders, their superficial religiosity and the political conservatism of the Order.

In the prim little town of Coleraine, where three Presbyterian churches represented tenant farmer, merchant and shop-owner constituencies, support for politicised forms of anti-Catholicism was not particularly strong. In Novem-

---

14. 'The Twelfth of July in and around Belfast,' *The Vindicator*, 14 July 1847.

ber 1844 one of the three Presbyterian ministers, William Magill, denounced the 'No Popery' cry as a slogan which sufficed as the passport to jobs and offices 'from the lowest scribbler in the land to the highest declaimer'.[15] He was convinced that nothing was gained from stirring up and manipulating unwarranted fears for party-political purposes. While he disliked Erastianism, Puseyism and Romanism, he had nothing to fear from such systems of thought. Evangelicalism, in his opinion, was bound to survive and, indeed, triumph. Presbyterian confidence and optimism, which would receive a huge boost from the revival, reflected an older postmillennial eschatology of hope and this prevented dissenters from sliding into a defensive negativity.

Presbyterians were, in addition, generally more generous of spirit and more liberal in politics than Episcopalians and far more supportive, for example, of tenant rights. In a debate in the House of Commons in 1850 Lord Londonderry actually attacked Presbyterian ministers for exhorting their people not to pay rents, but to resist unjust laws on tenant rights.[16] While landlords sought to instil respect for the law in tenants, dissenting clergymen were concerned about justice. In September 1851, the Presbyterian minister Dr John Brown of Aghadowey, in an address before the Evangelical Alliance, spoke of the sin of developing a personal hostility to Catholics. If one wanted to further advance the Reformation, one could not erect barriers and proclaim a 'separation' from one's fellow men. He warned of the self-righteous 'holier-than-thou' attitude amongst his countrymen.[17] As an active member of the Coleraine Tenant Right Association[18] Brown was keen to see the development of a cross-denominational campaign which was to include Catholic labourers.

---

15. *Coleraine Chronicle*, 23 November 1844, pp. 2 3.
16. Ibid., 2 March 1850, p. 2.
17. Ibid., 6 September 1851, p. 1.
18. *Coleraine Chronicle*, 16 December 1848, p. 2.

The politics of Orange landlords alienated most Presbyterian ministers and their congregations from Orangeism.

Other dissenting churches, much smaller than the Presbyterians, were not as politically active as their co-religionists, but they were just as opposed to Orangeism. The reasons were generally of a more spiritual nature and were related to the general public misconduct and aggression associated with Orange parades. Otherwise opposed to certain doctrines and practices of Catholicism, the independents censured and dismissed from membership men who belonged to the Orange Society. One such case is recorded in March 1847. The excommunication of Robert Clarke[19] followed his 'continued adherence to the Orange Society and attendance at their meetings', even though fellow Congregationalists had remonstrated with him and he had promised to discontinue his connection with the Orange Institution. This Orangeman's 'walk and conversation have not seemed to the Brethren who were best acquainted with him to be such as to justify the Church in retaining him in full communion'. In particular, the man's 'almost total neglect of the ordinances of the Lord's House, accompanied with a prevailing worldliness of mind' necessitated his dismissal. The church members unanimously agreed to expel 'so unworthy a member' at a meeting on 21 March 1847. It was hoped the discipline would bring the Orangeman to a recognition of the 'evil of his conduct'.[20]

19. Robert Clarke was a confectioner and baker who owned property in Coleraine which had a total annual valuation of £25 and 10 shillings. *General Valuation of Rateable Property in Ireland. Union of Coleraine* (Dublin, 1859), pp. 185, 191, 196; *The Belfast and Province of Ulster Directory for 1858–1859*, vol. IV, p. 559.
20. Entry for March 23, 1847, in church Minute Book. Coleraine Independent Church (1844–1850), p. 27. The discipline is all the more surprising as Congregationalism was 'strongly' anti-Catholic at the time. James Miller Henry, 'An Assessment of the Social, Religious and Political Aspects of Congregationalism in Ireland in the Nineteenth Century' (Ph.D. thesis, Queen's University Belfast, 1965), p. 285.

In Baptist circles, too, a rather low view of Orangeism prevailed in the middle of the nineteenth century. Rev. Thomas Berry, a Baptist, spoke in 1838 of the matter. 'Abbeyleix, though small, has one of the largest Orange lodges in this country. Among this class, humanly speaking, there is not much good to be expected. I am happy that one or two of the church have ceased meeting in their lodge.' Elders of the Tobermore Baptist Church visited and reprimanded four members of the church who were seen walking in or alongside an Orange procession in 1861.[21] Some Baptist churches specifically prohibited members from joining the Order; others did not. Brethren assemblies, which began to be formed in Dublin at the end of the 1820s but which grew in number particularly as a result of the 1859 revival, unanimously rejected involvement in such 'worldly' organisations.

BANS ON PARADES

In the popular mind Orangeism was associated with sectarian singing, marches and not a little drinking.[22] The British government had decided that the only way out of the violence periodically engulfing Ulster from the end of the eighteenth century was to either ban the Order altogether or ban parades. In 1823 all oath-bound societies were declared illegal. From 1825 to 1828 the institution was a dead letter.[23] In 1832 party processions were outlawed for the first time.[24] In 1836 the complete dissolution was accepted in Grand Lodge by a majority of ninety-two.[25] Between 1839 and 1845 lodges still met in violation of the law and illegal

---

21. Norman Porter, 'Irish Baptists and Orangeism' in *Irish Baptist Historical Journal* 18 (1985–6), p. 12.
22. Many lodges, which had no rooms of their own in which to assemble, met in public houses or similar establishments.
23. Richard Niven, *Orangeism as it was and is. A concise history of the rise and progress of the Institution, with Appendix* (Belfast, 1899), pp. 21–5.
24. M.W. Dewar, J. Brown, S.E. Long, *Orangeism*, 126; R.M. Sibbett, *Orangeism in Ireland and throughout the Empire*, vol. 2 (London n.d.), p. 368.
25. Richard Niven, *Orangeism*, p. 32.

processions took place in different parts of the country in 1842, 1843 and 1844. Throughout Orange leaders supported government policy. In 1845 the Party Processions Act expired and the Order re-constituted itself. On 12th July 1849 serious disturbances took place at Dolly's Brae, a Catholic district near Castlewellan, when a procession of over one thousand Orangemen, several hundred of whom were armed with guns, marched from Ballyward Church to Tollymore Park, deliberately taking a different route from 1848.[26] Not surprisingly, the act outlawing Orange parades was renewed in 1850.

Surprisingly, perhaps, the anti-parade legislation received the support of most district and provincial leaders of the Order. This policy of the Order was maintained until the evangelical revival. The policy reflected the establishment mentality of the landowning class running the Order. The Earl of Roden, the owner of Tollymore Park, founding member of the Evangelical Alliance and leading Orangeman, said at the time he was sure Orangemen would be the first to obey the law by not marching.[27]

William Verner, a district grand master, in an address of the Grand Orange Lodge of Ireland (15 May 1850) stated: 'The Orange Institution was not founded for purposes of marching.[...] If there be among us brethren more ambitious of parades and display than of the substantial advantages which union ensures to society, we tell them that such ambitions are at variance with the spirit of our society, as set forth in its acknowledged rules.' At times such as the one they were living in, Orangemen were 'required to relinquish those public celebrations which are naturally

---

26. 'Papers relating to an Investigation held at Castlewellan into the Occurrences at Dolly's Brae on the 12th July, 1849,' in Richard Niven, *Orangeism*, pp. 55–163. William Beers admitted in the inquiry that followed the bloodshed that he could have used his authority to encourage the marchers to go home by a different route.

27. R.M. Sibbett, *Orangeism*, vol. 2, p. 368.

dear to us'. Obedience to the law 'for conscience sake' was a central Orange tenet, Verner insisted.[28]

In Coleraine there was in 1850 no attempt to hold a procession although the town was deemed to be 'the very focus of Orange feeling' in the region.[29] Protestants and Catholics went about their business as if party spirit had been 'buried for ever in the ocean of oblivion'. During the evening dinner celebrations, members pledged themselves to live in peace with all denominations of men. The following year, 1851, there were once again no marches or demonstrations of feeling. Robert Weir, the County Master, is actually said to have intervened to prevent a procession taking place. He seized a flag and drum and told his brethren to go home.[30] Weir was determined to enforce obedience to the law.

William Beers, Grand Master of County Down who had played a major role at Dolly's Brae, seems to have imbued the new spirit of peace and reconciliation. In a letter to Orangemen dated 26 June 1852, he stated: 'I need hardly say to you, brethren, that should any of your enemies taunt you to violate, either in letter or spirit, the anti-processions act, on the coming anniversaries, or taunt you for not doing so, your answer will be that it is the principle of an Orangeman to respect, not to trample on the law.'[31] In the same vein the Earl of Enniskillen advised Orangemen to 'avoid even the semblance of walking in procession' on the approaching Twelfth.[32]

In Coleraine, and many other places, few Orange marches had taken place in the 1850s.[33] The Conservative MP for the town, Sir H. H. Bruce, a key figure in the life of the area throughout this period and Grand Master of Orangemen in

---

28. *Coleraine Chronicle*, 25 May 1850, p. 4.
29. Ibid., 13 July 1850, p. 2.
30. Ibid., 19 July 1851, p. 2.
31. *Coleraine Chronicle*, 10 July 1852, p. 4.
32. Ibid.
33. Ibid., 17 July 1852, p. 2.

County Derry, had reminded his brethren on 10 July 1857 that the Twelfth was to fall on a Sunday that year. He told them to honour that day by attending worship services in their respective churches 'without parade and without display'.[34] No special Orange services were held in Coleraine and 'out of respect for the sanctity of the Sabbath' no demonstration of any kind was undertaken. People of all religious persuasions were said to be agreed upon the propriety of that decision. The Twelfth passed 'very quietly, without riot or drunkenness'.[35] The scene was very similar the following year. There was no 'shrill cheering sound of the fife and the beat of the drum'. The almost complete absence of any kind of display of Orangeism was put down to the conciliatory address of Bruce and the admonitions of the County Chaplain, Rev. James O'Hara (of St. Patrick's, Coleraine).[36]

POLITICAL CORRUPTION

In 1857 some fifty members belonging to county Derry lodges were expelled for voting against their Grand Master, Sir H. H. Bruce, at the parliamentary elections.[37] Another fifty were suspended for seven years 'for using their influence against their Grand Master at the elections'. These expulsions and suspensions are said to have taken place as 'a personal favour' for Sir Hervey.[38] Orangeism was perceived to be an embodiment of establishment-minded political reaction. It was perhaps such blatant favouritism which persuaded Bruce to hand in his resignation as County Grand Master on 1 September 1858.[39] Rev. James O'Hara was unanimously elected Derry County Grand Master on 28 October.[40] Given

---

34. Ibid., 11 July 1857, p. 5.
35. Ibid., 18 July 1857, p. 6.
36. Ibid., 17 July 1858, p. 4.
37. H.W. Cleary, *The Orange Society* (London, 1899), p. 134.
38. *Coleraine Chronicle*, 5 November 1858, p. 4.
39. Ibid., 4 September 1858, p. 4.
40. Ibid., 5 November 1858, p. 4.

the open nature of elections such retaliatory actions were relatively simple to carry out. They were a further reason why Presbyterians were unlikely to support Orangeism. Only with electoral reform and the disestablishment of the Church of England and Ireland in the late 1860s were the prerequisites of Presbyterian involvement in the Order really in place.

Though a corrupt influence himself, Sir H.H. Bruce accepted the need for Orangemen to make compromises in the interests of societal stability. He maintained this position over many years. In November 1868 Bruce, after being returned unopposed to the House of Commons, addressed the thorny matter of the Party Processions Act and called on his Orange brethren to give up parading if 'they knew that such processions gave offence'. He hoped the Act would remain on the statute book as long as the government believed it was 'effective in preventing displays of rebellion and sedition'. Yet, nobody, he added, should impugn the loyalty of Orangemen for renouncing that tradition.[41]

Social Tensions

In the year of evangelical revival Lord Dungannon, Grand Master of County Antrim (but resident in North Wales), called on his brethren on June 28 1859 to 'abstain from any party procession, any outward display, anything, in a word, likely to cause irritation, or cause the slightest disturbance calculated to provoke a breach of the peace'. Orangemen were told to celebrate the Twelfth by attending public worship.[42] Like other Orange leaders, Dungannon sought to contribute to a relaxation of tensions in the province.

A propensity to violence and immoderate drinking amongst lodge members ensured that no prominent Presbyterians, let alone sober-minded, level-headed Presbyterian

41. Ibid., 21 November 1868, p. 4.
42. *Belfast News-Letter*, 6 July 1859, p. 1.

clergymen, became patrons of Orangeism in its formative years.[43] By mid-century this was beginning to change. The bloody riots of 1857 in Belfast actually point to the Order's growing significance over sections of the urban working class,[44] even though triggered by the open-air preaching of the Presbyterian Rev. Hugh Hanna, who was not at the time an Orangeman and in fact disagreed fundamentally with the politics of leading Orangemen,[45] and the two Anglican clergymen, William McIlwaine (who was not an Orangeman) and Thomas Drew (who was). Hanna, McIlwaine and Drew were not the first evangelicals to disclaim any responsibility for the consequences of fiery, polemical preaching. Nor would they be the last. However, the time for a close marriage between evangelicalism and Orangeism, which Dr Henry Cooke had been working towards, had not yet come.

Throughout the initial and middle decades of the nineteenth century, Presbyterians, and members of other dissenting bodies, were offended by the social snobbery of Orange leaders, the superficial religiosity and the reactionary politics of the Order as well as the 'uncontrollable displays' of working-class 'party animosity and hatred'. Each successive Twelfth of July, wrote William Gibson, a professor of Christian ethics and Moderator in 1859 of the General Assembly of the Presbyterian Church in Ireland, brought 'an ebullition of political and religious frenzy, often provocative of resistance, and terminating in violence and bloodshed'.[46] The commissioners of inquiry into the Belfast riots of 1857, David Lynch and Hamilton Smythe, concluded from their deliberations: 'The Orange system seems

---

43. Hereward Senior, *Orangeism*, p. 40.
44. Andrew Boyd, *Holy War in Belfast* (Tralee, 1969).
45. *Report of the Commissioners of Inquiry into the Origin and Character of the Riots in Belfast , in July and September, 1857* (Dublin, 1858), p. 170 (8055, 8058). Hanna pointed out during the inquiry that several Orangemen had left his church because of his political views.
46. William Gibson, *The Year of Grace: A History of the Ulster Revival of 1859* (Edinburgh, London and Belfast, 1860), p. 157.

to us now to have no other practical result than as a means of keeping up the Orange festivals, and celebrating them, leading as they do to violence, outrage, religious animosities, hatred between classes, and, too often, bloodshed and loss of life.' They wondered whether there was 'any controlling necessity' to keep the Orange Society alive, considering 'the evils that unfortunately attend its existence'.[47]

This ban of 1850 nevertheless seems to have led to a phase of introspection and bitter infighting within the Order. There were major disagreements over the degree of allegiance one should owe governments which portrayed Orangeism in such dark colours. In Ulster several lodges re-solved to discontinue sittings and resigned their warrants.[48] A number of lodges, particularly in the Armagh and Ty-rone area, including some in Loughgall and the Portadown district, piled up their banners, warrants, emblems and flags in the Diamonds of towns and turned them into bonfires.[49] LOL No. 948 in the Portadown district denounced the 'unjus-tifiable calumnies' poured upon their institution in the weeks leading up to the Party Processions Act and determined to 'appoint a day to assemble and burn our banners and other emblems of our order'. In part, this was in recognition of the hostility and, indeed, hatred festering amongst those in 'the humbler ranks of life' towards Catholics, because as an institution all they wanted was to live peaceably with all men, 'particularly with our Roman Catholic countrymen'.[50] In the Fintona and Dromore districts, masters of lodges resolved to dissolve their lodges, 'ceasing to act in future as

---

47. *Report of the Commissioners of Inquiry into the Origin and Character of the Riots in Belfast, in July and September, 1857*, p. 11.

48. *Coleraine Chronicle*, 30 March 1850, p. 3.

49. Ibid., 13 April 1850, 2 (Stewartstown); 11 May 1850, 1 (Portadown); 18 May 1850, 3 (Loughgall); 25 May 1850 (Derryscollop); 8 June 1850, 2 (Loughgall, Blundell's Grange). See also M.W. Dewar, J. Brown, S.E. Long, *Orangeism*, p. 137.

50. *Coleraine Chronicle*, 11 May 1850, p. 1.

a political body'.[51] Moneymore Orangemen resolved to dissolve their connection with the Orange Society and advised lodges 'instead of assembling for political purposes, as heretofore, to establish reading societies'.[52] Was this an outbreak of repentance? A more likely interpretation of these bonfires was deep anger at the instructions of the Grand Lodge and the Masters, reflecting not contrition, but rather the old die-hard spirit of disregard for those in authority and for the Party Processions Act in particular.[53]

Spiritual Changes

A legal ban at the start of the 1850s had led some Orangemen to give up their traditions; a religious awakening at the end of the decade temporarily shook the whole Orange institution. From June 1859 through to the autumn the north of Ireland was caught up in the wonders of revival. Numerous testimonies from this period reveal the apparently profound impact of evangelistic meetings on the tone of conversation and the way of life. In particular, the manner in which the Twelfth was celebrated is mentioned in glowing terms.[54] In the Strabane Primitive Methodist Society Rev. John White reviewed some of the fruit of the months of outreach. He drew attention to the decrease in drunkenness, the closure of pubs and the fact that Orangemen in Belfast, Killyman and many other places had 'instead of having processions on the 12th of July, held prayer meetings'. In the vicinity of Sandy Row alone he claimed fifty such prayer meetings

---

51. Ibid., 11 May 1850, p. 3.
52. Ibid., 15 June 1850, p. 2.
53. Tony Gray, *The Orange Order* (London, 1972), p. 143.
54. W.D. Killen, *The Ecclesiastical History of Ireland. From the Earliest Period to the Present Times*, vol. 2 (London, 1875), 531; Benjamin Scott, *The Revival in Ulster: Its Moral and Social Results* (London, 1859), 37 (quoting Dr Knox, Bishop of Down, Connor and Dromore); *The Revival Movement in Ireland. An Impartial History of the Revival Movement from its Commencement to the Present Time* (Belfast, 1859), pp. 59–61.

had been established.[55] A policeman in Sandy Row told the secretary of the Wesleyan Missionary Society, William Arthur, that even the most sanguine were astonished at the way the Twelfth passed that year. Arthur concluded it was 'the most striking effect produced upon national manners, in our day, in these islands, by the sudden influence of religion'.[56]

Elsewhere in Belfast, already a city of about 130,000 inhabitants, there were no Orange arches flung over the streets, no orange garlands, no 'irritating flags' displayed from lodge room windows, no firing of shots or beating of drums and, as the librarian of the Belfast Society recalled, 'no military or semi-military parade'.[57] There was in fact 'nothing in the town during the day to indicate that it was the "Twelfth" at all'.[58] 'Never, since the distinction of political partisanship stigmatised different classes of the community [of Belfast], was so little personal rancour exhibited,' concluded the Congregationalist James Massie.[59] A stipendiary magistrate of fifteen years noted that it had been the first 13th July in his experience that nobody had been brought before him on charges of drunkenness and

---

55. *Londonderry Sentinel*, 17 February 1860, p. 4. The Presbyterian historian James Seaton Reid remarks on the change in this part of town. 'Even in Sandy Row – a portion of Belfast long noted as the grand theatre for the orgies and broils of Orangeism – that day passed away without disturbance. No drums were heard; no drunken Protestants were seen staggering through the street cursing the Pope and breathing out threatenings and slaughter against Romanists; but in many of the dwellings were heard the notes of grave sweet psalmody and the voice of prayer'. He admits, however, that red-hot Orangemen desisted only for a time from their party cries. James Seaton Reid, *History of the Presbyterian Church in Ireland*, vol. iii (Belfast,1867), pp. 512–13.
56. Benjamin Scott, *The Revival in Ulster*, p. 75.
57. William Gibson, *The Year of Grace*, p. 160. Gibson's report contains eye-witness testimonies from Belfast, Lurgan, Newtown, Limavady, Clarkesbridge (County Monaghan), Clare (County Armagh) and from a town in County Tyrone. Most reflect the opposition of Presbyterian ministers to Orangeism.
58. *Belfast News-Letter* 13 July 1859; *Belfast Weekly News*, 16 July 1859; *Coleraine Chronicle*, 16 July 1859, p. 5.
59. Benjamin Scott, *The Revival in Ulster*, p. 38.

disorder. 'There was no drunkenness', B. Ranyard wrote to Benjamin Scott, Chamberlain of the City of London, on 5 November 1859, 'there were no "party cries", and there was no fighting.'[60] And there were certainly no 'religious riots', in spite of what Myrtle Hill has stated.[61] Only at the Maze Course did a large number of young men carrying Orange flags, some of the men wearing sashes (contrary to the law), interrupt and disturb the preaching of the Methodist New Connexion pastor Moses Mills.[62] They continued beating their drums throughout the religious service and their presence is said to have caused 'considerable annoyance' to all who wished to engage in prayer.[63]

In many towns a new spirit was abroad. Peace and sobriety and a lack of ostentation characterised the Twelfth celebrations in Larne.[64] In Newtownards no Orange display of any kind was made. 'There was not one drunken man to be seen during the day.'[65] In Portglenone sectarianism became much less acute. Orangemen held their traditional parade on the Twelfth, yet without the accompaniment of fifes and drums. At Tully Hill they were addressed by one of the Presbyterian ministers at the epicentre of the revival, David Adams of Ahoghill.[66] The day, one writer recalled, was 'more like a Sabbath than the occasion of a popular celebration, not one in the large assembly showing the least sign of intoxication'.[67] In Randalstown 'no political demonstration hurtful to the feelings of any section of the community' was made throughout the day. No flags were exhibited, no sectarian

60. Benjamin Scott, Ibid., p. 40.
61. Myrtle Hill, *Ulster Awakened*, p. 459.
62. *Belfast Weekly News*, 16 July 1859, p. 1.
63. *Banner of Ulster*, 14 July 1859, p. 2.
64. Ibid., 16 July 1859, p. 2.
65. *Belfast Weekly News*, 16 July 1859, p. 1.
66. Rev. David Adams, *The Revival at Ahoghill: Its Narrative and Nature. With Suitable Reflections* (Belfast, 1859).
67. R.M. Sibbett, *The Revival in Ulster or The Life Story of a Worker* (Belfast, 1909), p. 83.

comments made, no drums were beaten. Markers in the Bibles of some of those who attended the Twelfth celebration in Randalstown 'were almost, if not altogether, the only articles displayed at all approaching an orange tinge'.[68]

Pettigo Orange Lodge No. 321 filled the church of the Rev. John Farrar, 'each member with the Bible in his hand'.[69] In Dundrod Rev. William Magill reported exactly the same scene in the Orange Hall. 'Here was another glorious triumph – the name of Jesus was exalted above every other name. The name of the "glorious, pious and immortal" William was not heard from a single lip; the Pope escaped his usual malediction; the publicans and sinners bit their lips in disappointment, for their "occupation" was gone. Satan seemed to have fallen like lightning from heaven, and the Prince of Peace reigned throughout the day.'[70] From Dromara in County Down came a similar report. Rev. William Craig was astounded: 'There is no party spirit now – no Orange parades – no beating of drums – no exclamations, to hell with the Pope or King William, and on the part of the Protestants, no wickedness towards Roman Catholics.'[71]

At Tobermore a stranger would hardly have guessed that it was the anniversary of the battle of the Boyne. Orange insignia were worn by no more than half a dozen people.[72] In Ahoghill itself there were none of the usual 'political and inflaming harangues' on the Twelfth, but rather 'very solemn and deeply interesting religious services' conducted by the Revds Gass, Cowan and Buick. Instead of fife and drum, there was peace and quiet. Instead of 'political and

68. *Belfast Weekly News*, 16 July 1859.
69. *Belfast News-Letter*, 14 July 1859; *Belfast Weekly News*, 16 July 1859.
70. *Banner of Ulster*, 16 July 1859, p. 2; William Gibson, *The Year of Grace*, p. 164.
71. John Weir, *The Ulster Awakening: its origins, progress and fruit: With notes of a tour of personal observation and inquiry* (London, 1860), p. 207.
72. *Coleraine Chronicle*, 16 July 1859, p. 5.

inflaming harangues' psalms were sung. A collection was taken up to buy Bibles and clothes for the poor.[73] There was no drinking, no disorder and no provocations. Everybody seemed agreed that they had 'never spent such a 12th of July before'. 'This is a glorious change,' wrote a correspondent in the Presbyterian Banner of Ulster.

At Ballymena quiet praise and thanksgiving services took place. 'We neither saw a policeman nor a single badge of Orangeism during the entire day!' wrote a correspondent to the *Ballymena Observer*. There was not a single arrest for drunkenness or disorder.[74] At Finvoy the Presbyterian Church was used for an Orange service. There, where in the past nothing was heard but fife and drum, 'music associated with the psalms of the sweet singer of Israel resounded in the neighbourhood'.[75] George V. Chichester, curate of Portrush, wrote of the 'remarkable and unusual way in which the last 12th of July passed'. He continued, 'I had not a single drunken or disorderly person in the lock-up. On the whole, politically as well as morally, the face of society is greatly changed.'[76] Rev. Park of Ballymoney remarked that the duty paid on spirits for the month of July for the whole of the Coleraine area had dropped by a total of £400. 'Not a few public houses are actually shut. The 12th of July, a day of celebration on which party spirit was wont to run high, and on which not seldom blood was shed, was consecrated by prayer meetings and spent with the decorum and solemnity of a Sabbath.'[77] Of the meetings in Glenavy and Crumlin several 'respectable persons' were quoted as saying they had 'never during their life spent a 12th of July with so much real pleasure and

---

73. Ibid., 16 July 1859, p. 5; *Banner of Ulster*, 14 July 1859, p. 2.

74. Alfred Russell Scott, *The Ulster Revival of 1859. Enthusiasm emanating from mid-Antrim* [Mid-Antrim Historical Group: 22] (Ballymena, 1994), p. 76.

75. *Coleraine Chronicle*, 16 July 1859, p. 5.

76. Benjamin Scott, *The Revival in Ulster*, p. 56.

77. *Coleraine Chronicle*, 6 August 1859, p. 3.

happiness'.[78] In Garvagh there was no procession or any of the usual signs of Orangeism.[79] 'Nothing short of the Spirit of God could have effected such a blessed change,' as was evident in Macosquin. Instead of Orange songs, hymns and psalms were sung by the brethren marching soberly and orderly to and from church: 'A feeling of reverence and adoration was manifest in every countenance.'[80]

Visitors from over the water noticed the difference too. The Irish-born Rev. Hugh McNeile reported a similar tale following a visit to his native country: 'What do you think the Orange lodges did on the 12th of July? Instead of going about with banners flying, and playing party tunes, and drinking "the glorious, pious and immortal memory", and exciting the bad passions of their Roman Catholic neighbours, they left the banners and drums and fifes behind, and they went every man with his Bible in his hand, and, instead of attracting hostile attention by perambulating the neighbourhood, they went to church and worshipped God; and peace and quiet reigned on the 12th of July in that district.'[81] Rev. Weir of London describes an encounter with young men as he returned from a meeting with Rev. Macdonnell:[82]

> As my friend and brother, Mr. M'D., conducted me towards his house in the country, there suddenly fell on my ear the sound of singing at a distance. I thought, from old remembrances, that it must be a band returning from a drinking party, who were singing Bacchanalian and party songs. But my friend knew better, and as we ascended a rising-ground on our way, distant, clear,

---

78. *Belfast Weekly News*, 16 July 1859, p. 1. The same report is carried by the Belfast News-Letter on 14 July 1859.
79. *Coleraine Chronicle*, 16 July 1859, p. 5.
80. Ibid., 16 July 1859, p. 5.
81. *The Times*, 13 October 1859.
82. John Weir, *The Ulster Awakening*, p. 110f.

solemn, and beautiful there was wafted us from the valley westward, the choral harmony of an air, familiar as it was sacred. The words could not be distinguished, and night threw her sable mantle over the singers. I longed to come in contact with them, and so traversing a country lane rapidly, and just as we reached the cross-yards, lo! We came upon the head of a column of about thirty young men, marching four or five deep, with steady, regular tramp, and filling the listening woods around, and the solemn starlit heavens above, with the high praises of Jehovah. This was a band of 'United Irishmen', indeed. In 1798 such a band might have been seen marching in military order, with firm tread, with gleaming pikes, in silence, under the stimulus of mistaken love of country. But now the Author of peace and Giver of concord had been welding all hearts together by the Grace of His Holy Spirit, and inspiring these hymns of praise. These are some of the converts whom I saw two hours ago in the upper [school-]room at Coleraine. They are returning home, and, like thousands more over Ulster, they beguile the way with songs of rejoicing. And see! There is a coloured young man (who had been at the meeting, and who had since addressed them separately), and two of them, with their arms entwined in his, bear him on to a night's hospitable reception and repose. […] they gather around us. They are then briefly addressed as to the importance of watchfulness, prayer and holy self-denial, that so they may retain the fervour and freshness of 'first love'. […] At length we part, to meet, I trust in glory. That scene I can never forget – those voices still ring in my ears. Here was one of the many bands, who all through the summer and autumn, have nightly, and ofttimes till near the dawn, poured out their gratitude to God with a kindred fervour and continuance to those seraphs before the throne, 'Who all night long unwearied sing high praise to their eternal King'.

From County Tyrone the Presbyterian Moderator received a report from Rev. J. Geddes who was grateful that 'the leading Orangemen meet and pray for the Romanists, whom a little ago they hated'.[83] In Portadown, too, a 'marked change in the tone of feeling' was noticed throughout the town.[84] The editor of the local newspaper was astounded. 'We never recollect seeing on such an occasion [the Twelfth] so great a number of people together with less disturbance. All was harmony and goodwill.' The same paper went on to quote the *Lurgan Gazette* ('no disturbance whatsoever') and the *Newry Telegraph* ('no displays of any description ... no party emblems even on Orange walls').[85] Moira reported no demonstration of Orange sentiment; nor did Armagh.[86] No marching took place in Derry.[87] Rev. William McClure and Rev. Richard Smyth refused, moreover, to allow Apprentice Boys to use their meeting-houses prior to or after demonstrations.[88]

Only the parish churches in Coleraine and Killowen were flagged on the Twelfth. No dissenting meeting houses were granted for Orange services, as was true for nearly all districts in Ulster. The *Coleraine Chronicle* noted that, in Coleraine, drunkenness was almost wholly absent and that more drank the toast to the 'Glorious Memory' with cold water than ever before.[89] There was no traditional procession of 'ragged boys and enthusiastic musicians with fife and drum, whose acquirements in the instrumental department of music might be comprehended in the two tunes of the "Protestant Boys" and "Boyne Water".' 'The streets were as quiet as on an ordinary day', the reporter added. The local newspaper recorded an entire

83. William Gibson, *The Year of Grace*, pp. 164–5.
84. *Banner of Ulster* 16 August 1859, p. 2; C.H. Crookshank, *History of Methodism in Ireland, vol. 3: Modern Development*, (London, 1888), p. 517.
85. Alfred Russell Scott, *The Ulster Revival*, p. 88.
86. J. Edwin Orr, *The Second Evangelical Awakening in Britain* (London and Edinburgh, 1953), p. 206.
87. *Belfast News-Letter*, 13 July 1859.
88. H.W. Cleary, *The Orange Society*, p. 89.
89. *Coleraine Chronicle*, 16 July 1859, p. 5.

absence of levity in lodge rooms in the evening. Drunkenness had been replaced by an atmosphere of solemnity.[90]

CATHOLIC RESPONSES

Some Catholic clergymen were very critical of revivalism and as angry as Episcopalian critics.[91] However, according to one revivalist activist, William Montgomery Speers, although most Catholics stood aloof from the movement, their attitude remained throughout one 'free from any offence'. The majority 'spoke respectfully' of the changes taking place within the Protestant community.[92] The Methodist William Arthur wrote to the *London Daily News* on the matter: 'Many Roman Catholics spoke of it [the revival] with dread and aversion, but all took it as a settled point, that the love of whiskey, and the habit of cursing the Pope and "Papishes" [*sic*], had got such a check as never was known in Ireland.'[93] James W. Massie, secretary of the Irish Evangelical Society, was told wherever he went that very little sectarianism had been exhibited that Twelfth of July. 'Roman Catholics have thankfully and significantly acknowledged to myself and others, in private, how acceptable a fruit this has been of the Revival, and how likely to win the hearts of all. It seems as if the law of love would bind men formerly arrayed in hostile factions.'[94] Catholics were quite willing to correct the official Church position on the revival virus. One Catholic in Ballynahinch was quoted as saying: 'You can talk of the revival as you like, but it has done more against the public houses here than ever Father Mathew could do.'[95] Another critic concluded: 'If the divil [*sic*] has done all this, there must be a NEW DIVIL [*sic*]; for I'm very sure the 'oul

---

90. Ibid., 16 July 1859, p. 5.
91. Alfred Russell Scott, *The Ulster Revival*, p. 176.
92. R.M. Sibbett, *The Revival in Ulster*, p. 40.
93. John Weir, *The Ulster Awakening*, p. 192; Benjamin Scott, *The Revival in Ulster*, pp. 74–5.
94. Benjamin Scott, *The Revival in Ulster*, p. 38.
95. *Coleraine Chronicle*, 24 September 1859, p. 3.

one wouldn't do it at all.'[96] The Ballymena Presbyterian minister quoted an Orangeman as saying that, rather than throw stones at Catholics, he would now rather embrace them.[97] One fruit of revival enthusiasm was particularly un-devilish. The Rev. John Venn, rector of Hereford, in a letter to the *London Daily News* on 20 October 1859, quoted the stipendiary magistrate for the county of Antrim and claimed not a few Orangemen had begged their Catholic neighbours for forgiveness for the manner in which they had been treating them.[98] In districts where there had been sectarian trouble, as Professor Norris Wilson, of the Reformed Presbyterian College, Belfast, has reported, 'expressions of kindness were peacefully exchanged between the sides'.[99] It truly was the oddest Twelfth of July.

From all over Ulster there were reports of astonishing changes being effected in the lives of men and women.[100] Instead of the shouts of revelry and drunkenness, crowds sang hymns and met for prayer. Typical Twelfth music was abandoned. Few emblems of Orangeism were displayed. What laws on party processions had only partially been able to effect, the revival movement seems to have accomplished. It is astonishing that 12 July 1859 apparently passed off without a single street fight or 'Macadam missiles' being thrown.[101] The revival seems to have passed the very practical test of improving community relations, even in those areas where

---

96. Samuel J. Moore, *The History and Prominent Characteristics of the Present Revival in Ballymena and its Neighbourhood* (Belfast, 1859), p. 31; Benjamin Scott, *The Revival in Ulster*, p. 59.

97. Samuel J. Moore, Ibid., p. 22.

98. *The Revival Movement in Ireland. An Impartial History of the Revival Movement from its Commencement to the Present Time.* Belfast: George Phillips and C. Aitchison 1859, xvi; John Weir, *The Ulster Awakening*, p. 196; Benjamin Scott, *The Revival in Ulster*, p. 80ff.

99. Norris Wilson, 'Covenanters and the Orange Order' in *Lion and Lamb*, no. 13, Summer 1997, p. 14.

100. Maurice F. Day, *A Letter on the Religious Movement in the North of Ireland*, Dublin 1859, pp. 7–8; Benjamin Scott, *The Revival in Ulster*, p. 105.

101. *The Times*, 23 September 1859.

strife and rioting were endemic. This was welcomed by those Catholics who knew better than most what Orangeism in the past had meant. At the July 1859 Assizes for County Down a Catholic judge on the bench, the Right Hon. Chief-Baron Pigott, used the occasion to speak in the most favourable terms of the revival in Ulster. Pigott expressed his hope that the revival would extend over the whole country and influence society at its lowest depths.[102]

Animosity can take many forms. Take for example some of the 'heavenly' visions reported during the revival. Some of these were redolent of the political and religious animosities that characterised the north of Ireland. One Ballymoney lady saw a deceased Presbyterian minister driving a bread cart through hell. Another saw the recently deceased Pope dancing on a red-hot griddle while yet another former occupant of the papal chair was seen cutting turf in order to keep the fires going. The lady overheard the turf-cutting Pope arguing with the Devil about the heavy labour. Men too had their visions. Whenever they were favoured with a glimpse of heaven, noted a cynical reporter for the *Northern Whig*, 'it is found quite filled with orange lodges in session'.[103] Blinded to their own deceits and delusions, the visionaries clothed their deep-felt wishes in religious verbiage and projected the venom at anyone willing to pay attention. It would be unwise to ascribe to a divine spirit all that took place during the 1859 revival.

On the other hand, a close reading between the lines of a paper like the *Coleraine Chronicle* (which, more than most, promoted revivalism) reveals the deep-seated animosity felt within the Protestant community towards Catholics. It would have been truly miraculous if age-old thought patterns had changed overnight. Nevertheless, a certain improvement was clearly ascertainable, though the nature

102. William Gibson, *The Year of Grace*, p. 166.
103. *The Weekly Northern Whig*, 18 June 1859, p. 3.

of inter-community relations was as yet far from, say, the pattern of interaction between Catholics and Protestants in any Prussian town. Normality had not been attained.

TEMPERANCE

The revival does, nevertheless, seem to have led to a rethinking process amongst some ultra-Protestant Orangemen. As the archives of lodges are not open to public scrutiny it is difficult to make a final judgment on the full impact of revivalism. Yet we do know that some lodges resolved to give up the use of intoxicating drink.[104] Some such as Dromore Orange Lodge No. 519 used the money thereby saved to purchase forty Bibles, which were then handed over to the different Sunday schools in the town to be given away as prizes for good knowledge of the Scriptures. Elsewhere, instead of traditional balls, some lodges began to hold soirées at which speeches were delivered on religious subjects.[105] In Monaghan, where party feuds had ceased, Orange Lodge No. 1 had held a prayer meeting on 12th July and raised a subscription for the Bible Society. Similar prayer meetings were reported taking place in other lodge rooms.[106]

Other lodges (such as Glenmanus Orange Lodge) moved over to teetotal principles at this time. The rejection of alcohol was not limited to Orangemen, of course. The temperance movement, which had been growing over the previous decades, generally received a strong impetus from the revival.[107] 'Temperance and the Revival are twins,' said John Edgar, who claimed that most of the converts joined temperance societies.[108] A correspondent of the *Belfast News-Letter*

104. William Gibson, The Year of Grace, p. 165 (Clarkesbridge, County Monaghan).
105. *Coleraine Chronicle*, 17 March 1860, p. 6.
106. John Weir, *The Ulster Awakening*, p. 201.
107. Elizabeth Malcolm, *'Ireland Sober, Ireland Free'. Drink and Temperance in Nineteenth-Century Ireland* (Dublin, 1986), pp. 153–181; Alfred Russell Scott, *The Ulster Revival*, pp. 192–4; John W. Lockington, 'Dr. John Edgar and the Temperance Movement of the Nineteenth Century', *Bulletin of the Presbyterian Historical Society*, no. 12 (March 1983), pp. 2–15.
108. Isaac Nelson, *The Year of Delusion: A Review of 'The Year of Grace'* (Belfast, 1861), p. 181.

noted 'a great change in the manner of holding the meetings at Orange societies'. Rev. Robert Dunlop (Newbliss) reported, months after the high point of the revival, that four Orangemen had been 'led to cry for mercy' during the singing of a sectarian song in their hall.[109] Most lodges had given up using intoxicating liquors, and some now opened and closed meetings with singing and prayer.[110] As members of other lodges became increasingly sober, many are said to have deserted the Order. Others left precisely because alcohol was now disdained.

Whole communities were probably affected by these changes. Robert Brown, of Kells, in a letter to the *London Times* dated 6 November 1859, spoke of the changes in the parish of Connor, where the Ulster revival had been ignited. The revival had 'annihilated party spirit', he said. 'I may state, that up to the revival our population was out-and-out Orange, and on every 12th of July, up to the last one, paraded regularly and drank galore. On the last 12th of July I did not see a man in a public house in either the village of Kells or Connor, nor did I see a man in the bounds with the appearance of drink; and I assert that, a few years ago, all the police force in the province of Ulster, had it been concentrated in this parish on a 12th of July, could not have maintained the same peace and quiet that I observed on the last one. It is not many years since a young man was shot dead in a savage riot out of the police barracks in Connor, on a 12th of July evening.'[111] As Brown pointed out, a number of pubs had actually closed and others were losing their regulars. Some of these were clearly Orangemen. It is significant that Grand Lodge received returns from only two lodges in the Connor area in 1859, a fact which the Orange

---

109. William Gibson, *The Year of Grace*, p. 166.
110. *Londonderry Guardian*, 20 September 1859, p. 1. LOL No. 245 is named in this article.
111. *The Times*, 26 October 1859.

historian John Brown believes was at least partially a fruit of the revival. Many lodges in the area had closed down.[112] In other words, where the revival was strongest, Orange influence waned.

Even critics of revivalism accepted that the law was, in 1859, obeyed more strictly than in any of the preceding years. All agreed that abuses and objectionable aspects of the anniversary celebration had been done away with. Rev. H.M. Waddell claimed nothing but the power of God 'could have put down the Orange Society. Government had failed to suppress it; yet here we see it dying of itself under the influence of revived religion.' He hoped the gospel would turn their lodges into prayer meetings and their collections for banquets into missionary contributions, 'as I have heard of being done'.[113]

The striking practical effects of the revival were echoed throughout the Presbyterian community. 'What all the powers of parliament could not effect', claimed the *Coleraine Chronicle*, 'has been accomplished by the extinction of the malignant hatred entertained by Orangemen towards their opponents.'[114] One is led to disagree with Myrtle Hill's view that the revival had 'little direct impact on day-to-day relations between the two religious communities' in Ulster.[115] All the evidence suggests it most certainly did. Orangemen, those who perhaps felt most vulnerable and threatened, succumbed to the subduing effects of revivalist evangelicalism. The Orange mindset had been softened, as had the

---

112. John Brown, *Orangeism Around Ballymena. Articles on Warrants 115 to 515 in Ballymena District Orange Lodge No. 8* [Mid-Antrim Historical Group] (Ballymena, 1990), pp. 8, 27, 41. Brown points out that LOL No. 594 (Craigywarren) ceased to work in 1860, LOL No. 221 (Ballymena) became dormant in 1859, and LOL No. 453 ceased to meet in Ferniskey. Ibid., pp. 11, 18, 29.

113. William Gibson, *The Year of Grace*, pp. 165–6.

114. *Coleraine Chronicle*, 24 September 1859, p. 3.

115. Myrtle Hill, *Ulster Awakened*, p. 459.

rigid Calvinism prevailing in some Presbyterian circles. If Presbyterianism was becoming more emotional in tone, it seemed the revival had the opposite effect on Orangemen. Presbyterians might feel triumphalist and favoured by the deity, yet the fiery zeal and fervour so characteristic of many respectable working-class lodge members had apparently abandoned them. While Catholicism was resurging and becoming ever more politicised, violent emotions had ebbed away from one section of the Protestant community. Orange traditions had been abandoned as a result – for one year at least.

The 1850s were years in which the Twelfth had passed relatively peacefully, even if sobriety had rarely featured prominently. The revival reinforced trends which government legislation had been fostering for years. In 1859, however, thousands of Orangemen seem to have been impacted by evangelicalism in a unique way. The contagion of enthusiastic Protestantism, which may have impacted thousands of women,[116] had a similarly powerful effect among men of all ages in all parts of Ulster[117]. There is some evidence at least, suggesting that bases of Orange influence were undermined as a result.

Presbyterian Opposition to Orangeism

The influence of the Presbyterian Moderator and his work on the revival, *The Year of Grace*, no doubt helped to galvanise opposition to Orangeism. He acknowledged in this influential work that Orangeism had for a number of years been 'falling

---

116. Peter Gibbon, *The origins of Ulster Unionism. The formation of Popular Protestant Politics and Ideology in Nineteenth-Century Ireland* (Manchester, 1975), pp. 44–66.

117. The Coleraine doctor, J.C.L. Carson, a supporter of the revival, emphasised at the time that, in the Coleraine district, males, especially working-class males, made up the vast majority at all revival meetings he had attended. In particular, 'an important portion of society who had hitherto considered religion beneath their notice, had now turned their attention to the matter'. *Coleraine Chronicle*, 18 February 1860.

to pieces', even in those areas where its 'baneful influence' had once been exercised. He believed the system had been on the wane before revival broke out. This he ascribed to the vigorous enforcement of the anti-procession laws, the spread of knowledge and a concomitant improvement in community relations in many places. He attacked the Orange parsons who continued to fan 'the dying embers of religious discord' and welcomed the revival as a gracious divine intervention. Never before had Orangeism 'received such a fatal blow as since, within the last few months, the Spirit from on high descended on the community of Ulster'.[118] Aiken McClelland states that in 1860 the Order was in fact practically moribund. However, it doubled its membership in the following ten years.[119] Orange praxis had received a body blow in 1859, though not, as Gibson thought, a knock-out punch.

Still, William Gibson looked confidently into the future. 'Let us hope', said Gibson, 'that the happy experiences of 1859 will be repeated in all future years, and that the Orange confederacy, if it exists at all, will be found subserving some better purpose than any for which it has hitherto been celebrated.' 'The Orangemen of Ulster', he concluded, 'have been taught a solemn lesson in the revival; who will not hope and pray that it may never pass out of their remembrance.'[120] The Moderator's hopes were dashed, his prayers left unanswered. For decades to come Catholics would be pressured into conversion by the 'abundant use of brickbats and bludgeons'.[121]

After disestablishment in 1869, the end of state support in the form of the *regium donum*, the repeal of the Party

---

118. William Gibson, *The Year of Grace*, p. 158.
119. Aiken McClelland, 'The Later Orange Order' in T. Desmond Williams (ed), *Secret Societies in Ireland* (Dublin and New York, 1973), p. 126.
120. William Gibson, *The Year of Grace*, p. 166.
121. Andrew Boyd, *Holy War in Belfast*.

Processions Act in 1872 and Gladstone's conversion to Home Rule in 1886, Presbyterians in fact began to join lodges in increasingly large numbers, though it was not until the twentieth century that Presbyterian ministers took up office in the Order as county chaplains and it was only in 1908 that a Presbyterian minister, Alexander Gallagher, was elected Grand Chaplain.[122] Presbyterians certainly failed to learn the lessons their moderator hoped they would learn from 1859. The sectarian riots in Belfast in 1872, 1880, 1884, 1886 and 1894 do not seem to have dented their growing enthusiasm for Orangeism.

Orangeism had been politically and religiously anathema to most Presbyterians in the first half of the nineteenth century. Presbyterian tenant farmers in Coleraine, of liberal persuasion, were proud to be the first in Ireland to set up a Tenant Right Association. Tenant Right was the main political issue of the day and it was fought against the power and privileges of the established church. Roman Catholic priests and Presbyterian ministers shared platforms in the campaign to improve the conditions of rural communities. Liberal politics and friendly attitudes to Roman Catholics were mutually reinforcing. The temperance crusade of Father Matthew also attracted much Presbyterian respect and support. Thus it was not surprising that Orangeism was resisted by Presbyterian ministers. Yet the time had not yet come for a marriage of Presbyterian blue and High-Church orange. Rev. Dr John Edgar, the great temperance reformer, summed up majority opinion when he said that no honest or enlightened Presbyterian could possibly support societies like the Orange Order which had done 'unutterable mischief' and widened the rift between the two main branches of Western Christendom. The intemperance – in

---

122. W. Warren Porter, 'Orangeism – a force for Protestant unity', in Billy Kennedy (ed), *Steadfast for Faith and Freedom. 200 Years of Orangeism* [Bicentenary Publication of the Grand Orange Lodge of Ireland], p. 103.

speech and drinking habits – of Orangemen seemed to be diametrically opposed to the spirit of Christ. The fruit of their marching was abundantly clear: they had fostered 'the worst feelings among the lower classes of the population'.[123] The fires of revival, which received far more support from the dissenting Protestant churches than from the Church of England and Ireland, had consumed sectarian bitterness, though sectarianism emerged once again from the ashes.

The very way the revival of 1859 was reported by contemporaries gave abundant testimony to the widely held view amongst Nonconformists that Orangeism was a force for evil in the region. Sectarianism had been temporarily suppressed. True repentance was perceived to have led to a diminution of Orange feelings; this, for most Presbyterians, was a reason to rejoice. Laws on processions and emblems had, earlier in the same decade, held in check sectarian passions and even triggered a temporary implosion of Orangeism in some districts.

Contemporary Presbyterian clergymen were, however, certainly wrong in seeing some kind of radical revolution taking place under the force of religious convictions. Their exuberance, while understandable, was ill-founded. In August 1859, at the height of revival, the *Londonderry Sentinel* gave voice to the discomfort felt at the time by the Orange party.[124] An article on 'Revival and Party Feeling' aimed to correct what the paper perceived to be 'errors' in the way other newspapers and clergymen had described the change in community relations. 'We do not see any necessity for blackening the prior character of our province,' it said, as if Ulster did not have a bad reputation abroad. In fact, the paper claimed, with some justification, that 'the law was more strictly obeyed in external modes of celebration; the display of emblems was abstained from; sacred music was substituted for the old spirit-stirring music of the fife and drum, which may be wanted again in

---

123. W.D. Killen, *Memoir of John Edgar, D.D., LL.D.* (Belfast, 1867), p. 19.
124. *Londonderry Sentinel*, 5 August 1859.

its proper place; prayers were always read at the meetings referred to, these have been supplemented since the revival movement commenced; the Bible was always read, but is now read with more earnestness and attention; and sermons were heard, as they always were, whenever an opportunity of hearing them was afforded.' Orangeism had profited from the revival. The 'defensive organisation' – which the *Sentinel* did not name – had been purified by the fires of revival. In reports on a supposed annihilation of party feeling some had implied that the Orange Order had actually encouraged hatred and strife. This was, in the paper's view, patently wrong. 'The revival has done away with abuses, cut off excrescences; it may have destroyed party feeling of an objectionable nature; but it has served to deepen that party feeling which should be cherished – attachment to the Throne, and the Protestant institutions of the country.' It was not a time to give up the 'No Surrender' motto, as Orangemen had been told by visiting pilgrims, but to apply it more faithfully. 'As the brave men of 1689 would not surrender to James, but were loyal subjects of William, so it becomes revived Christians not to surrender to the usurper who claims the sovereignty of this world, but to be loyal subjects of the "Prince of Peace"…The revival has done great things for Ulster, but its light may be painted without throwing the previous character of the province, or any of its political institutions, into a deeper shade than facts would warrant.' Here then was an attempt to direct the revival streams into traditional, party-political channels.

This attitude found an echo in Coleraine. The rector of St. Patrick's Coleraine, Rev. O'Hara[125], had held over a number of decades various offices of responsibility within the Orange Order at district, county and national level. He had no great wish to turn his back on that history, let alone

125. On the incumbency of James O'Hara in St. Patrick's Coleraine, see Hugh Alexander Boyd, *The Succession of Clergy in the Parish Church of St. Patrick Coleraine in the Diocese of Connor from the Londoners' Plantation 1609 to the Disestablishment of the Church of Ireland 1871: A Biographical Study* (Master's thesis, New University of Ulster, 1983), pp. 352–8.

consider it as worthless. O'Hara, born into an old aristocratic family in Ireland, was a conservative evangelical and a hard-line Orangeman.[126] His experiences of the revival may well have softened his Orange attitudes a little.[127] He had no doubt witnessed the impact of the revival on some of the lodge members in his parish. Some had no doubt resigned membership. This trend needed to be counteracted. At a soirée held in the Town Hall on 28 February 1860 to promote the interests and union of all Protestants, O'Hara, wearing an Orange emblem, insisted there was nothing in Orangeism that could persuade a man who had experienced evangelical conversion to leave the institution. Yet he admitted he would like to see Orangeism lose 'its political aspect' and expressed his hope that the day would come when every Orangeman's life adorned the doctrine of the gospel.[128] One perceives a sense of uneasiness on his part about elements within the Order and its public function. James O'Hara was one of many Anglicans who saw no reason in 1859, or at any time thereafter, to cease nourishing sectarianism.

The 'foul demon' of ascendancy had not in fact been exorcised by revivalism, though it had been bound for a while. In March 1871 a Presbyterian elder fumed that Episcopalian clergy were still clustering around the Orange standard as 'the last relic of an exclusive ascendancy'.[129] Another ten years later, at an Orange meeting in Coleraine Town Hall in December 1880, the main orators were all Episcopal clergymen and 'the principal subjects of abuse', according to the *Chronicle*, were Presbyterian ministers – 'the natural enemy'.[130] The cultural and religious solidarity of Ulster Protestants has been much exaggerated; for much of the period under consideration, it is difficult to demonstrate. The

---

126. *Coleraine Chronicle*, 1 April 1848, p. 2; 8 April 1848, p. 2; 5 November 1858, p. 4; 19 August 1893, 1, p. 5.
127. Ibid., 10 September 1859, p. 4.
128. Ibid., 31 March 1860, p. 6.
129. Ibid., 4 March 1871, p. 4.
130. Ibid., 8 January 1881, p. 8.

Evangelical Alliance, the functioning of which was one of the prerequisites of revivalist activity in 1859, failed to make deep inroads into Ulster. It was only towards the end of the following century that some clergymen began to worry about the nature of Orangeism and the impact it was having on the church's witness to the God of peace and justice.[131]

---

131. Lord Eames, a former Primate of the Church of Ireland, has questioned whether Orangeism is a Christian movement and a small group of clergy recognise its divisive sectarian function in society. 'Dr Eames questions if Orangeism is Christian movement,' *Irish Times*, 24 July 1998; 'Problems and opportunities,' *Church of Ireland Gazette*, 7 August 1998; 'Church must confront sectarian poison,' *Irish Times*, 18 July 1998. See also Earl Storey, *Traditional Roots. Towards an appropriate relationship between the Church of Ireland and the Orange Order* (Blackrock, 2002); Brian Kennaway, *The Orange Order. A Tradition Betrayed* (London 2006).

Chapter 6: The Fruit of the Revival

It was estimated by the chamberlain of the City of London, and repeated by many a clergyman involved in the Ulster revival, that about a hundred thousand men, women and children were swept into the Kingdom of God in 1859.[1] It is virtually impossible to provide strong evidence to back up such claims. At the time contemporaries claimed that hundreds of inhabitants of Coleraine had been impacted in some way by the revival. In August 1859 one non-local newspaper, the *Morning Advertiser*, said there had been more cases of conversion in the previous three months in Coleraine than there had been in the previous fifty or 'perhaps we should say hundred years'.[2] No doubt this was a faithful representation of the *impressions* left by the wave of religious enthusiasm through the summer. Obviously, there was no statistical survey carried out at the time. No names of converts were given by the *Chronicle*. The Advertiser does quote one former Member of Parliament, then a member of the Court of Aldermen and of the Court of Common Council of London, who had visited the Irish Society's school in Coleraine, as stating: 'Out of the 200 young people belonging to that school, no fewer than 40, whose ages varied from 12 to 16, were found one day on their knees in prayer, when the room was unexpectedly

---

1. *Coleraine Chronicle*, 12 November 1859.
2. Ibid., 3 September 1859.

entered.'[3] That young people, even children, were impacted by the revival was witnessed by Dr Weir of London and, based on the M.P.'s observations, perhaps as many as 20 per cent of teenagers had some kind of religious experience in 1859. Similarly, the one thousand people who 'nearly filled' the Town Hall at the times of the morning prayer meeting would represent roughly 20 per cent of the town's population, even taking into account the fact that many visitors also took part in these meetings.

All social classes were represented at these times of prayer: 'merchants, ladies and gentlemen occupying the same seats with labourers, porters and artisans'.[4] To some degree at least the world of business was noticeably affected by the revival; any class antagonisms were covered with a veneer of fraternal Christian love. On 26 December 1859 Edward Gribbon, the Baptist businessman, entertained about one hundred and fifty of his employees from the weaving factory, the yarn department and the soap manufactory. Banners festooned the room: 'Success to the Linen Trade,' 'Coleraine for Ever' and 'All are Welcome'. Gribbon talked of the mutual dependence of the owner and the worker, that all were one 'large family'. Labourers and mechanics had never been so well paid, he said on this occasion. At the end of the evening thanks were offered to Gribbon and his family for their 'long-continued and unwavering attention to the wants of their work people'. Henry Gribbon then invited all present to a prayer meeting inside the main factory taking place on the following Saturday evening—in other words, outside of the normal working hours. The goal of the meeting was to thank God for His mercies during the past year and ask for His blessing in the year to come.[5] Wages were not increased and the structure of economic relations remained untouched.

3.   *Coleraine Chronicle*, 3 September 1859
4.   Ibid., 30 July 1859.
5.   Ibid., 31 December 1859.

This increased attention given to spiritual and religious matters was, in part, the fruit of the patient labours of many simple unnamed believers and many unsung heroes such as the Town Missionaries John Mills[6] and Mr Topping[7]. The ministers of the various evangelical churches all played significant roles in seeking to channel the enthusiasm into the traditional denominations.

FELLOWSHIP MEETINGS

Christians began to pray earnestly and meet with one another for fellowship on a scale hitherto scarcely seen. These meetings had preceded the revival itself; some said they were a prerequisite of the movement. The pan-denominational prayer meeting was established in the summer of 1858, probably in July – sixteen months before the hardware merchant John Horner, the builder Thomas Boyd, the woollen and linen draper James Thompson and the grocer John Young approached the Commissioners to ask them to grant them the use of the Town Hall for the purpose of an all-saints prayer meeting.[8] The first meetings were in private homes, later moving to the Infant School building, then to the Baptist chapel in Meetinghouse Street. As some had objected to the meeting taking place in the house of worship of a particular denomination, a neutral venue was sought and attained. The Scottish version of the Psalms was used to praise God at these meetings.[9]

Weekly Bible classes were speedily organised to give the largely uneducated converts some knowledge of Scripture. Rev. Weir has provided an account of such a class:

> I might dwell also on other prayer-meetings held that evening in different places of worship, at which addresses were delivered by various ministers from a distance.

6.   *Coleraine Chronicle*, 13 March 1858.
7.   Ibid., 27 August 1859 and 3 September 1859.
8.   Ibid.,12 November 1859.
9.   William Richey, *Connor and Coleraine; or, scenes and sketches of the last Ulster Awakening*, vol. I, Belfast 1870, p. 163.

But sweeter still was the closing and special meeting with converts, in a large upper school-room connected with one of the Presbyterian churches. It was crowded to the doors. A pious citizen presided, and around and immediately before him were gathered ministers and lay gentlemen – pilgrims to Ulster, that they might see what God had wrought. As I had marked elsewhere, so at this meeting, the sweetness and jubilant exultation of the song and shout of praise was delightful, and proceeding as it did from a host of recently awakened and rescued ones, it was like the echo of the blessed symphony of adoring gratitude of the upper sanctuary, 'Salvation unto our God that sitteth on the throne, and unto the Lamb.' Mingled with the prayers and singing was a very impressive and touching address from Dr Murray Mitchell, Free Church missionary at Bombay. [...] he dwelt on the 67th Psalm, 'God be merciful to us' – the church seeking mercy, and quickening for herself; – why? 'That Thy way may be known on earth, and Thy saving health among the nations.' Never did I feel so strongly or perceive more clearly, that the revival of the church itself, and the awakening and conversion of the dead in sin, are the destined presages and pioneers of the salvation of the race.

In each of the churches and meeting houses in town, classes were held on two evenings of the week. Classes of on average forty to fifty converts gathered for example in the three Presbyterian meeting houses and the Congregational church.[10] In Rev. Richey's meeting house attendance ranged, however, from two hundred to three hundred over a period of several months. Significantly, most of these participants had previously been attending Sabbath schools and Bible classes linked to the church.[11] The Parish church of St. Patrick's organised similar Bible classes.[12]

---

10. *Coleraine Chronicle*, 25 June 1859 and 9 July 1859.
11. William Richey, *Connor and Coleraine*, p. 176.
12. *Coleraine Chronicle*, 23 July 1859.

CHRISTIAN LITERATURE

These converts added to the growing demand for Christian literature. There was a hunger for the Bible and other devotional literature. The year 1859 saw the birth of the Bible and Colportage Society of Ireland, which opened depots in Londonderry, Belfast and Dublin.[13] By 1873, 470 book agents and 56 colporteurs reported total sales of over £7,361. In the months from June to September 1859 the Edinburgh Bible Society sold 19,641 copies of the Bible to Irish booksellers which represented nearly a fourfold increase over the same months in 1858.[14] The actual numbers of copies of Bibles sold to Irish booksellers in the months of revival, compared with the data from the previous year, are as follows:[15]

	1858	1859
June	1,482	2,575
July	1,673	6,133
August	1,003	5,485
September	1,171	5,443
Total	5,329	19,636

The Coleraine Auxiliary of that Society received £118 from sales in those four months, representing a tenfold increase in receipts over the same period in any other year in the past.[16] A large parcel of books and tracts reached Coleraine from London, to be distributed free of charge to the poor townspeople. Many Bibles and tracts were distributed in 1859 by the town missionary, Mr Topping, whom the *Chronicle* described as 'an indefatigable worker in the revival movement'.[17]

---

13. *Bible and Colportage Society of Ireland. Abstract of the Report for 1873*, p. 1.
14. *Coleraine Chronicle*, 22 October 1859.
15. Ibid., 22 October 1859.
16. Ibid., 15 October 1859.
17. Ibid., 27 August 1859.

Apart from reading and studying the Bible together other religious exercises received momentum from the revival. Coleraine bookshops sold large numbers of the *Ulster Revival Hymn Book* (published by Phillips & Sons, Belfast) and McComb's *Revival Hymn Book*. There was an outpouring of poetry and new songs. The anthem of the 1859 revival, *What's the News?*, was actually imported from America, where it had been penned by a young man converted in the revival there.[18]

> Where'er we meet, you always say,
> What's the news? What's the news?
> Pray, what's the order of the day?
> What's the news? What's the news?
> Oh! I have got good news to tell;
> My Saviour hath done all things well,
> and triumphed over death and hell,
> That's the news! That's the news!
> The Lamb was slain on Calvary,
> That's the news! That's the news!
> To set a world of sinners free,
> That's the news! That's the news!
> 'Twas there His precious blood was shed,
> 'Twas there He bowed His sacred head;
> but now He's risen from the dead,
> That's the news! That's the news!
> To heav'n above the Conqueror's gone,
> That's the news! That's the news!
> He's passed triumphant to His throne,
> That's the news! That's the news!
> And on that throne He will remain,
> Until as Judge He comes again,
> Attended by a dazzling train,
> That's the news! That's the news!
> His work's reviving all around –

---

18. According to Clifford J.M. Marrs the man was a Scot. Clifford J.M. Marrs, *The 1859 Religious Revival in Scotland: A Review & Critique of the Movement with Particular Reference to the City of Glasgow*, Ph.D. Dissertation University of Glasgow, 1995, p. 74.

That's the news! That's the news!
And many have redemption found –
That's the news! That's the news!
And since their souls have caught the flame,
They shout Hosanna to His Name;
And all around they spread His fame –
That's the news! That's the news!
The Lord has pardoned all my sin –
That's the news! That's the news!
I feel the witness now within –
That's the news! That's the news!
And since He took my sins away
And taught me how to watch and pray,
I'm happy now from day to day –
That's the news! That's the news!
And Christ the Lord can save you, too –
That's the news! That's the news!
Your sinful heart He can renew –
That's the news! That's the news!
This moment, if for sins you grieve,
This moment, if you do believe,
A full acquittal you'll receive –
That's the news! That's the news!
And now, if anyone should say –
What's the news? What's the news?
Oh, tell them you've begun to pray,
That's the news! That's the news!
That you have joined the conquering band,
And now with joy at God's command,
You're marching to the better land –
That's the news! That's the news!

The song speaks of the joy of knowing one's sins are
forgiven, the freedom from the power of sin, and the power
of prayer, all key elements in the revival's theology.[19] At
the centre of the revival message stood Christ, the eternal

---

19. Cp. *Coleraine Chronicle*, 20 November 1858.

Son of God, and His work of redemption on the cross of Calvary – His saving works then, His sanctifying work now, His work of judgment in the future. Jesus is portrayed not simply as a good teacher or prophet, but as the Lord of history who is coming back soon. He is the one who has conquered death and the devil; His followers are part of a conquering band, marching to a better land. Throughout the song there resounds a joyful note because the good news of salvation has not simply been understood; it has been appropriated and trusted. The one rather un-Presbyterian note, perhaps, is the line, 'I feel the witness now within.' Yet, nobody seems to have taken umbrage at the idea of experientially knowing the witness of the Holy Spirit.

The weekly paper *The Revival* outlined and detailed the progress of the revival in the north of Ireland and Britain.[20] The local Coleraine newspaper was also a good source of encouraging reports on the further spread of the movement. John McCombie, editor of the *Chronicle* and one of the signatories of the 1859 Memorial Bible, noted that sales of his paper had increased greatly since the revival started and this had not a little to do with the extensive reports on the movement. It had been suggested to him that the paper be renamed the 'Revival Chronicle'. As far as McCombie was concerned the revival had been good for his business.

Church Growth

Did the revival actually add many new families to the rolls of the churches? The 1860 returns for the Presbyterian churches reveal only a moderate increase in members at First and Third Coleraine and a small drop in the numbers of families in fellowship at Second Coleraine (New Row). Altogether there was an aggregate increase of twenty-three families. Between 1858 and 1861 the membership figures reveal an overall

---

20.   *Coleraine Chronicle*, 3 September 1859 and 10 September 1859.

decline in the number of families on the membership rolls of the three churches. In November 1859 a good number of names were added to the rolls of communicants: 76 at First Presbyterian, 100 at Second Presbyterian and 56 at Terrace Row.[21] Rev. Canning said 'a great many' had been added to his church. In particular, the number of young communicants had been about four times the usual number.[22] Some of these new communicants were not unknown to the churches and most probably took part for the first time.

This is not the full picture however. The actual numbers of families in communion with the Presbyterian churches of Coleraine were as follows:

	First Presbyterian	New Row	Terrace Row
1856	200	330	225
1857	200	260	225
1858	200	302	224
1859	220	306	226
1860	230	300	245
1861	220	280	225
1863	194	270	263
1866	185	220	300

Source: *Coleraine Presbytery Book. Minutes of Coleraine Presbytery 1842–1869*

The number of communicant members of First Presbyterian actually fell from 209 in 1855 to 185 in 1866. In addition, the actual number of stipend payers there fell from 150 at the visitation in 1855 to 136 in 1866. One should not forget, however, that this was a time when the population of the town was declining. On the other hand, whereas there were no prayer meetings in 1855, two elders led prayer meetings in

---

21. *Coleraine Chronicle*, 12 November 1859. Figures for First Presbyterian are taken from the *Records of the Coleraine Presbytery* 1855 and 1866.
22. *The Presbyterian Magazine*, January 1860, p. 21.

1866 and the minister's stipend had been increased from £84 and 5 shillings to £150 over the same period even though the congregation was somewhat smaller. On the positive side, the number of Sabbath schools connected with this church rose from two to fifteen in the same time period. Given the vast numbers of people who attended revival meetings one must conclude that many backslidden or unregenerate Presbyterians who were only formally members of their church were restored or reborn at this time. The revival seems to have impacted families already connected with the Presbyterian churches.

Some Presbyterian churches in Ulster, including Terrace Row, felt the need to extend their premises due to increased attendances.[23] More Sabbath school accommodation was required by New Row. The Terrace Row Sabbath school also registered increased numbers in 1859:[24]

	Female Classes (Pupils)	Male Classes (Pupils)
1852	9 (103)	10 (88)
1853	15 (161)	11 (130)
1858	14 (111)	12 (96)
1859	14 (153)	12 (132)

These figures reflect an increase of nearly 38 per cent over the year. The reasons for the increase may, or may not, have been due to the revival since, in 1859, 34 females and 37 males were struck off the school rolls. In addition, the average attendance during the year of revival is said to have been small (142 pupils, taught by 27 teachers, in total). The bad weather was blamed for the relatively disappointing results. Numbers continued to fall. In 1861 only 243 children were still on the rolls.

Overall, however, Sunday schools experienced growth. The Sunday School Society for Ireland – the organisation

23. *Coleraine Chronicle*, 9 June 1860.
24. Ibid., 22 January 1853 and 11 February 1860.

which was established in 1815 as the successor of the Hibernian Sunday School Society – reported an increase in the number of Sunday schools throughout the island of Ireland in 1859, 29 new schools being established in Ulster alone with 15,329 additional scholars.[25] The report for 1860 noted also an increase in subscriptions to the society which enabled the committee to meet the increasing demand. The 1862 report reiterated this optimism: '[U]pon the whole a large amount of permanent good has resulted [from the revival] to the Sunday School system of instruction.'[26] Increasing numbers of people were making themselves available as teachers and as scholars. On the other hand, the pan-denominational character of the society suffered when, in 1862, the Presbyterian churches split off to establish their own Sabbath School Society.

The numbers attending Methodist chapels on the Coleraine Circuit grew by 23.6 per cent from 1855 to 1857 and by a further 35.6 per cent between 1858 and 1861, the 1860 figure alone revealing a 25 per cent growth over the preceding year. In 1863 Ballycastle became an independent circuit, leaving 172 on the Coleraine circuit. Membership grew slightly to 175 by the year 1869. The membership of the Methodist society in Coleraine developed as follows:

1856	298
1857	309
1858	250
1859	264
1860	330
1861	339
1862	332

Source: *Minutes of Several Conversations between the Methodist Ministers at their Annual Conference* (Dublin 1856–62)

---

25. Helen Clayton, *To School without Shoes. A Brief History of the Sunday School Society for Ireland 1809–1979*, n.p. n.d, p. 42.
26. Ibid., p. 45.

Some of the success was no doubt due to the labours of the Town Missionary, Mills,[27] and the Methodist General Missionary, Hewitt, who preached at seven open-air meetings in the area and at other meetings indoors. Hewitt wrote at the time of the state of religion in Coleraine: 'No pen can describe the work that is going on upon this Circuit. Some of the meetings were of an extraordinary character: so many struck down, crying for mercy, shouting for joy, with the clapping of their hands; others singing praises and so on; that the scene could hardly be conceived by those who had not seen it.'[28] The attraction of enthusiastic, exuberant Methodist meetings was reflected in the improving statistics. As elsewhere in the British Isles it was the Methodists who, more than other denominations, adopted the new measures of revivalist evangelism advocated by Finney and they reaped the rewards.[29]

The Independent chapel (Congregationalists) experienced quite astonishing growth as a result of the revival. The historian of Irish Congregationalism, James Miller Henry, calculated that the revival added 55 individuals to a church which only had 37 members.[30] The Minute Book of the church, however, clearly states that in 1859 only 45 people were added to the church. The membership figures are as follows:

1836	12
1857	56
1861	113
1871	55

---

27. *The Irish Evangelist*, March 1860, p. 46.

28. *The Wesleyan Methodist Magazine for 1859*, p. 953.

29. Cp. Kenneth S. Jeffrey, *When the Lord walked the land. The 1858–62 Revival in the North-East of Scotland*, Carlisle 2002, p. 38.

30. J.M. Henry, *An Assessment of the Social, Religious and Political Aspects of Congregationalism in Ireland in the Nineteenth Century*, Ph.D. Dissertation, Queen's University Belfast, 1965, p. 263.

The numbers admitted to the Congregational Church at the time were as follows:

1856	7
1858	0
1860	17

1857	2
1859	45
1861	6

Source: Coleraine Congregational Church. *Minute Book* 1854–77.

That growth made the building of a new chapel necessary. Its minister, the Rev. John Kydd,[31] in a June 1859 report to the Irish Evangelical Society, had expressed his belief that no other church in the town would 'gain so much, numerically' as the Congregational Church.[32] This proved to be a correct assessment of the situation. On 16 June of the 'year of grace' eleven individuals were admitted to membership of the Independent Church and two others were proposed for admittance; of these thirteen only three were the children of parents already attending the chapel, nine were recent converts.[33] By 1871, however, the number of members had once again fallen – not least due to emigration – to the 1857 level.[34] Indeed, even as the new building was being formally opened at the end of May 1862, it was clear that less permanent good could be ascribed to the awakening than was at first hoped.[35]

One church's gain seemed to be another church's loss. There were accusations, some published, of sheep-stealing. This was particularly true of Londonderry, but also for Coleraine, as the minute books reveal. Presbyterians such as Rev. Thomas Witherow and Independents such as Rev.

---

31. Dying in 1906, Kydd was the last surviving minister from the revival in Coleraine.

32. J.W. Massie, *Revivals in Ireland. Facts, Documents and Correspondence*, London 1859, p. 9.

33. J.W. Massie, Ibid., p. 9.

34. Coleraine Congregational Church. *Minute Book* 1854–77.

35. *Coleraine Chronicle*, 7 June 1862.

Robert Sewell (Derry) accused the Baptists of attempting to use the revival for their own sectarian, denominational ends.[36] In his *A Word with the Baptists about Baptising*, published in Coleraine in 1860, Rev. Sewell claimed the Baptists had 'taken advantage of the late Revival to press their particular views on the attention of the young'. They and they alone had caused divisions, perplexing the young, and had thereby 'stopped the Revival in some places'.[37] This inter-denominational strife, which erupted in October 1859, no doubt contributed to the quenching of the revival fire. Though the problem was more acute elsewhere, even in Coleraine there were many rumours and suspicions. There was a single case of a member of New Row Presbyterian Church being baptised by full immersion on being truly converted. The kirk session exercised discipline by demanding the return of the communion token.[38] As far as Coleraine Presbyterianism was concerned, however, this case remained an isolated event.

Figures for the Baptist Church prior to 1860 do not seem to have survived. This was due not least to the fact that prior to September 1860 the congregation had had no pastor for seven years. James Nelson, a Scripture Reader in the Baptist congregation, was for many years a most zealous evangelist and colporteur in the district and he signed the Memorial Bible.[39] Dr James Carson addressed some revival meetings in Coleraine and witnessed many others.[40] At the end of August 1859 several young men, converts from Roman Catholicism, were among a group of people baptised in the Baptist chapel.[41] Special prayer meetings were organised in that chapel, as well

---

36. J.M. Henry, *An Assessment of the Social, Religious and Political Aspects of Congregationalism in Ireland in the Nineteenth Century*, p. 273.
37. *Coleraine Chronicle*, 1 September 1860.
38. Public Records Office of Northern Ireland. *New Row Presbyterian Church Session Minutes* 1850–70. Entry for 28 October 1859.
39. *Coleraine Chronicle*, 23 April 1881.
40. Ibid., 27 August 1859.
41. Ibid., 3 September 1859.

as in the other church buildings in the town.[42] Membership steadily grew throughout the 1860s, which in all likelihood built upon growth during 1859. In 1838 there had been only 30 Baptists in Coleraine. Numbers grew as follows:

(September) 1860	72
(September) 1861	129
1862	165
1865	191

Source: *Record Book*, Baptist Church Coleraine from 1860.

Not only the local Baptists were trying to consolidate their own particular evangelistic work. Visiting Baptist ministers were also active in Coleraine in 1859. One English Baptist was responsible for starting a controversy which some young converts seem to have relished. He publicly stated that 'infant baptism was concocted in hell'.[43] The statement did not help to foster Baptist-Presbyterian relations. It did not win Baptists many friends. The phrase, expressed during a heated debate, was, it must be said, essentially a response to the 'exceedingly unfriendly' and hostile attitude of Ulster Presbyterianism to 'Anabaptist' principles at the time.[44] Throughout the autumn a controversy took place in Coleraine over the issue, and a number of tracts were published giving guidance to the respective camps. In an editorial the *Chronicle* quite rightly referred to 'a most useless warfare' being waged over the issue of baptism, which was only undermining evangelical unity. Rev. Kydd, for example, published a series of *Tracts on Christian Baptism*,[45] which were praised by the Rector of Killowen, William W. Sillito, as proving that 'pouring is the better outward sign of the pouring forth of

---

42. *Coleraine Chronicle*, 10 September 1859.
43. Ibid., 24 September 1859.
44. Joshua Thompson, 'Irish Baptists and the 1859 Revival', in: *Irish Baptist Historical Society Journal*, vol. 17 (1984–5), pp. 8–9.
45. *Coleraine Chronicle*, 3 December 1859. Mr S. Eccles of Coleraine was selling Kydd's tracts. For references to other tracts on the subject of baptism see Ibid., 10 March 1860, 17 March 1860, 9 June 1860 and 1 September 1860.

the Holy Spirit'.[46] Both were concerned about inroads made by Baptists and Brethren. In his own *Address* to his parishioners Rev. Sillito refuted the arguments put forward by these groups which were perplexing members of his own congregation. Members of other churches, the Baptist-Brethren argument ran, had not really been baptised; infant 'sprinkling' was 'an awful lie, and hell its birthplace'.[47] By the beginning of October 1859 the controversy had died down somewhat. 'We hear less of the sectional and denominational spirit which called forth our caution last week,' stated the *Chronicle*'s editor on 1 October, emphasising that only a few individuals had been guilty of exhibiting a dogmatic attitude on non-essentials. Sillito's address suggests the matter was still simmering under the surface.

The arrival of Rev. T.W. Medhurst from Kingston-upon-Thames in 1860 led to a strengthening of the Baptist position in Coleraine. On the one hand Medhurst was appreciative of the Presbyterian witness in the area. To a man, the Presbyterian body was 'as sound as the Derry bells', he wrote in a letter to London in June 1860. His ministerial colleagues held to a 'pure gospel of the kingdom'. At the same time he was more than willing to immerse Presbyterians on confession of their faith in Christ. There was a particularly bitter conflict with the Rev. John Martin of Crossgar about such practices. Medhurst threw himself into open-air evangelism, preaching in barns, factories, chapels and the Town Hall – anywhere, in fact, where he could gather a crowd. And crowds turned up to listen.[48] The Presbyterians of Portstewart and Articlave opened their doors to him.[49] The revival of 1859 had, he claimed, created 'a large amount of hungering

---

46. William W. Sillito, *An Address on the Religious Revival, and Matters Connected Therewith, to the Parishioners of Killowen, especially those who worship in the Parish Church*, Coleraine 1859, p. 15.
47. William W. Sillito, Ibid., 13. Cp. *Coleraine Chronicle*, 24 December 1859.
48. *Coleraine Chronicle*, 7 July 1860, 17 July 1860 and 8 September 1860.
49. Ibid., 14 July 1860 and 24 May 1862.

and thirsting after the gospel'. The Baptists in Coleraine experienced a second harvest. Within two years the congregation had doubled in size.

Mention should be made of the Brethren, a relatively new group at the time which caused headaches in most of the other evangelical congregations in Coleraine. The census for 1861 reported that in Coleraine there were sixteen members of the 'Christian Brethren', 7 members of the 'Brethren' and five members of the 'Plymouth Brethren'.[50] Whether or not these twenty-eight individuals worshipped together in the Brethren's Room at 4, Church Street, is unclear. Most of them presumably did. There were also Brethren in the rural parishes of the north-east Liberties of Coleraine (five in Ballyaghran, for example) and the revivalist preaching, over a number of years, of Charles Mackintosh – the 'quondam leader of the Plymouth Brethren in Coleraine'[51] – attracted adherents in the region. Some of these had once fellowshipped with the smaller Nonconformist groups and this led to a public relations onslaught. Dr Carson, the Baptist controversialist, wrote a polemical treatise on the alleged 'heresies' of the Brethren. Among Congregationalists Rev. Kydd and the Derry Independent minister, Robert Sewell, attacked them. In spite of these polemics, the most recent evangelical group to emerge in Ireland actually grew in strength throughout the year of revival and beyond.

The revival had given credence and added impetus to lay preaching. Those groups such as the Brethren who did away with a salaried clerical caste altogether seem to have profited most from the revival. But the evangelical groupings within the Anglican denomination were consolidated during 1859. Many new Bible-reading adherents had been won to the evangelical cause. The average numbers of communicants at St. Patrick's Coleraine at the time were as follows:

---

50. *Census of Ireland for 1861*, Dublin 1863, pp. 450, 457.
51. *Coleraine Chronicle*, 24 May 1862.

1856	75
1857	57
1858	67
1859	110
1860	110
1861	101
1862	85
1863	88

The average number of worshippers grew in the period between 1850 and 1865, though a causal link with the revival cannot be demonstrated. Bearing in mind that there were 1,492 members of the established church in the Coleraine benefice in 1861 attendance was as follows:

	Morning Service	Evening Service
1850	400	200
1865	530	400

Source: *Preachers Book* (PRONI).

Killowen Parish Church, where Rev. Sillito was rector, does not seem to have benefited at all from the revival impetus. Here there were 310 members in 1856, rising to 454 members in 1865. In spite of growing numbers on the rolls, attendance dropped in these years:

	Average Morning Attendance	Sunday Evening Attendance	Children catechised	Sunday school scholars
1856	98	73	77	98
1865	80	29	63	100

The number of communicants also dropped at Killowen, as shown in the following table:

	Easter Day	Whitsunday	Christmas Day
1856	47	25	35
1865	20	14	22

Source: Diocese of Derry. *Reports of Rural Deans* June 1856 and June 1865 (PRONI)

Ulster Protestantism as a whole became less wary of emotionalism within the context of the church. The fervour and enthusiasm of revival meetings could obviously not be maintained for years on end. The synod of Ballymena and Coleraine, meeting at Ballymoney in May 1861, noted that the 'enthusiasm connected with the Revival of 1859 is gone' but that there remained 'so many gracious and blessed results as to give cause for devout thanksgiving and praise to God'. Ministers were still zealous in their duties. Very few prayer meetings had been discontinued, though the 'overflowing attendance' was no longer characteristic of them. Attendances at Sunday meetings had been sustained and it was claimed that the moral tone of society was considerably better than it had been in 1858.[52] But what were the social effects of revivalism? Contemporary writers all referred to the conversion of prostitutes, the increase in temperance and a drop in crime. The following paragraphs aim to offer some critical analysis of the argument that social life in Ulster radically changed in 'the year of grace' 1859.

PROSTITUTION

That prostitutes were converted in 1859 has already been mentioned. At least eight women are said to have left brothels in Coleraine and sought sanctuary elsewhere.[53] In

---

52. *Coleraine Chronicle*, 25 May 1861.
53. John T. Carson, *God's River in Spate. The Story of the Religious Awakening of Ulster in 1859*, Belfast 1958, p. 39.

all likelihood, this number represented a small percentage of the total number of women working in Coleraine brothels. None closed for good during the revival; the demand for their services actually grew over the next fifteen years. In 1877 there were numerous brothels in Killowen and the *Chronicle* complained of the 'unbridled license' and 'extreme youth' of the women working there. Soliciting was going on at all hours of the day and night and on most of the streets of Coleraine.[54] Certainly, the social conditions which fostered prostitution were not to change much in the second half of the nineteenth century.

TEMPERANCE

The revival not only added believers to churches, it also helped the temperance cause in Coleraine. The Christmas festivities in 1859 were said to have been celebrated with less levity and drunkenness and 'more sober seriousness' than ever before.[55] The Fair days in the town, 12 May and 12 November, never passed without hundreds being found 'the worse of liquor'.[56] In 1859 only a few young men over-indulged that November. A wholesale merchant in Coleraine told the *Banner of Ulster* that it was customary in the past for farmers to send into town for two, three or five gallons of whiskey to celebrate the harvest; in the year of revival, however, he had not received a single order from a farmer. He was now selling only about a tenth of the normal volume sold prior to the revival. One publican, the one who did most business in the town, had to close down his business as a result of the falling number of customers.[57] In the Coleraine district the excise duty paid on spirits for the month after the revival began in June is said to

---

54. *Coleraine Chronicle*, 27 August 1881; T.H. Mullin, *Coleraine in Modern Times*, Belfast 1979, p. 118.
55. Ibid., 31 December 1859 and 14 January 1860.
56. Ibid., 19 November 1859.
57. Ibid., 20 October 1860.

have fallen by £400 sterling.[58] There were other signs that Coleraine people were becoming more sober. In 1858 there were nineteen publicans and ten spirit merchants in the town; these numbers fell to fourteen and eight respectively by 1861.[59]

This is one side of the story. The other side is just as true. By 1865 trade in spirits had recovered from the temporary drop in sales. In that year there were thirty-one publicans and ten wine and spirits merchants in Coleraine. James Moore's distillery in Coleraine was finding it difficult to keep up with demand.[60] After a very quiet year in 1859, the Borough Magistrates Court, meeting in August 1860, had to deal with six cases of drunkenness and disorderliness: the first sign that some men were going back to their old ways.[61] The Quarter Sessions on 29 June 1860 also noted an increase in drunkenness in the town.[62] For working-class men, of course, there was still very little alternative to the amusements and comradeship experienced in pubs. With the passing excitement of huge revival meetings, full of expectation that many would be 'stricken' by the Holy Spirit, people returned to their old habits.

CRIME

The revival also led to a drop in crime in the town and neighbouring districts. The Superior Officer of Police, who had work experience in most of the counties of Ireland, claimed he had never seen such a quiet town. There had been, in his view, a 'complete reformation' in the habits of many people. The Head Constable, with eighteen years' experience in Coleraine, said the Petty Sessions held on 17 June 1859 was

---

58. *Coleraine Chronicle*, 6 August 1859; William W. Sillito, *An Address on the Religious Revival*, p. 4.

59. *The Belfast and Province of Ulster Directory* for 1858–9 and 1861–2.

60. Wynne's *Business Directory of Belfast* 1865–6.

61. *Coleraine Chronicle*, 18 August 1860.

62. Ibid., 7 July 1860.

the first he had ever attended where nobody was prosecuted for both riot and drunkenness.[63] This trend continued into 1860. At the January Quarter Sessions there were very few criminal cases that had occurred during the previous three months. The Assistant-Barrister put this down to the improved state of morality among the townspeople brought about by the revival.[64] Coleraine men – and, according to the Baptist Dr Carson, men had predominated at every meeting he had attended during the revival months[65] – had in large numbers turned their attention to religious matters.

Having said this, it has to be borne in mind that throughout the 1850s, as the country was prospering, there had been a fall in all kinds of crime. In March 1857 there had been only one person on trial and the Assistant-Barrister had congratulated the Grand Jury on the 'most peaceable and orderly state of your town'.[66] In June 1857 there were only six cases, and only one of these seems to have been serious.[67] The Quarter Sessions in June 1858 had only three cases to deal with.[68] The revival may have added an extra pacifying factor to the equation, but it was the underlying economic trends in the 1850s which were the key to the drop in crime in Ulster and, indeed, throughout the island of Ireland. Quietness characterised the district until the summer of 1862 when business at the Quarter Sessions became busy again. There was suddenly 'a very large amount of business', said William Armstrong QC. Indeed, there was an unusually high number of offences to be dealt with – higher than in any other part of Ireland. The cases involved a great variety of offences – assaults, violent as-

63. *Coleraine Chronicle*, 18 June 1859.
64. Ibid., 14 January 1860.
65. Ibid., 18 February 1860.
66. Ibid., 4 April 1857.
67. Ibid., 4 July 1857.
68. Ibid., 3 July 1858.

saults, robbery, pickpocketing, theft, forgery. In the words of the barrister there was 'every description of crime short of murder or manslaughter'. Three years after the revival Coleraine once again had an extraordinarily high crime rate.[69] By 1865 ministers in the town could be heard deploring the increase in all forms of wickedness.[70] The very scene of many of the revival meetings in Coleraine, the Fair Hill, had by that year become a rubbish tip.[71] The sense of awe that had once pervaded the area had disappeared for good.

MISSION TO SCOTLAND

The ripple effect of the revival in and around Coleraine was perhaps the most important fruit of the movement. The appendix lists the names of some of those ministers who crossed the Irish Sea to see for themselves what was taking place on the Causeway Coast. It was not long before Scotland and England heard about what was taking place in Coleraine. During the summer of revival a gentleman from Liverpool wrote to the chairman of the united prayer meetings in the Town Hall requesting prayers for his own city. He had heard that Coleraine was the place where 'the blessing seems to be most abundantly poured out'.[72] This 'Coleraine blessing', if we may call it such, was to impact other towns too. A Coleraine man went to visit his two sons in Port Glasgow that summer in order to specifically tell them of the revival in Ulster. In his son's kitchen a meeting was organised one Sunday morning. Three conversions took place, news of which spread quickly through the town. A hastily convened meeting in a hall drew in over two thousand people. Again, a number of these were physically affected by the preaching. Rev. Patterson of Dunoon, who

---

69. *Coleraine Chronicle*, 5 July 1862.
70. Ibid., 3 June 1865.
71. Ibid., 3 June 1865.
72. Ibid., 17 September 1859.

reported these incidents to the *Christian Witness*, said he believed God had begun a work in Port Glasgow and that, 'just as He began in Connor and Ballymena, and then carried the work to the large town of Belfast', so now He wanted the message to be taken from Port Glasgow to the city of Glasgow itself.[73] Now, on hearing this news, a Christian doctor in Coleraine exclaimed: 'Is not this an answer to the prayers of the people of Coleraine?' Apparently, one of the ministers in Port Glasgow, the Rev. McLachlan, had been in Coleraine a few weeks previously and had specially requested the prayers of the converts there on behalf of his own town. The Rev. Adam Blythe of the Free Church in Girvan related all this to a united prayer meeting in Coleraine Town Hall on a day in August. Blythe had learned, he said, that in 1857 two gentlemen from America had visited Coleraine to speak about the revival in their country. On arriving in Ireland, they were requested by their hosts to remember Coleraine in their prayers. That was, he added, 'a request which has ever since been complied with in the Fulton Street prayer meeting in New York'. Thus, 'we have three central links, as it were, in that invisible chain of prayer in connection with which God pours out His precious blessings on the children of men. New York prays for Coleraine, and Coleraine in turn prays for Port Glasgow, and Port Glasgow is speedily visited with an outpouring of God's Spirit! Truly, prayer moves the hand that moves the world.'[74]

One Scot who contributed in different ways to the revival in Coleraine was Peter Drummond (1799–1877).[75] Drummond, a seedsman from Stirling, had established the

---

73. *The Primitive Wesleyan Methodist Magazine for the Year 1859*, pp. 305–6.
74. *Coleraine Chronicle*, 3 September 1859.
75. Michael J. Cormack, *The Stirling Tract Enterprise and the Drummonds*, Stirling 1984; William Richey, *Connor and Coleraine; or, Scenes and Sketches of the Last Ulster Awakening*, vol. I, Belfast 1870, pp. 163, 180.

Stirling Tract Enterprise in 1848, initially to combat what he perceived to be the desecration of the Sabbath. Assisted by the development of the railways and the postal services, Drummond sent his tracts all over the United Kingdom. They were, for example, used to spread the gospel in Coleraine. He spent some time in the town in June and July 1859. His tracts did a lot to promote the movement and also induce Scottish clergymen to visit Ireland and see for themselves what was going on. The *Chronicle* lists for July and August the names of over two hundred and thirty clerical visitors from Scotland and these were only a fraction of the total number who visited Coleraine in those months. There were, in addition, 'huge numbers' of Christian laymen from other parts of the United Kingdom who had come over to help in some way.[76] Among the visitors were George Bain of Garioch and Rev. Robert Reid of Banchory, two pioneers of the revival in Aberdeenshire. The impact of events in Coleraine, and elsewhere in the north of Ireland, on the revival in Scotland and England requires more research, but it was clear to contemporaries that there was a close connection. On returning from a visit to Coleraine George Bain fuelled the revival fervour in his parish. He had specifically requested that prayer be offered for evangelistic meetings in Garioch and, on returning, found that 'a great awakening had occurred within his church that very same night' on which prayer had been offered.[77]

Just as Bain proved to be pivotal in awakening souls in a part of Aberdeenshire so some of the visitors from Glasgow – particularly Rev. Alexander N. Somerville (Anderston Free Church), Rev. Dugald M'Coll (Wynds Free Church), Rev. Andrew A. Bonar (Finnieston Free Church), Rev. Jacob Alexander (Stockwell Free Church) and Rev. John Williams

---

76. *Coleraine Chronicle*, 30 July, 6 August, 13 August and 3 September 1859.
77. Kenneth S. Jeffrey, *When the Lord Walked the Land*, pp. 118,128.

of the Baptist Church on North Frederick Street – hurried across the water and 'brought the flame back to Scotland'.[78] In addition to these Scots, unnamed converts from Ireland also spread the news of revival in Glasgow.[79] Rev. Thomas Toye (Great George Street Presbyterian Church, Belfast) spent a number of weeks in October and November 1860 and again in June and August 1861, preaching to crowds in Glasgow.[80] The Coleraine hardware merchant John Horner gave addresses in the Religious Institution Rooms and, later, in Wynds Free Church on Sunday 24 July 1859, as the city was awaiting the first wave of revival.[81] He passed on detailed accounts of his own experiences in Coleraine, leaving, the *Scottish Guardian* claimed on 26 July, scores of people 'in great distress':

> Many were seen weeping … between fifty and eighty remained, when an invitation was given to anxious souls… some found peace…In the case of those individuals… conviction was not produced for the first time on the evening in question. The parties had for the most part been long anxious about their souls, and gladly embraced this opportunity of unbosoming their minds. Rev. Mr. Taylor of the Wynds Mission has now appointed a meeting with anxious inquirers…

Two days later Taylor reported to a gathering in the Religious Institution Rooms the impact of Horner's speech:

> [M]atters did not come to what appeared to be a crisis till last Sabbath (24 July). On the evening of that day, Mr. Horner … address[ed] our … meeting, which

---

78. Clifford J.M. Marrs, *The 1859 Religious Revival in Scotland: A Review & Critique of the Movement with Particular Reference to the City of Glasgow*, Ph.D. Dissertation University of Glasgow, 1995, p. 219.

79. Ibid., pp. 219, 234.

80. Ibid., pp. 80, 272f, 298, 303f.

81. Ibid., pp. 218, 221f.

was attended chiefly by the mission people, but also by a number of the regular congregation. The meeting was largely attended … and the address of Mr. Horner must have taken effect … about sixty [anxious] persons waited [behind]…. A similar opportunity was given to inquirers last night (Monday 25 July). I saw that the people were evidently deeply affected …

Irish clergymen also sought to stir the minds and hearts of Scottish brethren. Among them was the Rev. Alfred Canning of Coleraine, who, as a member of a deputation from the Irish Presbyterian Church, spoke at a revival meeting in the City Hall in Glasgow on 11 August 1859. He emphasised that 'earnest prayers were every day put up for [the] people [of Glasgow] by crowded audiences in the public hall of [Coleraine]'.[82] Two years later, in August 1861, the Baptist Rev. T. W. Medhurst, then of Coleraine – he would later succeed John Williams as pastor of the North Frederick Street church[83] – appears to have laboured alongside the Presbyterian Toye in evangelistic campaigns in Glasgow in 1861 and 1862.[84] This was a very practical expression of the spirit and purpose of the Evangelical Alliance – a unity based not on denominational specifics, but on faith in the atoning work of Christ on Calvary.

---

82. Clifford J.M. Marrs, *The 1859 Religious Revival in Scotland: A Review & Critique of the Movement with Particular Reference to the City of Glasgow*, p. 224f.

83. *Coleraine Chronicle*, 25 October 1862.

84. Ibid., 27 September 1862; Clifford J.M. Marrs, *The 1859 Religious Revival in Scotland*, p. 306.

Chapter 7: The End of the Revival

Commemorative meetings were held in Coleraine in 1860, and every year thereafter for over forty years. The fiftieth anniversary meeting took place in the Town Hall when a vast audience heard Rev. G. W. D. Rea of First Presbyterian speak of his mother's conversion during the revival. He detected the need, in 1909, for an 'outburst' of the same fervour to sweep away the 'self-satisfied complacency, slackness and formality' that then characterised, in his view, church life. Sermons had become too general in content. Christians were no longer being discipled and disciplined. He encouraged his own congregation to look for a new revival: 'Let the people pray for it and wait for it, because it was bound to come.'[1]

In 1860 large crowds attended the commemorative event. People were described as 'earnest'; the atmosphere remained 'devotional'.[2] The movement had turned into a monument. It appears to be difficult, if not impossible, to explain why waves of religious enthusiasm suddenly or imperceptibly ebb away. Perhaps there was a rather banal cause of the decline: the weather. It seems to be as good a reason as any. In October 1859 the weather became wintry and cold.[3] Heavy showers of sleet and snow fell on 20 October. The snow was several inches deep the following day. Torrential rain followed on

---

1. *Coleraine Chronicle*, 12 June 1909.
2. Ibid., 9 June 1860.
3. Ibid., 22 and 29 October 1859.

the 29th. People were not totally deterred from attending morning and evening prayer meetings and there was no reduction in the number of meetings held. At the prayer meetings, however, calls were first heard for 'a renewal of the Revival'. In the middle of December heavy snows again covered the north of Ireland – hundreds had little fuel or warm clothing; others lost their employments as a result of the weather.[4] There were 186 people in the workhouse; the trend was upwards. It was a good season of the year, the *Chronicle* noted, to exercise benevolence and remember the poor. Attendance at prayer meetings slumped. Numbers were, the *Chronicle* lamented, not what they were at first or even what they were 'during the three or four months which immediately succeeded the first fruits of the awakening'.[5] The trend continued into the New Year. Very many people suffered privation due to the severe weather throughout the winter months. In a letter dated 10 February 1860 Rev. Canning drew attention to the miserable state in which the 'humbler operative classes' found themselves. Everywhere he went he found 'a cold hearth and a bare board' in the homes of the poor. Hungry children stared at him, making 'no complaint'. Unfortunately, he pointed out, many of those suffering did not belong to any church and could not count on Christian benevolence, yet he had no doubt that 'some means will be devised soon to meet the urgent necessities of the poor'.[6] It was apparently left to somebody else to devise them.

LACK OF COMPASSION
No doubt some individuals did respond to the needs of the poor. In an obituary to Alexander Cuthbert – he died in May 1860 – special mention is made of his concern for

---

4.   *Coleraine Chronicle*, 17 December 1859.
5.   Ibid., 10 December 1859.
6.   Ibid., 11 February 1860.

the suffering of those unemployed during the 'late severe and protracted winter' and in other periods of agricultural and business recession.[7] Such relief was only a drop in the ocean of suffering. The open-air preaching in Killowen, where most inhabitants vegetated in poverty, seems to have come to an end as worries returned that cholera would be, as in the past, the companion of poverty. A letter writer wondered why Presbyterians in the town felt 'incompetent or disinclined' to look after these poor people, most of them dressed in filthy rags.[8]

If the revival had been encouraged by the summer sun and economic optimism of people in Coleraine, the cold weather and sudden loss of employment helped to bring it to a standstill. The Clothworkers Company had had the mission station, renovated at a cost of £80, torn down a long time prior to the revival and continued to refuse the petitions from the synod of Ballymena and Coleraine that a place of worship be erected for Presbyterians in that vicinity.[9] 'Is not this time of revival a suitable time', a correspondent had asked in October, 'to rebuild that [mission] station and to afford accommodation to the roused multitudes?'[10]

The prosperity Presbyterians enjoyed, however, was not put to use in a manner that benefited poorer co-religionists. Two hundred Presbyterian families in Killowen were described by John Brown in May 1860 as 'poor, ragged and unwashed' – more numerous than he had even imagined.[11] The poor remained poor and, without a decent set of clothes, stayed away from meeting places. In fact, there was not even a mission station in Killowen, let alone a church building.

---

7. *Coleraine Chronicle*, 12 May 1860.
8. Ibid., 19 November 1859.
9. Ibid., 1 June 1850, 3 and 10 February 1855, 1 October 1859. The Baptist Edward Gribbon had granted use in the meantime of a very large room for worship services.
10. Ibid., 1 October 1859.
11. Ibid., 26 May 1860.

In the Nonconformist meeting places in town employers – merchants, manufacturers, shopkeepers – held sway, and they were not even in favour of subscribing to a modern sewerage system for the town, let alone a new church building. Critics noted the appalling living conditions of many of Coleraine's inhabitants, particularly in Killowen. The town's most influential families had repeatedly rejected Dr Macaldin's calls since 1845 for water pipes to be laid to ensure that all families had at least access to running water. One result was that whenever cholera came to the area – as it did in 1855 – the inhabitants of the poor sections of town were decimated. In this situation Brown wrote: 'Until the pious awakened people visit and purify its hovels, clothe its ragged population, and try to elevate the degraded masses, they will not aright discharge their duty. I do not venture to judge men's hearts, but until the Presbyterians of Coleraine undertake this task earnestly, I shall refer to their profession as transcendental, but lament their deplorable inconsistency. At the first visit of cholera there were as loud professions as during the late revival. I hope the tale will not vanish like the former, for they disappeared like the early cloud and morning dew. Until the Presbyterians of Killowen be visited and cared for I shall read essays on 'Home Heathenism' [published in 1855 by Rev. William Richey of First Coleraine[12]] and reports on the marvels of grace shown in Coleraine *cum grano salis*, although I shall not question the sincerity of the writers.' For revival to continue, Finney had argued years before, fervour had to feed into practical concern for people. Were Presbyterians so busy building their own homes and businesses that they had little time for building Christ's kingdom in the poor part of town? Certainly little seems to have been done for the two hundred Presbyterian families in Killowen. Another petition issued in May 1869 to erect

---

12.   *Coleraine Chronicle*, 19 May 1855.

a hall for meetings fell on deaf ears.[13] While 'persons more elevated and comfortable in their worldly circumstances' attended the three Presbyterian meeting houses on one side of the Bann, fellow Presbyterians on the other bank, lacking appropriate clothing, often ill or infirm, were left to meet their own spiritual needs.

Similarly, while few towns were thought to be as well supplied with good schools as Coleraine was, one inhabitant, Drummond Grant, a nephew of Peter Drummond of Stirling, noted in 1867 that there were still huge 'moral wastes' in the neighbourhood. He had recently met a completely illiterate fourteen-year-old Presbyterian girl who told him she had never even heard of Jesus. She certainly couldn't tell Grant where he lived.[14] The non-sectarian pan-denominational Coleraine Ragged School, which published its first annual report in 1859[15] though it had been running for over three years, was clearly unable to attract new scholars. The numbers in attendance there fell from an average of seventy in 1858 to an average of forty in 1859 and of thirty in 1861. In other words, fewer children of the poorest classes were receiving basic education, food and clothing in the school in the years following the revival. The reasons for this are unclear. The ministers of the various churches who superintended the school's operations and the ladies 'of the highest respectability and influence' in the community seem to have lost sight of the 'waifs and strays' who were left to fend for themselves on the streets of Killowen and other parts of town.

Charles Finney was one of the greatest evangelists in the nineteenth century. He left his imprint upon the United States, Britain and other countries. He was in his day, perhaps, the most important theorist of revival. His *Lectures*

---

13. *Coleraine Chronicle,*15 May and 22 May 1869.
14. Ibid., 17 August 1867.
15. Ibid., 1 September 1860.

on Revival, as has been mentioned already, were being sold in Coleraine years before a revival was even being considered. Some of the factors which Finney discusses in these lectures are a good starting place for a tentative appraisal of the reasons which may have doused the fires of revival in Ulster.

The conduct exhibited by clergymen at the General Assembly of the American Presbyterian Church in the revival year of 1831 was a red rag for the evangelist. Finney felt that it was inevitable that God would one day visit the denomination in judgment. He had an 'unutterable feeling of distress' and his soul was 'sick' on hearing of the carping and rebukes offered there to those ministers engaged in revival.[16] A *Pastoral Letter,* focussing on 'evils' attendant on the revival, added insult to the injury done to the Holy Spirit, he believed. Writing four years later, Finney said it was unmistakeable that 'the glory has been departing, and revivals have been becoming less and less frequent' within American Presbyterianism. It is dangerous for a church to quench the 'prophesyings' of men and women moved by God.

The revival ended as brotherly love was quenched.

LACK OF LOVE

Making distinctions between individuals was a further hindrance to revival, he believed. The *New York Tribune* carried a letter in the revival summer of 1858 which referred to the treatment handed out to a coloured man and woman who had turned up for a revival meeting in the North Dutch Church in that city. They were immediately led away to 'a room apart'. 'You know how it is,' said the man who led them away. 'Yes', said the coloured lady, 'I know all about it.' The 'revived' whites, noted the paper, clearly wanted to be saved by themselves. Charles Finney wrote that 'prejudice is one of the most detestable sins that disgraces the Church

---

16.   *Revivals of Religion. Lectures by Charles Grandison Finney,* p. 329.

and grieves the Holy Spirit'. Discrimination blasphemed the Maker of another human being. Those Christians who would be offended by the presence of another human being in a place of prayer and worship could not expect divine blessing. Love was an all-important virtue and any activity – whether it be political, social or religious in nature – which did not express in some way love to God and to other people was, in his view, a waste of time and energy. For a revival to continue, Christians must remain in a humble and broken spirit of love. Individual believers would automatically become lukewarm and backslide the moment they ceased devoting themselves to God and His work. This at least was one of the reasons Charles Finney gave in his lecture on why revivals were hindered or stopped.

It is clear that some of the publications on the revival were motivated by feelings of bitterness and anger. The most well-known in this regard was Isaac Nelson's *The Year of Delusion: A Review of 'The Year of Grace'*, published between 1860 and 1862. Nelson, a founding member of the Evangelical Alliance, found cause to denigrate the revival in its entirety. This had not a little to do with his resentment towards Rev. William Gibson, the author of the propagandistic work *The Year of Grace*. The resentment had not a little to do with unforgiveness, selfish ambition and hurt pride.[17] Nelson could not suppress personal jibes and insinuations. Unfortunately, this was not untypical of Ulster Protestantism.

There were, of course, issues of great theological and pastoral concern which motivated writers. The title of one tract – *Revivalism: Is it of God, or of the Devil?* – pointed to the key question in the debate, which was not conducted behind the closed doors of manses. Ministers publicly attacked ministers, in tracts and in sermons, for holding dif-

---

17. On the conflict between Nelson and Gibson surrounding the appointment to the chair in Greek at Assembly's college see *Coleraine Chronicle*, 22 September 1855.

ferent views on a specific aspect of the revival. Rev. Alexander McCreery of Killyleagh, for example, published *Satan's Devices and Dr Hincks's Fancies: A Review of a Sermon published by the Rev Edward Hincks, DD, entitled 'God's Work and Satan's Counter-Works'*, in which the charges of demonic interference made by an Episcopalian were rebutted in a most offensive manner. McCreery took offence at the suggestion made by the rector of Killyleagh that 'what is done by Episcopalians is "God's work", and what is done by Presbyterians is "Satan's counter-works".' He wondered whether Hincks was not 'lying and sinning against the Holy Ghost' and responded to the clergyman's attacks on the physical manifestations with the prayer: 'O, Holy Spirit, take what thou pleasest, adopt what seemeth good to thee, if only sinners are aroused and convinced.' Even if McCreery was substantially right in his arguments, he was wrong to launch such an attack on another created being loved of God. A bitter, prejudiced spirit, closed to the arguments of others, grieved many an observer. Denominational rivalry and bitterness seemed to quench the spirit of revival.

LACK OF UNITY

On the one hand, advocates boasted of the revival in a rather self-exalting manner. As has been pointed out, some ministers lamented the instrumentalisation of the revival for denominational reasons or in order to highlight a particular doctrine. This inevitably led to unresolved conflicts and rivalries which must have had an impact on worship and prayer meetings. There is even biblical precedent for suggesting that some of the physical weakness and illness and even death, which affected some congregations at the time, may have been psychosomatic expressions of underlying disunity. Writing in the *Adelaide Observer* on 26 July 1861, Rev. William Richey deplored the fact that the spiritual state of things in Coleraine had deteriorated so much since 1859. Ministers, he said, no longer displayed 'the same brotherly attachment to each other, nor did the same abstemiousness on the part of the people now obtain'.[18] People had rekindled old hostilities and returned to old habits of thought and behaviour.

LACK OF WISDOM

Charles Finney also makes mention of the importance of prudence and common sense in maintaining the revival momentum. It did not help a revival, he said, when people neglected to eat and sleep at proper hours. Rev. William Richey of First Coleraine, though a signatory to the inscription in the Memorial Bible, was unable to take part in meetings after the end of June. On 11 July it was reported to the union prayer meeting in Derry that Rev. Richey had died, 'causing great sorrow among the friends of the Revival'.[19] The following day Rev. Richard Smyth received a telegram from Coleraine saying that the news of Richey's death had been a little premature. The presiding minister at the Derry midday prayer meeting, Rev. Robert Ross, gave thanks to God that He had, after all, preserved 'His servant's life'. William Richey spent most of the summer in Harrogate, recuperating from the serious illness which some attributed to his overexertions during the initial weeks of revival. In an obituary, it was pointed out that Richey had frequently worked 'all hours of the night and day, comforting the stricken of heart, or helping the earnest seekers after peace'. He had sacrificed himself by incessant work during the year of grace and so ruined his health. Eventually, he felt the need to resign from his pastorate in July 1860[20] and sailed to the warmer climes of Australia, where he died and now lies buried.

One of Richey's elders, Alexander Cuthbert, is also said to have gone to an early grave by an imprudent lifestyle during

---

18. *Coleraine Chronicle*, 1 February 1862.
19. Ibid., 2 July, 9 July and 16 July 1859; *Londonderry Guardian*, 12 July 1859.
20. Ibid., 7 July 1860.

the revival. There are limits to what an individual man or woman can and should do. This is why Methodism expected every member of a congregation to be active in some area of the church's evangelistic outreach. Some ministers and laymen clearly failed to delegate responsibility in 1859 and suffered the consequences in body and soul. Apart from eating regularly and getting a good night's rest, as one letter writer in the *Chronicle* said, many believers needed to spend far more time with their own wives and children rather than going to every prayer meeting in the Town Hall. This, too, seems to have been a piece of good advice. Duties to one's family were at times neglected as people sought to serve God. Strong churches are, however, only built upon strong families rooted in prayer and God's Word.

LACK OF ZEAL

One tract discussed the issue of grieving the Holy Spirit as a cause of the decline of the revival. Rev. F.J. Porter of Donagheady published *The Spirit Resisted: A Revival Address* in 1860. It was an attempt to show how the Spirit was being resisted in the 'Pentecostal days' of revival in Ulster. Firstly, Rev. Porter noted that indifference and sloth were coming upon congregations. 'Monster meetings' were no longer being organised in town and country. Awe and fear were no longer being inspired by the church. Many professors of religion were filled only with 'disgust and fear' on witnessing the awakening for they believed 'a Church, as closely as possible, should resemble a cemetery', a place 'where there is deep silence', not life, activity, colour, warmth. Formality , not reality, was all they wanted. Too many people wanted to 'ornament a pew' or 'enjoy an intellectual feast'. They wanted 'the pleasing preacher' to 'prophesy smooth things' which would not challenge them radically to change their lifestyles. Many ministers had given in to this pressure. 'Wearied with labour which revivals imposed, are we preferring the ease and quietness of colder times, and getting fast, even the best of us, into the old routine of family worship and Sabbath sermonising?' He warned that 'unless we instantly bestir ourselves, the unclean spirit will return, and the last state of the Church and country be worse than the first'. The Spirit, he said, would go to other lands if He found no open channels in Ulster. At the same time God would bring judgment upon ministers unwilling to preach the whole counsel of God for the sake of an easy life.

LACK OF GENEROSITY

Secondly, Porter claimed the Spirit was being resisted by spiritual pride in some groups. Some people remained stationary as others grew in number and grace. Some remained selfish as others became loving and shared their possessions. Some remained cold as others burned with zeal. The key issue was the willingness to sacrifice. James McQuilkin and five others gave up their jobs and became full-time 'missionaries', receiving an annual income of £10 from a society in Connor set up specially to support those who were seen to be gifted evangelists. It may well be that McQuilkin was forced to leave Ulster at the end of 1859 because people had withdrawn that support. The revival called for a new commitment of resources to the task in hand. Printing placards, purchasing tracts, entertaining visitors and converts in one's home, paying assistants, supplying the temporal wants of working-class converts (who, as has already been noted, were often so enfeebled by the experience of conversion that they were unable to work), supplying the needs of converts who had no work – all this required finance and sacrificial giving, which, it seems, was not forthcoming. That niggardly spirit at a time of prosperity grieved Porter. The refusal to bring money into the house of God to meet human needs quenched the life-flow of the revival. On this point Finney would have agreed with his Presbyterian colleague. In a lecture in 1835 Finney warned that revivals would challenge habits of giving. Professor Holmes noted that no missionary was appointed in the six years following the revival.[21] Purses were not opened. For example, £200 less was contributed to the Roman Catholic Mission in 1861 than in 1858. Certainly, the annual stipends to the three Presbyterian clergymen in Coleraine were increased by their respective congregations in May 1860, partly because the number of communicants had greatly increased in all three churches. The annual financial statements for the congregations showed that they were all in a 'highly prosperous state'.

The inhabitants of Coleraine had received quite a lot of instruction on the matter of financial giving over the previous decade. Rev. G.L. Herman of Dublin had lectured in Coleraine Town Hall on 'Gold and the Gospel' on 18 April 1855. This was the title of a recently published book, which sought to impress on believers the duty and measure of Christian liberality. Its author, the Methodist Rev. R.G. Cather, had come to work in Coleraine in 1856. Hundreds of copies of the work had been sold in Coleraine before 1859. Presbyterians, too, had been alerted to the need to finance evangelism and mission. In May 1856 Rev. William Richey gave a lecture before the Coleraine Branch of the Evangelical Alliance on 'Reasons for Refusing to Rob God!' in which he asked Christians why they kept the Sabbath if they robbed God by holding back their 'full tithes'.[22]

Thirdly, Rev. Porter referred to one of Isaac Nelson's many criticisms of the revival, namely the role played by the laity. Lay preaching was, he said, seen in Presbyterian circles as a novelty, a human device 'disliked, despised and set aside' by congregations. People took offence at the 'humble life and questionable origin' of some of the preachers,

---

21. R.F.G. Holmes, 'The 1859 Revival Reconsidered', in: John T. Carson, *God's River in Spate* (Presbyterian Historical Society 1994), xiii.
22. *Coleraine Chronicle*, 3 May 1856.

their lack of experience, their 'incorrect' style and 'plain' manner. Porter recognised at once the unscriptural nature of much of these criticisms and wondered how Sunday schools would survive were they to be taken seriously. 'To despise lay agency', he said, 'is to do despite unto the Spirit of Grace.' It was a fact, he said, that where the lay preachers and converts were excluded, the revival had produced 'indifferent results' and the work was 'inefficiently done'. Where they had been totally absent, there had been 'symptoms of decline'. It was not for Christians to enquire why God had given so prominent a place to lay ministry in the revival, but to simply use the means God had provided. 'Is He rebuking idle and foolish shepherds, by setting before them, in the persons of their flocks, examples of activity and earnestness? Or is He showing the Laity that they are part and parcel of that Church, which was commissioned by His Son to "go into all the world and preach the Gospel to every creature"?' Rev. Porter asked why Methodism was progressing. It was because, he quotes a man who knew the secret of its power, 'they are all at it and always at it'. The branches of trees that bore no fruit were useless, he said, and were only good for making a fire.

LACK OF DISCERNMENT

Finally, attention is drawn by Rev. Porter to the outright opposition to the revival. To affirm, as some had done, that the work was largely the work of men or devils was tantamount to resisting the Spirit. Just because the way people were being converted and refreshed was at times 'unusual and striking' should not mislead people, he maintained, into misrepresenting the revival, as some periodicals and pamphlets had done. 'How comes it that every little extravagance which the inexperienced professor of religion runs into is adverted to, and the name of any convert, who has lost his first love, is paraded, and the *io triumphe* raised, when meetings for prayer are less numerously attended or more rarely held?' If one took away from the revival what everyone disliked there would be nothing left, he said. There were many deceivers in the church and many Achans in the camp who, he felt, were resisting the Holy Spirit for extremely superficial and self-deceiving reasons. He warned Presbyterians not to commit the sin of the antediluvians by striving with their maker. Fearful punishment awaited anyone who did despite to the Spirit of Grace – fearful judgment and fiery indignation. Reference is also made to Saul's fate, who was troubled by an evil spirit from the Lord when the Spirit of the Lord departed from him. 'When the Spirit and the Bride are saying "Come" as they have not spoken since the times of the Apostles – when invitations so freely given are so freely accepted – and "tongues of fire" are visible: Oh! beware, then, of committing the sin referred to, or any other, leading directly or indirectly to it.' He called on believers to pray daily – 'Create in me a clean heart, O God; and renew a right spirit within me. Cast me not away from Thy presence; and take not Thy Holy Spirit from me.'

In 1860 Rev. Robert Knox told the General Assembly that he was anxious that the Presbyterian Church did not fall into the habit of looking back to 1859 as an extraordinary year never to be repeated. Knox hoped annual celebrations would inspire and challenge each future generation to seek God's face for a time of refreshing and renewal.[23] Each generation of Christians has faced this challenge. Who would deny that there is need today for a revived church?

Hundreds of laymen and clergymen came from Britain, and further afield, to observe the astonishing events in Coleraine in the second half of 1859. One was the Rev. John Weir, D. D., minister of the Presbyterian Church in Islington, who in his 1860 work on *The Ulster Awakening* referred to Coleraine as 'this thrice-favoured town, where ministers, press, and

---

23. *Coleraine Chronicle*, 7 July 1860.

people, have all been baptised with the Holy Ghost'. On 6 October 1859 a copy of the Holy Scriptures, purchased by the voluntary contributions of Christians of all evangelical denominations, was committed to the custody and safe keeping of the chairman of the Town Commissioners of Coleraine. That Bible was an expression of gratitude to God 'for the times of refreshing with which he has been pleased to visit Coleraine'. It remains a silent witness to our own generation of 'how good and how pleasant it is for brethren to dwell together in Unity'. Revival services and anniversary meetings were organised in Coleraine from 1860 till the end of the century. On the occasion of Sir George White's visit to Coleraine in June 1900 Henry A. Gribbon, vice-chairman of the Urban Council, noted that Coleraine was 'the only town in Ireland that has continued down to the present year to commemorate the religious revival of 1859'. This reflected perhaps not so much the loyalty to God and the Saviour, as Gribbon suggested, as loyalty to tradition and convention. Unfortunately, there is nothing quite like religious traditions when it comes to killing a living faith.

Conclusion

All churches are always in need of change and reformation, whether they recognise this or not. The insight was gained at the time of the great revival in the fifteenth and sixteenth centuries which followed upon the rediscovery of fundamental biblical truths. In the postmodern, post-Christian twenty-first century that need has never been greater. According to Jim Packer, it was the conviction of Dr Martyn Lloyd-Jones that 'without revival in the Church, there is really no hope for the Western world at all'.[1] In 1859 most people would probably have accepted the existence of God; today, intelligent individuals publicly proclaim all belief in God to be a delusion and they find a large readership for their books. Radical Islam and powerful secularising forces operating within the European Union are seeking to quench the Christian testimony to truth.

But there are forces within the church, too, which are undermining that witness. Christian unity remains a central task facing all denominations. Unfortunately, denominationalism is still alive and well. Ministers' councils in the various towns and cities could and should be embodiments of an evangelical alliance of all Christians. With so many people either drifting away from mainstream denominations or firmly positioned outside the Christian fold, the need for combined prayer and effort has

---

1. Martin Lloyd-Jones, *Revival. Can We Make It Happen?* London 1992, p. 6.

surely not decreased. The revival on the Causeway Coast took place within a context of growing evangelical unity which was, in fact, further promoted by the revival. In the 1850s younger people formed themselves into non-denominational YMCAs. The Evangelical Alliance brought ministers and Christian men and women together in fellowship. Talks in the Town Hall and the churches given by representatives of the various missionary societies facilitated regular times of fellowship outside 'church hours'. In 1859 God took pleasure in blessing Calvinists and Arminians alike. Indeed, there are a good number of cases, recorded in the literature produced at the time, of God taking pleasure in meeting Catholics in their homes and chapels. In times of revival He does not seem to be a respecter of denominational barriers.

The revival of 1859 suggests that, in the divine providence, a spiritual revitalisation of communities took place as a result of prayer and Spirit-filled and Spirit-fuelled endeavour. The revival was prayed down, not worked up, as critics said. People did not, however, simply 'say their prayers'. Times of prayer were seen as times of meeting and hearing from the almighty God who has ever been calling out to humanity: 'Adam! Adam! Where are you?' In the 1859 prayer meetings the heart of God was discovered for sinful mankind. God's mind was revealed – and it was good news! Very good news for modern man! Awakened to the reality of God's presence men and women communicated that news, first, to their families and neighbours and took them along to the meetings being organised. Prayer helped bring about a climate of quiet expectancy and hopeful yearning.

Itinerant preachers were the catalyst of revival in Ulster, but they only appeared after the news of revival in the United States had caught public attention. When the message was preached, the awe-inspiring sense of what it means to fall into the hands of an angry God was, for some hearers, physically debilitating. The Coleraine Town Hall became, for a while, a spiritual hospital where grace was prayerfully ministered to the anguished. Those who were surprised by the wailing and crying and the 'prostrations' responded in different ways. The revival of 1859 cemented Christian unity but it also created divisions between those who stood and mocked and those who simply asked: What can this mean? As well as people being amazed by the awakening of interest in Christ, there were others who became (even more) cynical and dismissive. The revival broadened some people's horizons and expectations; it hardened others' hearts and confirmed their prejudices. The revival highlighted opposition to, among other things, lay preaching and extemporary prayer, particularly by uneducated individuals (nearly all men) who itinerated around Ulster. At times the opposition became almost rabid. Eternity will reveal whether the attribution of the revival's effects to demons, mass hysteria or other psychological disorders was akin to the sin of grieving, or blaspheming, the Holy Spirit.

But having been prayed down, the work of revival began. Outreach and evangelism was carefully organised and supervised by the ordained clergy. If not worked *up*, the awakening was certainly worked *out* and incarnated in small vibrant fellowship groups where mutual encouragement, centred on the Bible and prayer, could be confidentially practised. Northern Ireland today may be known as the religious part of the United Kingdom, but can it be said confidently that the majority of the population is still well versed in Scripture? How much teaching in churches is laced with entertaining stories and jokes, for fear of losing parishioners' attention? How much of the literature sold in Christian bookshops today is of a self-help variety aiming to improve people's feel-good factor? The soundbite, a thrill-a-minute, culture of today is helping to erode the biblical bedrock upon which the Christian communities in the north of Ireland have been established.

At the centre of the 1859 revival, and of all true revivals, was not the welfare of man, but the glory and honour of

God. This naturally led to a great desire to hear and read His Word. In the light of that Word denominational rivalries must wither as the true unity in the Spirit of all the children of God is manifested, as it seems to have been in 1859. In many ways the revival was a messy affair, as all times of birth tend to be. The so-called 'physical manifestations', about which so much was written at the time and ever since, were, if not central to the movement, a strange accompaniment of it, at least in the initial stages. As has been said, it was not the physical reactions that created a reformed character. Nor could such phenomena feed the new spiritual life of individuals. Again, only the milk and the meat of the Word of God, along with the discipline and fellowship of a community of believers, can foster such growth. In 1859 those who came under the influence of the revival were formed into instruction classes. No doubt there were some, then as today, who were simply entertaining themselves at the meetings; such is inevitable. How many people are filling pews today imagining that all is well with their souls? Only a sovereign move of God, patiently and prayerfully received, can awaken such pew-fillers from their slumbers.

History, as well as the Bible, plainly shows that God moves in mysterious ways. In times of revival He works in unusual ways indeed. God seems to like to surprise us with His creativity. In 1859 His choice instruments were unknown, insignificant men and women. Next time it could be you whom God chooses! The encouraging point is that one does not need to be a well-educated, rhetorically gifted individual to be used by God. A life of prayer and a willingness to serve and be used are the key prerequisites.

Moreover, these evangelists spoke a language all people could understand. This recalls Martin Luther's approach to Bible translation. Luther went out to the marketplaces and recorded the words he heard being used there (*dem Volk aufs Maul schauen*). This approach or principle of action result-ed in a translation not free from vulgarisms. All preachers must ensure that the message is understood – that people are getting it. Jesus' messages were not *linguistically* difficult to understand. Speaking over people's heads is probably a waste of breath. All preaching should be geared to reviving individuals and communities (in the sense the word is used above) and this is best done in the language and idiom common to one's hearers.

Who, 150 years after the 1859 revival, would deny that the Christian churches are in need of renewal? Are complacency, slackness and formality no longer features of church life in the year 2009? Is there not rampant materialism and hedonism within church circles? Do not homes and holidays come before friends and fellowship? Is there any individual Christian who thinks he or she is not in need of being spiritually revived and refreshed? Church statistics at the beginning of the twenty-first century tell a bleak story, for many denominations at least. The challenge of being freshly awakened to eternal responsibilities and realities remains. The so-called Coleraine Declaration of 1990 reminded Presbyterians that a new baptism of fire and power in the Holy Spirit was the key to guaranteeing healthy, vibrant congregations in the future. This surely should be, and perhaps is, the heart-cry of every Christian congregation, whatever the denominational attachment. What is required is a divine visitation, an outpouring of the Holy Spirit on the whole community which will lead, inevitably, to a deepened sense of the power and authority of God as well as a deepened sense of our own unworthiness to approach such a God. This is the real core of any revival. The study of the past can help and encourage us to pray and work accordingly.

Appendix: Pilgrims in Coleraine in 1859

From the end of June to the beginning of September the names of religious pilgrims – ministers and some laymen – were recorded on the pages of the *Coleraine Chronicle*. Twenty-two came from Glasgow, fifteen from Edinburgh. Even at the beginning of September, when the enthusiasm for revivalism was waning, the paper claimed that 'the influx of visitors to this town and district is not diminished' (3 September). The following people took part in a range of activities in Coleraine in the summer and autumn of 1859, often giving addresses and getting involved in the united prayer meetings. Only in a few cases were Christian names provided. What is important is that these gentlemen took the impressions and, in some cases, the flame of revival back to their own towns and congregations.

Alexander, W.B. (Edinburgh)
Anderson (Morpeth)
Anderson (Norham)
Arbuckle (Kirkoswald)
Arnot (Methil)
Arthur, William (London)
Baillie, John (London)
Bain, George (Garioch, Aberdeenshire)
Bain (Logieport, Forfarshire)
Bain (Coupar Angus)

Banks (Kilmarnock)
Barrett (Stirling)
Barron, A. (Edinburgh)
Barrow (Edinburgh)
Beattie (Belfast)
Beaumont, A. (Huddersfield)
Begg, Dr (Edinburgh)
Best (Stirling)
Bickersteth, Edward H. (Hamstead)
Blelloch (Crewe)

Blythe, Adam (Girvan)

Boarland (Glasgow)

Bonar, A.A. (Glasgow)

Bonar (Greenock)

Borwick (Dundee)

Bowden (Leeds)

Brannigan (Ballinglen)

Brown, Dr (Dalkeith)

Bryce, Dr (Belfast)

Burnett (Glasgow)

Burns (Dundee)

Burnside (Castleblaney)

Burton (Bective)

Cairns (Stewarttown)

Cameron, Andrew (Edinburgh)

Campbell (Southend)

Caven (Southampton)

Chancellor (Strabane)

Chute (Market Drayton)

Clarke (Bath)

Cooke (Perthshire)

Cooper (Fala)

Coventry (Malta)

Craig (Hawick)

Creich, Gustavus Aird (Sutherlandshire)

Crombie (Melrose)

Crooke (Ballymoney)

Crookshank (Donegal)

Crookshank (Glasgow)

Cullen (Leith)

Cuppage (Kilmegin)

Curry (Wick)

Davidson (Saltcoats)

Day (Dublin)

Demster (Renton)

Donald (Limavady)

Douglas (Alexandria)

Douglas (Inverkip, Greenock)

Drummond, Peter (Stirling)

Elder (Rothesay)

Elliot, Edward (Worthing)

Ewing (Dundee)

Farrington (Cork)

Feddes (Killarn)

Fellowes (Liverpool)

Ffolliot (Portrush)

Fleming (Kentish Town)

Forbes (Glasgow)

Fraser (Gourock)

Fraser (Kirkhill, Inverness)

Fraser (Rosskeen)

Fyfe (Chinsurah)

Galloway (London)

Gault (Glasgow)

Gillies (Edinburgh)

Graham (Liverpool)

Grant (Dunfermline)

Greet, T. (Annahilt)

Guinness, H.G.

Guinness, Wynham

Gullane (Town Missionary, Rothesay)

Gunn (Madderty)

Hamilton (Cockpen)

Hanna, Dr (Edinburgh)

Hannah, Dr (President of
   Didsbury College, Manchester)

Hannay (Dundee)

Hargreaves (Wolverhampton)

Hart (Ballylaggan)

Henderson (Glasgow)

Henderson, Dr (Glasgow)

Hill (Dundee)

Hope (Wamphrey, Dumfriesshire)

Hunter (Dublin)

Hunter (Tillicoultry)

Inglis (Manchester)

Ireland (Sliene)

Irvine (Bandon)

Irvine (Fivemiletown)

Jeffery (Torrington)

Johnstone (Glasgow)

Johnstone (Govan)

Jones, John (Milnesbridge)

Kay (Edinburgh)

King, W. (Buxton)

King (Woodville)

Laughton (Greenock)

Lees (Berwick-upon-Tweed)

Longhead, William (Glasgow)

Luke (Uphall)

MacDougall (Glasgow)

Mackay (Fordyce)

Mackay (Rhynie)

Mackintosh, Dr (Dunoon)

Magennis (USA)

Martin (Camus)

Massie (London)

Mayne, James

McAlister (Kennoway)

McArthur

McCaw (Manchester)

McCleish (Methven)

McClure (Derry)

McColl (Glasgow)

McConachie (Mosside)

McCrea (Arran)

McDonald (New Leith)

McDougal (Florence)

McFarlan (Greenock)

McGillivray (Glencoe)

McGregor (Kilwinning)

McGregor (Kinkurd, Peebleshire)

McGregor (Glasgow)

McKay (Glasgow)

McKee (Gogo)

McKeown (Roseneath)

McLachlan (Port Glasgow)

McLean (Falkirk)

McLennon (Crosshill)

McPherson (Dores)

McTaggart (Glasgow)

Middleditch (London)

Miller (Edinburgh)

Miller (Heynstown)

Milne (Perth)

Mitchell (Dunfermline)

Mitchell (Glasgow)

Moody-Stewart, A. (Edinburgh)

Munnis (Lawrencekirk)

Murray (Auchencairn)

Murray Mitchell (Bombay)

Noel, Baptist (London)

North, Brownlow

Orr, Holmes

Orr (Ballycastle)

Orr (Fenwick, Ayrshire)

Oulton, W. (Ballyrashane)

Palmer, Dr (New York)

Palmer, Mrs (New York)

Parrot, R. (Fitzroy Chapel, London)

Paxton (Musselburgh)

Pillans, J. (Perth)

Playfair, Balie (Glasgow)

Pratt (Bristol)

Prust (Northampton)

Reid (Banchory, Aberdeenshire)

Rentoul (Ballymoney)

Ritchie, W. (Dunse)

Robertson (Ayr)

Robertson (Hamilton)

Robertson (Lymington)

Robertson (Newington, Edinburgh)

Robertson (Woodside, Dunkeld)

Robinson (Leamington)

Rogers, G. Albert (Holloway)

Ross (London)

Ross (Aberdeen)

Russell (Hawick)

Rutherford (Newlands)

Sandeman, F. (Edinburgh)

Scott, R. (Dumbarton)

Sewell, R. (Londonderry)

Sherrard (Kilcullen)

Shewan (North Berwick)

Smith, Dr (Biggar)

Smith (Edinburgh)

Smith (Shotts)

Smith, Prof. Sydney (Trinity College Dublin)

Smyth (Derry)

Smyth, A.C. (Innellan)

Somerville (Glasgow)

Sowerby (Wick)

Stewart (Ardrossan)

Stewart (Leghorn)

Sutherland (Inverness)

Taylor (Glasgow)

Taylor, Dr Lachlin (Toronto)

Thomson, Dr A. (Edinburgh)

Thomson, Charles (Wick)

Thomson (Pitcairn Green, Perth)

Thornhill (Castle Billingham)

Trench, F.

Tullo (Paisley)

Turnbull (Eyemouth)

Turnbull (Ringsend)

Venn (Hereford)

Walker (Rochester)

Wallace (Paisley)

Wallace (Tottenham)

Wallis (Kenilworth)

Warner (Oakengate)

Weir, Dr (London)

Whigham (Ballinnsloe)

White (Heddington)

Williams, John (Glasgow)

Williamson (Ascog, near Rothesay)

Wilson (Bo'ness)

Wilson (Campsie)

Wilson (Cookstown)

Wilson (Dundee)

Wilson, J.H. (Edinburgh)

Wilson (Irvine)

Wood, Dr J. Julius (Dumfries)

Wood (Campsie)

Young (Castlewellan)

Yule (Glasgow)

Select Bibliography

Acheson, Alan R., *The Evangelicals in the Church of Ireland, 1784–1859*. Ph.D. thesis, Queen's University Belfast, 1967.

Armour, W.S., *Armour of Ballymoney*. London: Duckworth 1934.

Arthur, William, *The Revival in Ballymena and Coleraine*. London: Hamilton, Adams & Co. 1859.

Baillie, W.D., *The Six Mile Water Revival of 1625*. Belfast: Presbyterian Historical Society 1976.

Boyd, Andrew, *Holy War in Belfast*. Tralee: Anvil Books 1969.

Boyd, Hugh Alexander, *The Succession of Clergy in the Parish Church of St. Patrick Coleraine in the Diocese of Connor from the Londoners' Plantation 1609 to the Disestablishment of the Church of Ireland 1871: A Biographical Study*. Master's thesis, New University of Ulster, 1983.

Brief Memorials of the late Rev. Thomas Toye, Belfast, by His Widow. Belfast: S.E. McCormick 1873.

Brooke, Peter, *Ulster Presbyterianism. The Historical Perspective 1610–1970*. New York: Gill & Macmillan 1987.

Brown, John, *Orangeism Around Ballymena. Articles on Warrants 115 to 515 in Ballymena District Orange Lodge No. 8*. Ballymena: Mid-Antrim Historical Group 1990.

Brown, William, *An Army with Banners. The Real Face of Orangeism*, Belfast: Beyond the Pale Publications 2003.

Campbell, Flann, *The Dissenting Voice. Protestant Democracy in Ulster from Plantation to Partition*. Belfast: Blackstaff 1991.

Carson, James C.L., *Three Letters on the Revival in Ireland*. Coleraine: J. McCombie 1859.

Carson, John T., *God's River in Spate. The Story of the Religious Awakening of Ulster in 1859.* Belfast: Publications Board of the Presbyterian Church in Ireland 1958.

Clayton, Helen, *To School without Shoes. A Brief History of the Sunday School Society for Ireland 1809–1979.* n.p., n.d. [1979].

Coad, F. Roy, *A History of the Brethren Movement.* Exeter: Paternoster Press 1968.

Cormack, Michael J., *The Stirling Tract Enterprise and the Drummonds.* Stirling: University of Stirling Bibliographical Society 1984.

Crookshank, C.H., *History of Methodism in Ireland. Volume iii: Modern Development.* London T. Woolmer 1888.

Dewar, M.W., Brown, J., and Long, S.E., *Orangeism: A New Historical Appreciation.* Belfast: Grand Orange Lodge of Ireland 1967.

Edwards, Jonathan, *On Revival.* Edinburgh, Banner of Truth n.d.

Edwards, Ruth Dudley, *The Faithful Tribe. An Intimate Portrait of the Loyal Institutions.* London: HarperCollins 1999.

Finney, Charles Grandison, *Revivals of Religion. Lectures by Charles Grandison Finney with the Author's final Additions and Corrections. Newly revised and edited with Introduction and original notes by William Henry Harding.* London: Morgan and Scott 1913.

Gibbon, Peter, 'The origins of the Orange Order and the United Irishmen. A study in the sociology of revolution and counter-revolution' in *Economy and Society*, vol. 1, pt 2, 1972.

Gibbon, Peter, *The origins of Ulster Unionism. The formation of Popular Protestant Politics and Ideology in Nineteenth-Century Ireland.* Manchester: Manchester University Press 1975.

Gibson, William, *The Year of Grace: A History of the Ulster Revival of 1859.* [Edinburgh : Andrew Elliott; London: Hamilton, Adams, and Co.; Belfast: C. Aitchison 1860.] Belfast: Ambassador Productions 1989.

The Glasgow Revival Tract Society *Narratives of Revivals of Religion in Scotland, Ireland and Wales.* Glasgow: Collins 1839.

Gray, Tony, *The Orange Order.* London: Bodley Head 1972.

Gwynn, Stephen, *The Ulster Revival: A Strictly Natural and Strictly Spiritual Work of God. Being a reply to certain popular opinions, as to its supernatural and physical character.* Coleraine: S. Eccles 1859.

Haldane, Alexander, *The Lives of Robert Haldane of Airthrey, and his brother, James Alexander Haldane* [London 1853]. Edinburgh: Banner of Truth Trust 1990.

Hamilton, William, *An Inquiry into the Scriptural Character of the Revival of 1859* [Belfast, 1866]. Coleraine: Coleraine Printing Company 1993.

Hempton, David and Hill, Myrtle, *Evangelical Protestantism in Ulster Society 1740–1890.* London and New York: Routledge 1993.

Henry, Jack, A Door That Opened. Rev. John Galway McVicker and the Founding of Ballymena Baptist Church, Ballymena: J. Henry 1989.

Henry, James Miller, *An Assessment of the Social, Religious and Political Aspects of Congregationalism in Ireland in the Nineteenth Century.* Ph.D. thesis, Queen's University Belfast, 1965.

Hill, Myrtle, 'Ulster Awakened: The '59 Revival Reconsidered' in *Journal of Ecclesiastical History* 41 (1990), no. 3 (July).

Holmes, Andrew, 'The experience and understanding of religious revival in Ulster Presbyterianism, c. 1800–1930,' *Irish Historical Studies*, vol. xxxiv, No. 136, November 2005.

Holmes, Finlay, *Our Irish Presbyterian Heritage.* Belfast: Publications Committee of the Presbyterian Church in Ireland 1992.

Holmes, Finlay, *Presbyterians and Orangeism 1795–1995.* Belfast: Presbyterian Historical Society of Ireland 1996.

Holmes, Janice, 'The "World Turned Upside Down": Women in the Ulster Revival of 1859,' in Janice Holmes and Diane Urquhart (eds.), *Coming into the Light: The Work, Politics and Religion of Women in Ulster 1840–1940.* Belfast: Queen's University, Institute of Irish Studies 1994.

Holmes, R.F.G., 'The 1859 Revival Reconsidered,' introduction to John T. Carson, *God's River in Spate.* Belfast: Presbyterian Historical Society 1994.

Hoppen, K.T., *Elections, Politics and Society in Ireland 1832–1885.* Oxford: Clarendon 1984.

Jeffrey, Kenneth S., *When the Lord Walked the Land. The 1858–62 Revival in the North-East of Scotland*, Carlisle: Paternoster Press 2002.

Kennaway, Brian, *The Orange Order. A Tradition Betrayed.* London: Methuen 2006.

Kingdon, D. P., *Baptist Evangelism in 19th Century Ireland.* Belfast: Baptist Union of Ireland 1965.

Larkin, Emmet, 'The Devotional Revolution in Ireland, 1850–75,' *The American Historical Review*, Vol. 77, Nr. 3, June 1972.

Lloyd-Jones, Martyn, *Revival. Can We Make It Happen?* London: Marshall Pickering 1992.

Lockington, John W., 'Dr. John Edgar and the Temperance Movement of the Nineteenth Century,' *Bulletin of the Presbyterian Historical Society*, no. 12 (March 1983).

Malcolm, Elizabeth, *'Ireland Sober, Ireland Free'. Drink and Temperance in Nineteenth-Century Ireland.* Dublin: Gill & Macmillan 1986.

Marrs, Clifford J. M., *The 1859 Religious Revival in Scotland: A Review & Critique of the Movement with Particular Reference to the City of Glasgow.* Ph.D. Dissertation, University of Glasgow 1995.

Massie, James William, *Revivals in Ireland. Facts, Documents, and Correspondence.* London: John Snow 1859.

McClelland, Aiken, 'The Later Orange Order,' in T. Desmond Williams (ed), *Secret Societies in Ireland.* Dublin and New York: Gill & Macmillan 1973.

McClelland, Aiken, 'Occupational Composition of Two Orange Lodges, 1853,' *Ulster Folklife* 14 (1968).

McLaughlin, William, *Revivals, Awakenings and Reform: an essay on religion and social change in America, 1607–1977.* Chicago and London: University of Chicago Press 1978.

Moody-Stuart, K., *Brownlow North. His life and work.* London: Banner of Truth Trust 1961.

Müller, George, *Autobiography of George Müller.* London and Bristol: J. Nisbet 1905.

Mullin, Julia E., *The Presbytery of Coleraine.* Belfast: J.E. Mullin 1979.

Mullin, T. H., *Coleraine in Modern Times.* Belfast: Century Services 1979.

Norman, E.R., *The Catholic Church and Ireland in the Age of Rebellion 1859–1873.* London: Longmans 1965.

North, Brownlow, *The Rich Man and Lazarus.* London: The Banner of Truth Trust 1960.

Orr, J. Edwin, *The Second Evangelical Awakening in Britain.* London and Edinburgh: Marshall, Morgan & Scott 1953.

Paisley, Ian R. K., *The 'Fifty Nine' Revival.* Belfast: Free Presbyterian Church of Ulster 1981.

Porter, Norman, 'Irish Baptists and Orangeism,' *Irish Baptist Historical Journal* 18 (1985–6).

Porter, W. Warren, 'Orangeism – a force for Protestant unity,' in Billy Kennedy (ed), *Steadfast for Faith and Freedom. 200 Years of Orangeism.* Belfast: Grand Orange Lodge of Ireland, n.p., n.d.

Restoration in the Church. Reports of Revivals 1625–1839. Belfast: Ambassador 1980.

Richey, William, *Connor and Coleraine; or, scenes and sketches of the last Ulster Awakening, volume i.* Belfast: C. Aitchison 1870,

Roberts, David A., 'The Orange Order in Ireland: a religious institution?' *British Journal of Sociology* 22 (1971).

Scott, Alfred Russell, *The Ulster Revival of 1859. Enthusiasm emanating from mid-Antrim.* Ballymena: Mid-Antrim Historical Group 1994.

Scott, Benjamin, *The Revival in Ulster: Its Moral and Social Results.* London: Longman, Green, Longman & Roberts 1859.

Senior, Hereward, *Orangeism in Ireland and Britain 1795–1836.* London: Routledge and Kegan Paul 1966.

Sibbett, R.M., *The Revival in Ulster or the Life Story of a Worker.* Belfast: J.W. Boyd 1909.

Sillito, William W., *An Address on the Religious Revival, and Matters Connected Therewith, to the Parishioners of Killowen, especially those who worship in the Parish Church.* Coleraine: J. McCombie 1859.

Simpson, Jonathan, *Annals of My Life, Labours and Travels.* Belfast: William Mullan & Son 1895.

Stewart, Alexander and Rivington, George, *Memoir of the Life and Labours of the Rev. Adam Averell.* Dublin 1848.

Storey, Earl, *Traditional Roots. Towards an appropriate relationship between the Church of Ireland and the Orange Order.* Blackrock: Columba Press 2002.

The Principles of Christians called 'Open Brethren'. London and New York: Pickering & Inglis 1913.

The Revival Movement in Ireland. An Impartial History of the Revival Movement from its Commencement to the Present Time. Belfast: George Phillips and C. Aitchison 1859.

Thompson, Joshua, 'Irish Baptists and the 1859 Revival,' *Irish Baptist Historical Society Journal*, vol. 17 (1984–5).

Walker, Brian M. (ed.), *Parliamentary Election Results in Ireland 1801–1922.* Dublin: Royal Irish Academy 1978.

Westerkamp, Marilyn J., *Triumph of the Laity: Scots-Irish piety and the Great Awakening, 1625–1760.* New York and Oxford: Oxford University Press 1988.

Whelan, Kevin, 'The Origins of the Orange Order,' *Bullan 2*, pt 2, 1996.

Other titles from
Christian Focus Publications ...

Tom Lennie

"Just as Pentecost was desperately needed at the beginning of the Christian era, so another season of God-sent revival is the urgent need of this hour. A careful reading of "Glory in the Glen" will help in many ways."

Richard Owen Roberts
International Awakening Ministries

Glory in the Glen

A History of Evangelical Revivals in Scotland

1880–1940

Glory in the Glen

A History of Evangelical Revivals in Scotland
1880-1940

TOM LENNIE

"an intriguing, judiciously balanced, and often inspiring account of movements of the Holy Spirit in Scotland in a period that we do not normally think of as characterized by revivals (except for the 1949-52 Lewis Revival, which occurred later)… It has encouraged me to pray with new expectancy for God to revive His work among us."

Douglas F. Kelly,
Reformed Theological Seminary, Charlotte, North Carolina

"In this fair-minded and thorough book, Tom Lennie has shown that there were evangelical awakenings in many parts of the land down to the inter-war years."

Richard Owen Roberts,
International Awakening Ministries

"Spontaneous local revivals of religion in Scotland did not virtually disappear, Tom Lennie has shown that there were evangelical awakenings in many parts of the land down to the inter-war years."

David Bebbington,
University of Stirling

"… it is not new techniques or new schemes we need… It is what many nineteenth- and early twentieth-century Scottish Christians, whose experience of true revival is set forth in this well-documented book, knew: the awesome God of holiness himself drawing near to his people and setting mind and heart ablaze with glorious light. Read—and pray!"

Michael A. G. Haykin,
The Southern Baptist Theological Seminary, Louisville, Kentucky

ISBN 978-1-84550-377-2

CHILDREN
IN REVIVAL

300 YEARS OF GOD'S WORK IN SCOTLAND
HARRY SPRANGE

Children in Revival

300 years of God's work in Scotland

HARRY SPRANGE

Children in Revival tells the stories of children, some as young as four years old, who have been involved in revivals in Scotland over three centuries. Whole communities and indeed nations have been influenced by the power of God at special outpourings of his Spirit.

ISBN 978-1-85792-789-4

Colin & Mary Peckham

Sounds from Heaven

The Revival on the Isle of Lewis, 1949-1952

SY360

Sounds from Heaven

The Revival on the Isle of Lewis, 1949-1952

Colin Peckham

This is the best and most definitive study of the movement of the Spirit of God in the Hebrides during the middle of the twentieth century. There are people who sit and hear us year after year. They are loyal, orthodox, moral people but they lack vitality, discipleship, courage in witness-bearing, prayerfulness – they are rarely present in Prayer Meetings. One longs for a spark, a new insight that takes them over the edge into assurance and holy zeal. Reading the testimonies in the closing chapters of the book describing the radical transformation of the lives of ordinary church goers, gives hope for new life in those who faithfully hear us, but do little more. In matters of the Holy Spirit, never assume anything.

Geoffrey Thomas,
Alfred Place Baptist Church, Aberystwyth

…provides ringing affirmation that God is still on His throne and delights to make bare His mighty arm in revival when His people get serious with Him.

Richard Owen Roberts
International Awakening Ministries

I cannot recall any book on revival that I have read that has given me greater pleasure, held my attention more, and incited my longing for a new visitation from God more than this one.

Brian Edwards, Author

This is an awe-inspiring book. It must be, because it contains the testimonies of people converted in a time of revival.

Evangelical Times

ISBN 978-1-85792-953-9

Christian Focus Publications
publishes books for all ages

Our mission statement –

STAYING FAITHFUL
In dependence upon God we seek to impact the world through literature faithful to his infallible word, the Bible. Our aim is to ensure that the LORD Jesus Christ is presented as the only hope to obtain forgiveness of sin, live a useful life and look forward to heaven with Him.

REACHING OUT
Christ's last command requires us to reach out to our world with His gospel. We seek to help fulfil that by publishing books that point people towards Jesus and help them develop a Christ-like maturity. We aim to equip all levels of readers for life, work, ministry and mission.

Books in our adult range are published in three imprints:

Christian Focus contains popular works including biographies, commentaries, basic doctrine and Christian living. Our children's books are also published in this imprint.

Mentor focuses on books written at a level suitable for Bible College and seminary students, pastors, and other serious readers. The imprint includes commentaries, doctrinal studies, examination of current issues and church history.

Christian Heritage contains classic writings from the past.

Christian Focus Publications Ltd
Geanies House, Fearn, Ross-shire,
IV20 1TW, Scotland, United Kingdom.
info@christianfocus.com
www.christianfocus.com